CIMA EXAMINATION KIT

Intermediate Level

Paper 5

Business Taxation

Finance Act 2003

ISBN 1 84390 296 6

British Library Cataloguing-in-Publication data

A catalogue record for this book is available from the British Library.

We are grateful to the Chartered Institute of Management Accountants for permission to reproduce past assessment material. The solutions have been prepared by The Financial Training Company.

Published by

The Financial Training Company
4 The Griffin Centre
Staines Road
Feltham
Middlesex TW14 0HS

Contents

Questions and Answers

Syllabus

Syllabus aims

To test the student's ability to:

♦   Identify the rules imposed upon employers in relation to employee taxation
♦   Explain and apply the system of corporation tax self assessment, capital gains and VAT
♦   Identify and evaluate the impact of international aspects on a UK company's taxation
♦   Identify and evaluate the impact of different tax planning scenarios

Guidance introduction

The syllabus recognises that management accountants will not be expected to become experts in taxation, but rather that they will recognise the important role that taxation can have to play in the decision making process in business. It is expected that the management accountant should be able to raise relevant issues with their tax advisers from an informed point of view. For example, they should be able to prepare notes concerning taxation issues which are to be discussed at a meeting.

Having mastered the basic rules involved in each of the taxes included in the syllabus, candidates will be able to produce correct computations of the tax liabilities of the business on the basis of the information given. However, more than this will be required in the paper. In many cases, candidates will be required to compute the taxation liability in more than one scenario and to advise on the most tax-efficient course of action. In some cases, the question will contain a 'what if' element. In addition the scenario based question in the new examination paper will carry marks for demonstrating communication skills required in reporting information.

Candidates should be aware that commercial decisions are not driven by tax alone and that, at all times, the commercial considerations should take priority. The approach taken in this paper is that where more than one course of action can be used to achieve a desired commercial objective, then management should be aware of the respective taxation implications of the alternatives.

The examination paper

The three hour paper will be divided into three sections.

Section A consists of **ten** objective test questions (of the multiple-choice type (MCQs) worth two marks each. These questions will examine any knowledge based topic within the syllabus.

Section B comprises a **compulsory** scenario based question which could include any elements of the syllabus including planning and compliance aspects. This question will be worth a total of **40 marks** with six marks available for style, presentation and communication skills. The format of the required answer will be specified – report, memo, letter, etc, and it is important to produce your answer in the format specified.

Section C will require **two** technical questions to be answered from a choice of four questions, with each question carrying 20 marks. While these questions could test any part of the syllabus, they are more likely to come from sections (ii), (iii), (iv) and (v). It is not envisaged that a full 20 mark question on section (vi) – VAT – would be asked although VAT could be a significant part of a Section C question. Questions in this section could contain a planning element. Any administration aspects would be incorporated into a larger question.

The weightings in the syllabus are a guide to the level of study required. They do not necessarily represent the spread of the marks in any single examination paper.

A taxation information sheet showing tax rates, etc will be included with the examination paper. To reduce the need to remember standard information, the information sheet will give details of capital allowances rates and the size of qualifying companies.

Syllabus content

Note: For each section of the syllabus the published content is shown first. This is followed by a commentary which expands this content, showing specific areas which are examinable. There are also notes identifying those topics which are excluded from the syllabus.

5(i)   Tax administration – (study weighting 5%)

Learning outcomes

On completion of their studies students should be able to:

♦   Describe the system of Corporation Tax Self Assessment (CTSA)

♦   Identify the key dates for submission of returns

♦   Describe the Inland Revenue's powers of enquiry

♦   Identify the various penalties and interest charges in CTSA

♦   Identify the minimum record-keeping requirements

♦   Identify the compliance requirements imposed on employers in relation to employee taxation

♦   Identify the VAT registration/de-registration requirements and the rules and penalties in relation to VAT returns

Syllabus content

♦   Corporation Tax Self Assessment – all compliance aspects: returns; interest and penalties
♦   Returns required by employers in connection with employees' tax and NICs
♦   VAT administration

Commentary

In relation to CTSA, candidates would be expected to learn about deadlines for submission of Form CT600; appeals and time limits for making appeals and other claims; the nature of Revenue enquiries.

In relation to the VAT element, candidates would be expected to know about registration matters and the timing of returns.

Given a weighting of only 5%, there is little opportunity for asking a full question on this area. It is more likely that elements of this section will be incorporated in a larger question – for example, the date by which the Revenue may instigate an enquiry into a CT600 CTSA Return; the impact of EC regulations on VAT.

Questions on this area will tend to require a narrative response.

5(ii)   Employees' taxation – (study weighting 10%)

Learning outcomes

On completion of their studies students should be able to:

♦   Apply knowledge of the Benefits in Kind (BIK) system for employees

♦   Identify the rules for different types of employees

♦   Calculate the total assessable benefits of an employee and explain the effect on code numbers

♦   Evaluate the relative tax efficiency of different methods of rewarding employees

Syllabus content

♦   All aspects of the system of benefits in kind
♦   Contrast salaries with dividends
♦   Efficient methods of rewarding employees

Commentary

The only income tax questions in the paper could cover employee taxation under the Employment Income Rules (formerly called Schedule E) and the related employer's duties and responsibilities. Note that the relevant legislation is now contained in the Income Tax (Earnings and Pensions) Act 2003 (ITEPA 2003). Tax efficient methods of rewarding staff will be an important aspect. The syllabus is taken to include the following topics:

♦ Quantification of assessable benefits in kind for an employee. Including the new rules for motor car benefits and mileage allowances introduced from 6 April 2002.

♦ The treatment of employees' expenses under SS328-331 ITEPA 2003 together with relevant case law.

♦ The operation of the PAYE system including the operation of code numbers.

♦ Knowledge of the employers' compliance duties in respect of the PAYE system.

♦ Alternative tax efficient methods of rewarding employees, including dividends vs salaries for staff who are shareholders.

♦ Employee share option schemes (including SIPs and EMI).

♦ Status issues and an awareness only of the consequences for IR35 type 'employees'.

In relation to National Insurance contributions (NIC), knowledge will be required of employer's class 1, class 1A and class 1B (on PSAs) only. The new rules for the application of class 1A to certain benefits will be required knowledge. There will be no questions on non-standard earnings or on the special arrangements for directors.

5(iii)   Corporation tax – (study weighting 25%)

Learning outcomes

On completion of their studies students should be able to:

♦ Calculate the Schedule DI profit for taxation purposes, showing knowledge of case law and statute

♦ Calculate the total profits of a company for CT purposes

♦ Calculate the capital allowances entitlement of a company

♦ Calculate the CT liability of a company (including that of small and intermediate companies)

♦ Prepare a schedule of CT payments of a large company covering a two year period under the quarterly payment system

♦ Identify the effect of all forms of loss relief on a company's, group's or a consortium's CT liability

♦ Explain the effect of the loan relationships rules on a company's CT liability

♦ Explain the operation of shadow advance corporation tax (ACT). No computation of ACT will be required

Syllabus content

♦ Adjustment of trading profits for taxation purposes – underlying principles and legislation

♦ Computation of total income and CT liability

♦ Quarterly payment rules

♦ All forms of relief for losses including Groups, Consortia and joint ventures

♦ Capital Allowances

♦ Loan Relationships

♦ Shadow ACT – an awareness only

Commentary

This is the largest single topic within the syllabus, reflecting the fact that most chartered management accountants will be employed by limited companies. The knowledge required is extensive and it is the area to which most study time should be devoted.

The FA 1996 introduced new rules for dealing with interest paid and received by companies under the generic heading 'loan relationships'. This area will be examined in every future corporation tax question and it must be learned.

It is important to distinguish between trade and non-trade loans and to be able to show how non-trade deficits can be relieved.

The syllabus is taken to include knowledge of the following topics:

♦ The method of computing the chargeable income and total income of a company (most frequently the adjusted profit figure will be given). Note that the total income determines the status of the company (large, small or intermediate – note that from 1 April 2000 there are two new categories: very small and small intermediate). If the company is large – taking into account associated companies – it may be required to pay its CT under the quarterly arrangements.

♦ Candidates should be aware of the effect of any brought forward surplus ACT on dividend policy. No ACT calculations will be required. Note that surplus shadow ACT will not be examined nor will any group aspects of shadow ACT.

♦ Full knowledge of accounting periods for CT purposes including the treatment of long periods of account.

♦ The detailed schedule of payment dates and amounts of CT under the quarterly payment arrangements – bearing in mind that the system is being phased in over a four year period.

♦ Full knowledge of the treatment of loan interest receivable and payable and of the treatment of corporate debt under the loan relationships rules. Be able to deal with non-trading deficits in the most tax efficient manner.

♦ Full knowledge of the treatment of patent royalties from 1 April 2002 under the FA 2002 legislation dealing with intangible assets. Note that, apart from rollover reliefs, no other aspect of the intangible assets rules will be examined in 2004.

♦ Detailed knowledge of the reliefs available for trading losses under present legislation and of the interaction between charges and trading losses. No questions will be set on the effect of a loss carried back to 1999 which creates surplus ACT prior to 6 April 1999.

♦ Detailed knowledge of all aspects of group and consortium reliefs, including the treatment of capital gains, including the treatment of pre-entry losses. Knowledge of the FA 2000 rules involving the role of non-UK resident companies in groups is required. No questions will be set involving 'link companies'. 'Group consortium' companies are examinable from 2004. Occasionally, narrative questions on group situations may be set.

♦ Knowledge of close companies and close investment-holding companies. Generally narrative questions will be set, although examination questions could involve calculating shareholdings to establish whether a company is close. Be aware of the principal members' rule. The consequences of close company status should be understood, including loans and benefits in kind to participators and the arrangements for paying any resulting tax.

♦ The method of calculating a company's Schedule A assessment under the FA 1998 rules and how to deal with Schedule A losses.

♦ Knowledge of the capital allowances system relating to plant (including short life assets and motor cars with low CO_2 emissions) and industrial buildings only. (Knowledge is not required concerning long life assets nor such items as patents and agricultural buildings.) The new relief for research and development expenditure in both FA 2000 and 2002 is examinable from May 2004 onwards.

5(iv)   International aspects – (study weighting 20%)

Learning outcomes

On completion of their studies students should be able to:

♦   Evaluate the taxation implications of alternative methods of running an overseas operation

♦   Identify the significance of company residences for tax purposes

♦   Calculate the CT liability of a UK company which has overseas income, using the rules of double tax relief (but excluding knowledge of Treaties)

♦   Identify transfer pricing problems, calculating any adjustment required and state how this will be reported in its CTSA return

♦   Identify a controlled foreign company (CFC)

♦   Calculate the CT liability arising as a result of the presence of a CFC

Syllabus content

♦   Foreign operations – Subsidiary vs Branch
♦   Company Residence
♦   Double Taxation relief (DTR)
♦   Transfer Pricing
♦   Controlled Foreign Companies (CFC)
♦   International Trading

Commentary

The present syllabus for IBTX is the first to include a separate section on overseas matters. However, since this is a first level tax paper, a number of the complex matters involved are not examinable. A list of these exclusions is shown at the end of this section.

The syllabus is taken to include knowledge of the following topics:

♦   Identifying the residence of a company for UK tax purposes. The effect of location of management on residence status.

♦   The taxation in the UK of overseas income received by a UK resident company.

♦   The alternative methods that a UK company may adopt in running an overseas operation.

♦   Basic double tax relief (DTR) – unilateral relief only – not treaty reliefs.

♦   The treatment of excess foreign tax credits under the FA 2000 rules (but not involving 'on-shore pooling' – see below).

♦   Identification of controlled foreign companies (CFC) and the consequences for UK companies.

♦   Fundamental aspects only of transfer pricing (no APAs).

♦   The role of non-UK resident companies in forming groups or consortia.

It is equally important to be aware of those aspects which are not in the IBTX syllabus and which will not be examined and are:

♦   Foreign companies trading in the UK.

♦   The use of 'mixer' companies.

♦   'Capping' of the rates of DTR.

♦   'On-shore pooling' of foreign dividends and the calculation of 'eligible unrelieved foreign tax' (EUFT) involving on-shore pooling.

♦   The calculation of 'exit charges' where a company ceases to be UK resident.

Questions could be set in any of the following areas:

♦ The completion of a CT computation involving double tax relief (DTR). Minor aspects of DTR may appear in the compulsory sections of the paper, including the scenario-based question (Section B), but any full question on this topic would be an optional question in Section C of the paper.

♦ Candidates should be able to identify a CFC from information supplied; know the consequences of this status for CTSA purposes; compute any CT due on CFC income and be aware of any exemptions.

♦ An awareness only of the fundamental aspects of transfer pricing as required under the CTSA reporting rules. No questions will be set on advance pricing agreements (APA).

♦ The important taxation differences under the different methods by which a UK company could run an overseas operation. Branch or subsidiary. Candidates would be expected to give advice on the choice.

5(v) Capital gains (for companies only) – (study weighting 10%)

Learning outcomes

On completion of their studies students should be able to:

♦ Identify chargeable assets for taxation as capital gains

♦ Apply rollover and holdover reliefs for tangible and intangible business assets

♦ Identify the CGT reliefs available in a group situation and the anti-avoidance rules relating to pre-entry assets

♦ Calculate the gain arising on the disposal of quoted securities using the pooling system

♦ Apply the substantial shareholding exemption rules (SSE)

Syllabus content

♦ Scope
♦ Reliefs for Business Assets
♦ Groups of Companies
♦ Shares and securities
♦ The substantial shareholding exemption (SSE)

Commentary

In this topic, computations of chargeable gains will always be required and the topic could be examined in the scenario-based question in Section B of the paper. ONE of the questions in Section C will always be wholly on CGT issues.

The syllabus is taken to include the following topics:

♦ Detailed knowledge of rollover relief and hold over relief on tangible business assets, including deferred gains on assets sold between 1985 and 1988.

♦ Knowledge of the new form of reinvestment rollover relief for intangible assets introduced in the FA 2002.

♦ Full knowledge of the reliefs for investments in Venture Capital Trusts (VCT) and in enterprise investment schemes (EIS). (See note below.)

♦ A knowledge of the new Corporate Venturing scheme introduced in the FA 2000 is required.

♦ A knowledge of basic planning in capital gains tax, for example which asset to sell; identification of planning opportunities within a group structure.

♦ Full knowledge of such areas as indexation allowance, re-basing at 31 March 1982 and the pooling of quoted shares.

♦ The anti-avoidance legislation on pre-entry capital losses in groups.

♦ Re-allocation relief in respect of a gain arising on a company leaving a group (within 6 years of an asset transfer). FA 2002. 'De-merging gains'.

♦ Relief for disposals of substantial shareholdings. Conditions for qualifying.

While no questions involving the calculation of a CGT liability for an individual will be asked, EIS and VCTs are examinable. The context of questions on these areas would be that a company was trying to raise finance and would require to explain to potential shareholders the taxation benefits (and disadvantages) of EIS and VCTs.

The following items are not examinable:

♦ Disposals by individuals in any circumstances.
♦ Disposals of agricultural quotas.

5(vi)   Value Added Tax – (study weighting 10%)

Learning outcomes

On completion of their studies students should be able to:

♦ Identify the significance of Standard rate, Zero rate and exempt supplies and those supplies outwith the scope of VAT

♦ Identify the correct tax point of a supply and understand its significance

♦ Identify the significance of EU and non-EU countries when dealing with VAT

♦ Discuss the problems and opportunities inherent in a VAT group registration

Syllabus content

♦ Scope
♦ Zero rating; exemption; partial exemption
♦ Tax point; payment and refunds
♦ The concept of a group registration and the consequent VAT regulations
♦ Transactions with foreign companies
♦ Groups of companies
♦ VAT treatment of basic transactions in property

Commentary

This section has a 10% weighting and a full 20 mark question in the optional Section C is unlikely. However, VAT will be examined in some form in every paper; either as an element within the scenario-based question or in the MCQs in Section A.

The syllabus is taken to include the following topics:

♦ The registration/de-registration rules; penalties; default surcharges.

♦ Knowledge of VAT in relation to basic property transactions – 'opting to tax' elections.

♦ Knowledge of the VAT regulations in connection with exports and imports, including trading with EU and non-EU countries.

♦ The planning opportunities available in a group context. Separate registrations.

♦ An understanding of VAT in property transactions.

♦ An understanding of the partial exemption rules.

The following items are not examinable:

♦ Fully computational questions on VAT, although occasionally some computation may be required as a minor aspect of a question, including compulsory ones.

♦ No questions will be set on any anti-avoidance provisions relating to groups of companies.

5(vii)   Tax planning – (study weighting 20%)

Learning outcomes

Students are reminded that 'Tax Planning' is not a discrete area of taxation. It is the application of the knowledge you gain while studying each section of the syllabus. Try to grasp the planning opportunities when studying each section.

On completion of their studies students should be able to:

♦   Calculate the form of loss relief which will minimise the CT liability in either a single company or in a group or consortium

♦   Evaluate the tax efficiency of alternative methods of acquiring other businesses

♦   Contrast the tax implications of financing a company by debt or equity

♦   Demonstrate the planning aspects of maximising the use of surplus ACT existing at 6 April 1999 for a company

♦   Demonstrate the most efficient method of disposing of assets to third parties by a group of companies

♦   Discuss the most efficient method of arranging VAT registrations for groups of companies

♦   Demonstrate how to maximise DTR

♦   Demonstrate the importance of timing in tax planning

Syllabus content

♦   Optimum use of trading losses
♦   Capital allowances and R&D expenditure
♦   Company acquisitions – assets or shares?
♦   Alternative methods of financing a company
♦   Shadow ACT
♦   Sales of Group assets
♦   VAT – Groups
♦   Charges and losses in DTR computations
♦   Loan relationships

Commentary

Although this subject has been allocated a separate section of the syllabus, it must be treated as an integral part of all areas covered in the syllabus. Within each section of the syllabus there have been references made to planning approaches.

All of the tax planning aspects inherent in any situation should be considered when candidates are studying a particular topic. For example:

♦   Whether to acquire other companies and the methods of acquisition; consider when studying groups and associated companies.

♦   Whether (or not) to have a group VAT registration; consider when studying VAT.

♦   When to buy an asset; consider when studying capital allowances.

♦   Whether to finance a company by debt or equity; consider when studying loan relationships.

♦   Whether or not to pay a dividend; consider when studying shadow ACT.

♦   Whether to provide employees with motor cars or let them buy their own.

Planning aspects will always be a feature of the scenario-based question in Section B. Every report asked for will contain some requirement to give advice on taxation matters. In Section C some planning could be examined in any question, often as a second requirement. Planning questions often require candidates to perform a computation and then to give advice based on the computation. It is therefore important to master the basic computational rules.

TAX RATES

TAX TABLE

The following table of tax rates should be used in answering this paper. The capital gains tax indexation factors for use with question 5 are given in the question.

Corporation tax

| | Financial years | |
| | 2002 | 2003 |
	Year ended 31/3/2003	*Year ended 31/3/2004*
Upper threshold	£1,500,000	£1,500,000
Standard rate of tax	30%	30%
Lower threshold	£300,000	£300,000
Small company rate	19%	19%
Taper relief fraction	11/400	11/400
Upper threshold for starting rate	£50,000	£50,000
Lower threshold for starting rate	£10,000	£10,000
Starting rate	Nil%	Nil%
Taper fraction for starting rate	19/400	19/400
Shadow ACT rate	20%	20%
FII tax credit rate (for calculating shadow ACT)	20%	20%
Rate for grossing up net dividends received for small company threshold purposes	100/90	100/90
Rate of income tax suffered/retained on receiving/paying debenture or loan interest	20%	20%

Rates of income tax to be used in dealing with UFII and charges   22% for 2003/04
(22% for 2002/03)

Income tax and NIC

Income Tax rates:

First £1,960	10%
Next £28,540	22%
Balance	40%

Employer's NIC, Classes 1A and 1B NIC   12.8%

VAT

Registration threshold from April 2003   £56,000

Meaning of CIMA's examination requirements

CIMA use precise words in the requirements of their questions. In the schedule below we reproduce the precise meanings of these words from the CIMA syllabus. You must learn these definitions and make sure that in the exam you do precisely what CIMA requires you to do.

Learning objective	Verbs used	Definition
1 Knowledge What you are expected to know	List	Make a list of
	State	Express, fully or clearly, the details of/facts of
	Define	Give the exact meaning of
2 Comprehension What you are expected to understand	Describe	Communicate the key features of
	Distinguish	Highlight the differences between
	Explain	Make clear or intelligible/state the meaning of
	Identify	Recognise, establish or select after consideration
	Illustrate	Use an example to describe or explain something
3 Application Can you apply your knowledge?	Apply	To put to practical use
	Calculate/compute	To ascertain or reckon mathematically
	Demonstrate	To prove with certainty or to exhibit by practical means
	Prepare	To make or get ready for use
	Reconcile	To make or prove consistent/compatible
	Solve	Find an answer to
	Tabulate	Arrange in a table
4 Analysis Can you analyse the detail of what you have learned?	Analyse	Examine in detail the structure of
	Categorise	Place into a defined class or division
	Compare and contrast	Show the similarities and/or differences between
	Construct	To build up or compile
	Discuss	To examine in detail by argument
	Interpret	To translate into intelligible or familiar terms
	Produce	To create or bring into existence
5 Evaluation Can you use your learning to evaluate, make decisions or recommendations?	Advise	To counsel, inform or notify
	Evaluate	To appraise or assess the value of
	Recommend	To advise on a course of action

Approach to objective test questions

The objective test questions will comprise a question with four possible answers. For example,

1   What is the world's tallest mountain?

     A   Ben Nevis

     B   K2

     C   Mount Everest

     D   Mount Snowdon

You have to select the correct answer (which in the above example is of course **C**).

In the examination, however, the incorrect answers, called distractors, may be quite plausible and are sometimes designed if not exactly to mislead you, they may nevertheless be the result of fairly common mistakes.

The following is a suggested technique for answering these questions, but as you practise for the examination you have to work out a method which suits you.

Step 1

Read all the questions, but not necessarily the answers. Select the ones which you think are the most straightforward and do them first.

Step 2

For more awkward questions, some people prefer to work the question without reference to the answers which increases your confidence if your answer then matches one of the options. However some people prefer to view the question with the four answers as this may assist them in formulating their answer.

This is a matter of personal preference and you should perhaps practise each to see which you find most effective.

Step 3

If your answer does not match one of the options you must:

(a)   Re-read the question carefully to make sure you have not missed some important point.

(b)   Re-work your solution eliminating any mistakes.

(c)   Beware the plausible distractors but do not become paranoid. The examiner is not trying to trip you up and the answer should be a straightforward calculation from the question.

Step 4

Time allocation. As with all questions you must not overrun your time. The questions are technically worth only two marks each which is about three to four minutes per question. It is very easy to get bogged down. If you cannot get one of the right answers then move on to the next question.

Step 5

When you have finished all the questions go back to the ones you have not answered.

Keep an eye on the clock – don't overrun the time allocation.

If you really cannot do it, **have a guess**. You are not penalised for wrong answers. **Never leave any questions unanswered.**

Analysis of past papers

Pilot Paper 2000

1   Multiple choice questions.

2   (a)   Estimation of corporation tax liability. Schedule of tax payments. CTSA scheme.

        (b)   Calculation of actual CT liability and dealing with the under/over payment of tax.

3   Schedule E benefits and employer compliance requirements.

4   Capital allowances.

5   Capital gains tax.

6   Double taxation relief.

May 2001

1   Multiple choice questions.

2   Estimation of corporation tax liability and subsequent calculation of actual CT liability. The question included group relief and capital gains tax computations.

3   Benefits in kind and Class 1A National Insurance Contribution rules.

4   Capital allowances, including treatment of Car Pools.

5   Group relief, including consortium relief.

6   Capital gains tax; opportunities to defer tax payable.

November 2001

1   Multiple choice questions.

2   Calculation of corporation tax liabilities for group companies, involving group reliefs, consortium relief, relief for capital losses, rules on non-resident companies.

3   (a)   Tax and NIC implications of providing benefits to employees.

        (b)   Partial exemption in VAT.

4   Effect on Schedule D Case 1 profit and taxation treatment of seven items of expenditure and income.

5   Corporation tax liability of a UK-resident company with foreign company investments.

6   Capital gains tax, including crystallisation of a gain on sale of shares in a subsidiary, sale of rights to shares.

May 2002

1   Multiple choice questions.

2   Corporation tax liabilities for a company with a 15-month financial accounting period, divided into two chargeable accounting periods.

3   (a)   VAT partial exemption rules.

        (b)   Tax treatment of AESOP and EMI share option schemes.

4   Capital allowances: industrial buildings allowances.

5   (a)   Loan relationship rules.

        (b)   Group relief rules and the roles of non-resident companies.

6   Capital gains tax: sale of a sub-lease; sale of a portion of a plot of land; holdover relief.

November 2002

1   Multiple choice questions.

2   Adjustment of profits, capital allowances, capital gains, calculation of corporation tax liability. Report on loan relationship rules.

3   Class 1A National Insurance Contributions.

4   Treatment of losses for corporation tax. Involving a company whose first period of trading was longer than 12 months (therefore two CAPs).

5   (a)   Schedule A: tax treatment of premiums on leases and sub-leases; interaction between Schedule A and capital gains treatment of premiums.

        (b)   Group registration for VAT.

6   Capital gains tax, involving a non-resident company with several UK subsidiaries.

May 2003

1   Multiple choice questions.

2   Calculation of corporation tax liability. Implications of the son of the majority shareholder receiving interest free loan. Tax implications of R&D. Tax effects of overseas branch or subsidiary. Joint venture with overseas company.

3   Benefits in kind on cars and fuel.

4   Capital allowances including industrial building allowances. Tax treatment of low emission cars and computers.

5   Capital gains tax including intra-group transfers.

6   Double tax relief and controlled foreign companies.

November 2003

1   Multiple choice questions.

2   Calculation of corporation tax liability including CGT and R&D expenditure.

Quarterly payment system.

Effect of moving company management to Switzerland.

Surplus ACT.

3   Adjustment to profits.

4   Analysis of the structure of a group. Computation of income chargeable to CT taking group reliefs.

5   (a)   Calculation of benefits in kind.

(b)   Calculation of Code Number.

6   Capital gains when a company ceases to be a group member.

Objective Test Questions

1   Go Forth Ltd leases a second-hand Volvo estate car which is used exclusively for its fruit importing business. Its second-hand market value was £13,000 (cost when new £16,000). The accounts for the year ended 30 April 2004 show lease rental payments of £5,000.

How much is allowable for tax purposes?

A   £625

B   £3,750

C   £4,375

D   £4,808

2   A company leases a car in 2004 costing £14,000 for use by one of its employees at an annual rental of £3,600. The car is used 75% for business purposes and the employee makes no reimbursement for private use.

The expenditure not allowable for Schedule D Case I purposes is:

A   £3,600

B   £3,343

C   £257

D   £193

3   A company's bad debts account for the year ended 30 September 2003 is as follows.

	Dr £	Cr £
Specific provision for bad debts (b/f)		150
General provision for bad debts (b/f)		750
Bad debts recovered		100
Trade debts written off	500	
Loan to former employee written off	400	
Specific provision for bad debts (c/f)	300	
General provision for bad debts (c/f)	1,000	
Profit and loss account		1,200
	2,200	2,200

The bad debts disallowed in the adjustment of profits computation are:

A   £250

B   £400

C   £650

D   £800

4 The entertaining account of Henry (Feeds) Ltd, a feed wholesaler which employs 10 people, is as follows.

	£
Gifts to customers	400
Entertaining staff at Christmas party	300
Entertaining local customers at trade shows	140
	840

The gifts were ballpoint pens, purchased wholesale at £8.00 each (retail value £11.00); all had an advertisement for the feed business on the side.

The amount allowed in the Schedule D Case I computations is:

A   £300

B   £400

C   £540

D   £700

5 Thompson (Office Supplies) Ltd's accounts for the year ended 31 May 2003 included a deduction in the profit and loss account for sundry expenses of £5,700.

These comprised the following.

	£
Christmas turkeys packaged with an advertisement for Thompson's business, given to customers (cost £25 each)	3,250
Seminar for customers to launch new product	1,650
Christmas party for all members of staff	800
	5,700

The sundry expenses allowable for tax purposes are:

A   £800

B   £2,450

C   £4,050

D   £5,700

6 Bob the Builder Ltd made a profit of £142,350 for the year ended 30 September 2003 after the following expenses.

	£
Rent	8,625
Depreciation	4,850
Legal expenses, comprising:	
(a) dispute with the local council over a rates bill	300
(b) acquisition of a new lease	250
Loss on sale of Ford transit van	835

What is the company's adjusted trading profit (ignoring capital allowances) for the year ended 30 September 2003?

A   £146,215

B   £147,200

C   £147,450

D   £148,285

7   Which of the following is an allowable deduction in calculating the Schedule D Case I profits of a business?

    A   Leather bound diaries costing £52 each, bearing the business name

    B   Gift Aid payment to a charity

    C   General provision for bad debts

    D   Legal expenses for renewing a lease for 19 years

8   On 1 June 2003 Kenton plc leased a car, which originally cost £16,000, for £6,000 rental per annum.

How much of this will be disallowed per annum for Schedule D Case I purposes?

A   £750

B   £1,000

C   £5,250

D   £6,000

9   The following legal costs were incurred by Opera Ltd during the year ended 31 March 2004.

	£
Employment contracts	1,000
Abortive work on prospective property purchase	2,000
Debt collection	750
	3,750

What expenses will be allowed for tax purposes?

A   £750

B   £1,750

C   £3,000

D   £3,750

10   The legal fees account of Quainton plc contains expenses in connection with the following.

	£
Acquisition of a 20 year lease	10,200
Renewal of a 60 year lease	4,600
Renewal of a 25 year lease	5,900

How much of this expenditure will be disallowed in computing Quainton plc's Schedule D Case I profit?

A   £4,600

B   £10,200

C   £10,500

D   £14,800

11   Oakham Ltd has incurred the following legal expenses in its first accounting period.

	£
Preparation of memorandum and articles of association	3,500
Issue of share capital	1,000
Obtaining an injunction against a trading competitor	2,000
	6,500

The legal expenses allowed for tax purposes are:

A   £2,000

B   £3,000

C   £5,500

D   £6,500

12   When preparing its accounts for the year to 31 December 2003, Icon Ltd, a retailer, provided for bad debts as follows.

	£
Debtors in liquidation	600
Specific debtors outstanding for more than six months	200
50% provision on other balances outstanding for between three and six months	350
Loan to John Williams, a former employee	125
	1,275

How much will be allowed when computing Icon Ltd's Schedule D Case I profits?

A   £600

B   £725

C   £800

D   £1,150

13   Cheer Ltd incurred the following expenditure in the year to 30 June 2004.

(1)   £500 allowance to a salesman to cover general travel expenditure.
(2)   £1,000 on entertaining its 15 employees at the annual staff dinner.

How much will be disallowed in computing the company's Schedule D Case I profits for the year?

A   Nil

B   £500

C   £1,000

D   £1,500

14   Juniper Ltd has the following items in its profit and loss account.

	£
Costs of registering a patent	150
Theft by cashier	200
Loan to ex-employee written off	250
	600

What amount would be disallowed for Schedule D Case I tax purposes?

A   £150

B   £250

C   £450

D   £600

15   The following is an extract of the detailed analysis of the entertaining expenses account of Bow Ltd for the year ended 30 June 2004.

	£
Gifts of industrial trade samples to UK customers	820
Staff Christmas party	570
Gifts to UK customers (one diary each)	
Pocket diary bearing company logo costing £6.50	650
Entertaining major supplier of components from France	410

What is the total amount of these expenses allowed in the Schedule D Case I computation?

A   £2,040

B   £1,630

C   £1,390

D   £410

16 York plc employs Simon as a salesman. He receives a salary of £22,000 and a round sum allowance of £2,750 to cover expenses. Simon has spent his allowance as follows.

	£
Travelling on company business	2,320
Entertaining customers	280
Business telephone calls	150
	2,750

What amount may York plc deduct in arriving at its assessable profits?

A £2,320

B £2,470

C £2,600

D £2,750

17 James plc has the following legal and professional charges in its profit and loss account.

	£
Costs of conducting a successful appeal to the Special Commissioners	2,150
Costs of defence of title to fixed assets	1,830

How much is allowable for tax purposes?

A Nil

B £1,830

C £2,150

D £3,980

18 Johnson Ltd has the following items charged to its profit and loss account.

	£
General bad debt provision increase	1,742
Provision against 50% of debt owed by Williams Ltd	2,086
Write-off of loan to ex-employee	1,200

What is the amount disallowed for Schedule D Case I purposes?

A £1,200

B £1,742

C £2,942

D £5,028

19   Phantasm plc has the following items charged in arriving at its profits before taxation for the y/e 31 October 2003.

	£
Cost of private health care plans for directors	4,000
Donation to Oxfam (gross)	1,000
Defalcation by a junior employee	800
Legal costs re negotiation of a new 21 year lease	300

What amount will be disallowed in arriving at the Schedule D Case I profit?

A   £1,300

B   £1,800

C   £4,000

D   £4,300

20   On 6 November 2003 Reydon Ltd, publishers, acquired a new motor car costing £29,610 (including VAT) for the sales director. Subsequently the company purchased a stereo for the car costing £1,175 (including VAT). The car was used 75% for business purposes.

What is the maximum input VAT reclaimable?

A   £131.25

B   £175.00

C   £3,438.75

D   £4,585.00

21   Acorn Antiques Ltd wishes to claim capital allowances in respect of a set of antique trade source books used to value and date European furniture. Pastas R Us Ltd is a restaurant operator which has had a false ceiling constructed to hide unsightly pipes in the restaurant; the company also wishes to claim capital allowances.

Who, if either, will succeed in its claim?

A   Neither

B   Acorn Antiques Ltd only

C   Pastas R Us Ltd only

D   Both companies

22   Fairbrother Ltd commenced trading on 1 July 2003. On 1 September 2003 the company bought two cars costing £6,000 and £14,000 respectively.

What are the maximum capital allowances available for the accounting period ended 31 March 2004?

A   £2,250

B   £3,375

C   £3,750

D   £4,500

23 On 1 January 2004 Lion Ltd acquired a car (costing £24,000) under a hire purchase agreement. Instalments in the first year amounted to £9,600 which included finance charges of £3,200.

What may be deducted in arriving at the Schedule D Case I profits for the year to 31 December 2004?

A £3,200

B £6,200

C £9,200

D £12,600

24 Wainwright Ltd, which operates a garage, incurred the following expenditure on plant and equipment.

	£
Canopy over the petrol filling station	10,500
Car ramp for the car repair workshop	3,800
Moveable partitions for the sales and accounts offices	8,400
	22,700

How much is eligible for capital allowances?

A £3,800

B £12,200

C £18,900

D £22,700

25 Foodchain Ltd owns two restaurants. During the year to 31 December 2003 it incurred the following expenditure on electric light fittings.

(1) £800 was spent on one restaurant in order to improve its general illumination.

(2) £1,000 was spent on the other restaurant on special lighting in order to create a romantic atmosphere.

How much, if any, of the expenditure will be eligible for capital allowances?

A Nil

B £800

C £1,000

D £1,800

26   Feldman Ltd (a small company) has been trading since 1 May 2002 and prepares accounts to 30 April. The tax written down value of plant and equipment on 1 May 2003 was £2,800.

On 4 September 2003 the company sold a machine for £3,600 which had cost £2,300. On 15 August 2003 the company purchased office equipment for £1,500. The costs exclude VAT.

What are the net capital allowances or balancing charges for the year ended 30 April 2004?

A   Capital allowances £175

B   Balancing charge £200

C   Capital allowances £500

D   Capital allowances £725

27   Time Trails Ltd (a small company) began trading on 1 May 2002 preparing accounts to 30 April.

The company bought machinery costing £40,000 on 1 June 2002.

What are the maximum capital allowances for the year to 30 April 2004, assuming that all allowances are claimed as early as possible? (Ignore VAT.)

A   £10,000

B   £7,500

C   £6,000

D   £2,500

28   Which one of the following items could beneficially be 'de-pooled' and treated as a short life asset following acquisition?

A   A motor car (no private use) to be disposed of in three years for less than written down value

B   Plant to be sold in six years for less than written down value

C   Machinery to be scrapped (nil proceeds) in three years

D   Plant to be traded-in after two years for 90% of its original cost

29   A large shipping business has incurred the following expenditure.

Dockside crane	£18,000
Portacabin office	£6,000
Dockside grain silos	£260,000

How much expenditure will qualify as plant for capital allowances purposes?

A   £18,000

B   £24,000

C   £278,000

D   £284,000

30   Faustus Ltd (a small company) commenced business on 1 August 2002 and will prepare accounts to 31 July each year. In its first year the company incurred the following capital expenditure.

23 August 2002	Motor car	£15,000
3 December 2002	Office equipment	£1,500
17 April 2003	Computer	£2,400

The capital allowances available as a deduction in the computation of assessable profits for the period ended 31 July 2003 is:

A   £3,390

B   £4,560

C   £5,310

D   £6,000

31   McCann (Soaps) Ltd commenced trading on 1 June 2003 and prepared accounts to 31 January 2004 and annually thereafter. The company bought plant costing £14,100 (inclusive of VAT) on 1 August 2003.

The company was registered for VAT from commencement. It is a small business and has only five employees.

What capital allowances will be available for the first accounting period?

A   £3,000

B   £3,525

C   £4,800

D   £5,640

32   Flore plc, whose year end is 31 December, starts to use two industrial buildings on 1 July 2003.

(1)   Melton, which the company constructed itself, the costs incurred between 1 January 2003 and 30 June 2003 being as follows.

	£
Construction costs of factory	229,750
Construction costs of integral offices	71,250
Architect's fees	74,000
	375,000

(2)   Stilton, a second-hand building purchased for £400,000. This building has been used continuously as an industrial building since it was first brought into use on 1 July 1988. Its original cost in 1988 was £255,000.

What are the maximum industrial buildings allowances which the company may claim for the year ended 31 December 2003?

A   £15,000

B   £55,000

C   £40,500

D   £115,500

33   On 1 October 2003 Hove Ltd purchased for £73,500 an industrial building from Ryde Ltd which had always used the building for industrial purposes.

Ryde Ltd purchased, and took into use, the building on 30 September 1999 for £42,000 and the written down value before sale was £35,280.

Both companies draw up accounts to 31 December.

What is the writing down allowance that Hove Ltd can claim in its accounting period for the year ending 31 December 2003?

A   £1,680

B   £2,000

C   £2,940

D   £3,500

34   Royton plc, which prepares accounts to 31 December, sold an industrial building on 1 March 2003 for £220,000. The building had cost £200,000 on 1 March 1986 and was brought into industrial use immediately.

Royton plc had claimed maximum capital allowances including a 25% initial allowance.

The balancing charge on the disposal is:

A   £20,000

B   £162,000

C   £186,000

D   £200,000

35   Henry Homes Ltd constructed a factory on land it already owned. The building cost £180,000 including both a staff canteen which cost £25,000 and offices which cost £43,000.

How much of the expenditure will qualify for industrial building allowances?

A   £112,000

B   £137,000

C   £155,000

D   £180,000

36   A manufacturer constructs a factory at a total cost of £105,000 made up as follows.

	£	£
Purchase of freehold land		20,000
Clearing of land		5,000
Building:		
Factory	30,000	
Drawing office	15,000	
Canteen	10,000	
General office	25,000	
		80,000
		105,000

On what figure would industrial buildings allowances be given?

A   £55,000

B   £60,000

C   £80,000

D   £85,000

37   Docklands plc incurred expenditure of £10 million during the year to 31 December 2001 on the construction of a commercial building in an enterprise zone. The land on which the building stood had cost a further £1 million.

Docklands plc claimed an initial allowance of 40% on the building in the year to 31 December 2001.

Assuming that maximum allowances were claimed in 2002 what is the maximum capital allowance that can be claimed for the year to 31 December 2003?

A   £400,000

B   £440,000

C   £1,000,000

D   £1,100,000

With reference to the following information answer questions 38 and 39.

Reginald Ltd, which prepares accounts to 31 January, purchased a new industrial building on 30 November 2003 and moved into the building on 1 April 2004. The cost of £250,000 was made up as follows.

	£
Land	40,000
Factory	210,000
	250,000

The costs attributable to showrooms and general offices within the factory were £40,000 and £20,000 respectively.

38   What is the expenditure qualifying for industrial buildings allowances?

    A   £150,000

    B   £170,000

    C   £190,000

    D   £210,000

39   For the year ended 31 January 2004 Reginald Ltd was entitled to claim:

    A   No allowances

    B   4% writing down allowance only

    C   40% initial allowance only

    D   4% writing down allowance $\times \frac{2}{12}$

40   Forres plc purchased two industrial buildings on 1 December 2003 both of which it immediately occupied for a qualifying purpose.

    (1)   Building 1, a newly erected unused building purchased for £400,000 from a trading company that had never used it. The original construction cost was £280,000.

    (2)   Building 2, a newly erected unused building purchased direct from a builder for £350,000. The builder's costs of construction were £290,000.

What is the maximum writing down allowance in respect of these two buildings which the company may claim for the year ended 30 November 2004?

    A   £30,000

    B   £27,600

    C   £25,200

    D   £22,800

41   Haldane Ltd owns a property which it lets for the first time on 30 June 2003 at a rent of £4,000 per annum payable quarterly in advance.

The first tenants left on 30 March 2004 and the property was re-let to new tenants on 31 March 2004 at a rent of £5,000 per annum payable yearly in advance.

Haldane Ltd's allowable expenditure was £1,000 for its accounting period to 31 March 2004.

What is the Schedule A assessment for the year to 31 March 2004?

    A   £1,667

    B   £2,000

    C   £4,000

    D   £7,000

42 Germaine Ltd owns four properties, all let at full rent, for which it receives the following rents for its accounting period to 31 December 2003.

Property		£	
1	Tenant repairing lease	5,500	profit
2	Tenant repairing lease	(8,600)	loss
3	Landlord repairing lease	10,000	profit
4	Landlord repairing lease	(2,000)	loss

What is the Schedule A assessment for the above accounting period assuming that loss relief is utilised as soon as possible?

A £4,900

B £5,500

C £6,900

D £8,000

43 Muxton Ltd has charged the following items in arriving at its net trading profit for the year ended 31 December 2004.

	£
Goodwill purchased 1 January 2004 written off	5,000
Amount written off stock to reduce it to net realisable value	8,000
Interest on late payment of corporation tax	1,000

What amount should be disallowed in calculating the Schedule D Case I profits?

A £1,000

B £5,000

C £6,000

D £9,000

44 Hammer Ltd has the following items in its general expenses account for the year ended 31 March 2004.

	£
Legal fees re renewal of 20 year lease	520
Donation to BBC 'Children in Need' appeal	100
Interest on repayment from Customs	(85)
	535

What amount should be disallowed in computing the Schedule D Case I profit?

A £15

B £100

C £535

D £620

45   The legal costs shown in the tax computation of Stathe plc are analysed as follows.

		£
(1)	Costs involved in unsuccessful attempt to raise long-term finance	1,050
(2)	Acquisition of a short lease	720
(3)	Cost involved in making a rights issue of shares	500
		2,270

What are the total allowable legal expenses?

A   £720

B   £1,050

C   £1,220

D   £1,550

46   Julian Ltd commenced trading on 1 January 2004 and purchased a motor car for £9,200 for the use of a salesman (20% private use).

What are the company's capital allowances for the nine month accounting period ended 30 September 2004?

A   £1,380

B   £1,500

C   £1,725

D   £2,300

47   Fly Ltd commenced trading and made up its first set of accounts for the 16-month period to 31 March 2004.

Its trading profits for the period will be assessed to corporation tax as:

A   4 months to 31 March 2003
        12 months to 31 March 2004

B   4 months to 5 April 2003
        12 months to 31 March 2004

C   12 months to 30 November 2003
        4 months to 31 March 2004

D   16 months to 31 March 2004

48   On 1 June 2003 Lewes Ltd was granted a 20-year lease for new business premises at a premium of £10,000.

How much of the premium will be allowed to Lewes Ltd as a deduction from trading profits for the year ended 31 May 2004?

A   Nil

B   £190

C   £310

D   £500

49 Which of the following statements most accurately describes the profits of a company which are chargeable to corporation tax?

  A   The total amount used to determine the appropriate rate of tax to charge on the company's taxable profits

  B   The total amount of profits upon which the corporation tax liability is computed

  C   A total amount comprising all income received by the company plus chargeable gains

  D   A total amount comprising all income received by the company, less charges on income, plus chargeable gains

50 Shadow ACT may best be defined as:

  A   The amount of unrelieved ACT brought forward which a company is able to use in an accounting period ending after 5 April 1999

  B   The amount of ACT which a company pays on dividends paid after 5 April 1999 following the abolition of ACT

  C   The excess of dividends paid over dividends received after 5 April 1999 multiplied by 25%

  D   The ACT on dividends received by a company which is deducted from that on any dividends paid after 5 April 1999

51 Foreign Affairs Limited has surplus ACT brought forward as at 1 July 2003 of £34,000. During the year ended 30 June 2004 it paid total dividends of £75,000 and received dividends of £18,000. Its profits chargeable to corporation tax are £238,600. The ACT set off for the year ended 30 June 2004 is:

  A   Nil

  B   £530

  C   £33,470

  D   £34,000

52 Neon Ltd has the following results in respect of the year ended 30 September 2004.

	£
Trading profit, as adjusted for taxation purposes	1,502,000
Bank deposit interest accrued and received	48,000
Local Authority Stock interest accrued and received (gross)	80,000
Gift Aid paid	20,000

The company also paid a dividend of £18,600 on 30 June 2003.

The Local Authority Stock interest was received gross.

Assume FY 2004 rates are unchanged from FY 2003.

What is Neon Ltd's corporation tax payable?

A   £469,200

B   £471,000

C   £471,400

D   £483,000

53   The frequency with which CT61 returns (of income tax) are required to be completed by a company is most accurately described as:

A   Monthly

B   Quarterly

C   Annually

D   When requested by the Inland Revenue

54   Mutter plc makes up its accounts to 30 November each year. The following receipts and payments arose in the year to 30 November 2003.

25 March 2003	Received patent royalties of £15,600 from individual traders.
9 June 2003	Made a Gift Aid payment to the local cathedral - £780.
30 November 2003	Paid annual interest on £100,000 5% debenture stock. (All the debenture holders were private individuals.)

What is the income tax available for set-off against Mutter plc's corporation tax liability?

A   £2,010

B   £2,830

C   £3,400

D   £4,400

55   Sage Ltd has the following results for the eight months ended 31 December 2003.

	£
Schedule D Case I profit	720,000
Schedule D Case III	6,000
Chargeable gain (after indexation)	8,900
Gift Aid to Save the Children Fund paid gross	20,000
Dividends paid to ordinary shareholders December 2003	17,980
Dividends received from UK companies August 2003	32,040

What are Sage Ltd's profits for determining the rate of corporation tax payable?

A   £714,900

B   £715,650

C   £750,500

D   £754,950

56 For the six months ended 30 September 2003, Hilley Ltd, a trading company, has trading income chargeable to corporation tax of £209,000 after adjusting where necessary for the following items of income and expenditure.

	£
Income	
Local Authority Stock interest accrued and received (gross)	3,000
Dividends from UK companies (amounts received on 1 September 2003)	42,129
Expenditure	
Patent royalties paid to individuals (gross)	1,000
Gift Aid (gross)	300
Dividends paid	
Final dividend for six months ended 30 September 2003 (paid on 18 December 2003)	67,580

What is the amount of corporation tax payable on 1 July 2004?

A £52,061

B £52,441

C £53,165

D £53,448

57 Manston Ltd has always prepared accounts to 31 May each year. It was decided to change the accounting date and accounts were prepared to 31 December 2003. Figures for the last two accounting periods were as follows.

	Year ended 31 May 2003 £	Period ended 31 December 2003 £
Schedule D Case I	39,000	-
Adjusted trading loss	-	(36,000)
Schedule D Case III	6,000	6,000
Gift Aid paid (gross)	500	500

The company will claim all available reliefs at the earliest opportunity.

The profits chargeable to corporation tax for the year ended 31 May 2003 are:

A £8,500

B £13,000

C £14,500

D £15,000

58   Wombourne Ltd has incurred an adjusted trading loss in its accounting period for the 12 months ended 31 December 2003. It wishes to make a claim under S393A ICTA88 to carry back the loss against the taxable profits of an earlier year.

The latest date for making the claim is:

A   31 December 2004

B   31 December 2005

C   31 December 2008

D   31 December 2009

59   Schott Ltd has had the following profits and (losses) since it began trading on 1 April 1999.

	Sch D Case I profit(loss) £	Sch D Case III £	Patent royalties paid (gross) £
12 m/e 31.12.99	10,000	3,000	-
12 m/e 31.12.00	20,000	3,000	2,000
12 m/e 31.12.01	25,000	3,000	2,000
9 m/e 30.09.02	6,000	2,250	2,000
12 m/e 30.09.03	(73,000)	4,000	-

The patent royalties were paid on 31 March each year and the loss for the year ended 30 September 2003 requires no adjustment.

What is the total amount carried forward on 30 September 2003 assuming all possible claims are made against total profits?

A   £12,500

B   £54,750

C   £56,250

D   £62,750

60   Gray Ltd commenced trading on 1 January 2002. Its results since then have been as follows.

	Year ended 31 December 2002 £	Six months to 30 June 2003 £
Trading profit/(loss)	100,000	(150,000)
Schedule D Case III	20,000	10,000
Gift Aid paid	2,000	1,000

Assuming that Gray Ltd claims relief under S393A for its loss to be relieved against total profits, what is the total amount carried forward at 30 June 2003 to be set-off against future trading income?

A   £20,000

B   £21,000

C   £23,000

D   £140,000

61 What is the latest date by which a claim for loss relief under S393A ICTA88 must be made in respect of a loss suffered in the year ended 31 December 2003?

A 31 December 2005

B 5 April 2006

C 31 December 2009

D 5 April 2010

62 Jay Ltd had no unrelieved losses brought forward at 1 October 2002. Its results since then have been as follows.

	Year ended 30 September 2003 £	Nine months to 30 June 2004 £
Schedule D I profit/(loss)	60,000	(250,000)
Schedule D Case III	20,000	10,000
Gift Aid paid	3,000	2,000

Assuming that Jay Ltd claims relief for its losses as early as possible, what is the total amount carried forward at 30 June 2004 to be set-off against future trading income?

A Nil

B £70,000

C £160,000

D £180,000

63 Sims plc has had the following results.

	Year ended 31 December		
	2001 £	2002 £	2003 £
Schedule D I profit/(loss)	54,000	(116,000)	59,000
Schedule D III	2,000	2,000	4,000
Patent royalties paid (gross)	(3,000)	(3,000)	-

The royalties are paid each year on 31 March. From 1 April 2002 patent royalties payable have been correctly treated as a trading expense.

Assuming losses are relieved as early as possible, profits chargeable to corporation tax in the year ended 31 December 2003 will be:

A £2,000

B £9,000

C £4,000

D Nil

64   Saul Ltd has had the following results.

	Year ended 30 June	
	2003	*2004*
	£	£
Schedule D I profit/(loss)	16,000	(59,000)
Schedule D III	7,000	14,000
Gift Aid to Oxfam	(2,000)	(2,000)

What are the total amounts unrelieved that may be carried forward at 1 July 2004 assuming losses are relieved as early as possible?

A   £44,000

B   £42,000

C   £22,000

D   £13,000

65   Yardley plc changed its accounting date to 30 June 2004, having previously made up its accounts to 31 December. The company incurred a trading loss in the six month period.

What is the earliest date to which these losses may be carried back under the loss relief provisions?

A   1 July 2000

B   1 January 2001

C   1 January 2003

D   1 July 2003

66   Tunbridge Ltd, a company with 10 associated companies, commenced trading on 1 January 2001 and had the following results.

Year ended 31 December	*2001*	*2002*	*2003*
	£	£	£
Schedule D Case I profit/(loss)	3,000	(10,000)	500
Schedule D Case III	1,500	2,000	1,000

The company claims relief for the loss sustained in y/e 31 December 2002 as early as possible.

What is the unused loss carried forward at 31 December 2003?

A   £3,000

B   £3,500

C   £7,000

D   £8,000

67   Smith Ltd has unrelieved trading losses at 1 January 2003 of £20,000. Its corporation tax computation for the year ended 31 December 2003 shows the following.

	£
Schedule D Case I	14,000
Schedule D Case III	1,000
Gift Aid paid	(2,000)

How much of the loss brought forward will be utilised in the period?

A   £12,000

B   £13,000

C   £14,000

D   £15,000

68   Chip Ltd had trading losses brought forward at 1 January 2003 of £110,000. Its corporation tax computation for the year ended 31 December 2003 shows the following.

	£
Schedule D Case I profits	90,000
Schedule D Case III	10,000
Dividends from UK companies (inclusive of related tax credit)	20,000
Chargeable gains	5,000
Gift Aid paid	3,000

The amount of the trading loss which will be carried forward at 1 January 2004 is:

A   £2,000

B   £5,000

C   £10,000

D   £20,000

69   Heel Ltd, which started trading on 1 January 2002, has suffered a trading loss in its year ended 31 December 2003. The company wishes to claim under S393A ICTA88 to carry back the loss to the previous year ended 31 December 2002.

By what date should the claim be made?

A   31 December 2004

B   31 December 2005

C   31 December 2008

D   31 December 2009

70   Brass Taps Ltd submits its CT return for the year to 31 October 2002 on 1 October 2003.

Until what date must the company retain all records used to complete that return?

A   30 September 2004

B   30 September 2005

C   31 October 2005

D   31 October 2008

71   Portly plc (established in 1980) had total profits chargeable to corporation tax as follows for its year ended 31 December 2003.

	£
Schedule D Case I	1,800,000
Patent royalties received net (312,000 × $^{100}/_{78}$)	400,000
	2,200,000

The patent rights were held as an investment and the gross equivalent of the amount received equals the amount accrued for the period.

How much corporation tax is payable on 14 April 2004?

A   £572,000

B   £165,000

C   £143,000

D   £125,840

72   Rita works for Penton Ltd and receives an allowance of £2,500 on condition that it is spent on entertaining customers. In addition to the allowance Penton Ltd reimbursed Rita £1,700 for other expenditure on customer entertaining.

How much may Penton Ltd deduct in arriving at its taxable profit, and on what amount will Rita be assessed?

A   Penton Ltd £2,500   Rita £2,500

B   Penton Ltd £1,700   Rita £1,700

C   Penton Ltd Nil   Rita £4,200

D   Penton Ltd Nil   Rita Nil

73   Joseph is a director of Weston Ltd and has the sole use of a 3-litre motor car, which was bought a year ago for a list price of £19,000. The car has a carbon dioxide emission rating of 277 gms/km.

During the year ended 5 April 2004 Joseph's total mileage in the car was 16,000 of which 14,500 miles were for private purposes. All expenses including petrol relating to the car were paid by the company.

What is Joseph's assessable benefit for 2003/04?

A   £11,690

B   £8,820

C   £7,950

D   £6,650

74   Joshua is an employee of Mumbles plc, earning £12,000 per annum. He received the following benefits in the year ended 5 April 2004.

	£
Luncheon vouchers (£1 per day for 240 days a year)	240
Expenditure on company credit card	
Annual subscription	25
Goods purchased for own use	272

What are Joshua's taxable benefits in 2003/04?

A   £476

B   £501

C   £512

D   £537

75   Cushing is employed at a salary of £11,640 by Hammer Ltd. The following details are provided for 2003/04.

	£
Employer's contribution to company pension scheme	840
Company car – taxable benefit	2,140
Repair to company car paid for by Hammer Ltd	300
Professional subscription paid by Hammer Ltd	85

What is Cushing's 2003/04 assessable employment income net of any allowable expenses?

A   £13,780

B   £13,865

C   £14,080

D   £14,620

76   Albert, who has been employed by Roberts Tools Ltd as a part-time salesman for several years, earned a salary of £6,800 in 2003/04 and had the use of a two year old 1,100cc car with an original list price of £6,160 and an emission rating of 172 gms/km. He drives 1,000 miles each month on his employer's business. No private petrol was paid for.

Albert was also given an expense allowance of £80 each month to cover incidental costs of travelling. At the end of the tax year he calculated that, of this, £750 would be allowable for tax purposes.

The amount assessable on Albert in respect of benefits for 2003/04 was:

A   Nil

B   £1,319

C   £1,884

D   £2,069

77   A company gives luncheon vouchers of 60p per working day to its employees earning less than £8,500 per annum.

How much may the company deduct in arriving at its profit, and on what amount will the employee be assessed?

A   Company 60p; employee 45p

B   Company 60p; employee 60p

C   Company 45p; employee 45p

D   Company 45p; employee 60p

78   In the year to 5 April 2004 Roger Brown, a director of Brown Ltd, received director's fees of £18,000 together with a bonus of £15,000 paid in September 2003. Roger pays Class I National Insurance contributions at the contracted-out rate.

What are Roger's primary Class I National Insurance contributions for the year to 5 April 2004?

A   £1,488.52

B   £1,729.70

C   £2,485.37

D   £2,916.35

79   Luke is an employee of Walton Ltd. During the year to 5 April 2004 he received a gross salary of £23,000 and BUPA private medical insurance was paid on his behalf, totalling £800.

Luke has private use of a 1,000cc one-year old company car which cost £7,200 two years ago and has an emission rating of 148 gms/km. The company pays for all petrol. No business miles are travelled.

On what amount are Luke's primary Class I National Insurance contributions computed for 2003/04?

A   £23,000

B   £24,080

C   £24,880

D   £27,120

80   Nomatat Ltd purchased an antique table for £8,200 in February 1992. In September 2003 the company sold it for £5,200 at an auction and incurred selling costs of £150.

Indexation allowance based on £8,200 is £3,900.

What is the company's allowable loss?

A   £2,350

B   £3,150

C   £6,250

D   £7,050

81   Which of the following investment assets could give rise to a chargeable gain?

A   Krugerrand

B   Gold sovereign minted in 1840

C   9% Treasury Loan 2002

D   1912 vintage car

82   Which of the following disposals will not give rise to a capital gains tax charge?

A   Sale of a diamond brooch

B   Sale of a thoroughbred racehorse

C   Grant of a lease with a term of 25 years

D   Sale of an antique table

83   Spock plc purchased shares in Bones plc on 4 March 1985. On 30 May 2003 Bones plc announced a rights issue and on that date sent provisional letters of allotment to its shareholders. The rights had to be taken up by 4 July 2003 and Spock plc paid for them on 20 June 2003.

From what date will indexation run on the amount paid for the rights issue?

A   March 1985

B   May 2003

C   June 2003

D   July 2003

84   Jonathan Ltd had the following transactions in Swift Ltd shares.

18 July 1980	bought 400 shares for £320
21 July 1998	bought 400 shares for £360
23 July 2003	bought 500 shares for £410
25 July 2003	sold 200 shares for £200

With which acquisition will the shares sold on 25 July 2003 be matched?

A   Acquisition on 18 July 1980

B   Acquisition on 21 July 1998

C   Acquisition on 23 July 2003

D   A pool of the shares acquired in 1998 and 2003

85   Comfy Homes Ltd owns the following securities as investments.

(1)   2% Indexed Linked Treasury Stock 2006
(2)   9% Debentures in Cableway plc
(3)   Ordinary shares in BG plc

Which of these investments is exempt from a charge to tax under the capital gains rules?

A   All of them

B   (1) and (2) only

C   (1) and (3) only

D   (2) and (3) only

86   Abraham Derby (Jugs) Ltd prepares accounts to 31 December and sold a business asset in March 2003 for £200,000 realising a gain after indexation of £50,000.

The company bought the following assets for use in its business.

October 2002	Land	£10,000
June 2003	Earth Mover	£180,000
February 2004	Weighbridge	£160,000

How much of the gain will be included in PCTCT for the year to 31 December 2003 assuming all possible claims are made in good time?

A   Nil

B   £20,000

C   £30,000

D   £50,000

87 In September 2003 a company sold a freehold building for £80,000, giving rise to an indexed gain of £44,300. In August 2003 the company had purchased another building for £72,000.

How much of the gain can be rolled over?

A   Nil

B   £36,300

C   £39,870

D   £44,300

88 On 1 September 2003 a company disposed of a freehold property used exclusively for its trade.

The period during which reinvestment of the proceeds should take place in order for capital gains rollover relief to be obtained is:

A   1 April 2002 to 31 March 2006

B   1 April 2003 to 31 March 2007

C   1 September 2000 to 31 August 2004

D   1 September 2002 to 31 August 2006

89 Basil Bond Ltd sold one of the hotels which it had been using within its business on 17 July 2003. The company wishes to claim rollover relief if possible. It purchased the following assets for use within its business.

5 May 2002	Aeroplane
9 March 2003	Fork life truck
10 July 2005	99 year lease on an amusement arcade
20 August 2006	Freehold shop

Against which purchase may it claim rollover relief?

A   Aeroplane

B   Fork lift truck

C   Lease

D   Shop

90 Conway Ltd sent taxable goods to Payne Ltd on a sale or return basis. The goods were despatched on 1 July 2003 and Payne Ltd accepted them on 30 September 2003. A tax invoice was issued on 3 October 2003 which was settled by Payne Ltd on 5 November 2003.

What is the tax point for this transaction?

A   30 September 2003

B   3 October 2003

C   5 November 2003

D   1 July 2004

With reference to the following information answer questions 91 and 92.

On 30 April 2003 Sparks Ltd ordered a new printing machine and on 16 May 2003 paid a deposit of £10,000. The machine was despatched to Sparks Ltd on 31 May 2003. On 13 June 2003 an invoice was issued to Sparks Ltd for the balance due of £45,000. This was paid on 20 June 2003.

91 What is the tax point for the £10,000 deposit?

    A   30 April 2003

    B   16 May 2003

    C   31 May 2003

    D   13 June 2003

92 What is the tax point on the balance of £45,000?

    A   16 May 2003

    B   31 May 2003

    C   13 June 2003

    D   20 June 2003

93 A taxable person supplying goods under £100 (including VAT) direct to the general public need only issue a tax invoice if requested. This invoice need only show a limited amount of information.

Which one of the following must be shown upon the invoice?

    A   The customer's name and address

    B   An identifying number

    C   The rate of VAT in force at the time of the supply

    D   The VAT payable

94 Mr Arnold, a manufacturer, sells a machine to Mr Big for £10,500 (VAT exclusive) and offers a 2.5% cash discount for payment in seven days. Mr Big pays 28 days later.

For how much VAT output tax should Mr Arnold account?

    A   £1,524.73

    B   £1,563.83

    C   £1,791.56

    D   £1,837.50

95 The following is the structure of the Romney group.

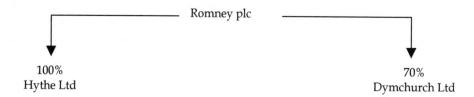

The other 30% of Dymchurch Ltd is owned by Dover Ltd, an unrelated company. For the year to 31 March 2004 Romney plc has profits of £100,000 and Dymchurch has a trading loss of £80,000.

Provided the election is made, Romney plc's maximum claim for Dymchurch Ltd's loss is:

A   Nil

B   £56,000

C   £70,000

D   £80,000

96 Risca plc holds the following ordinary shares in Shotts Ltd.

80 of the 100 'A' shares
60 of the 100 non-voting 'B' shares

Both classes of shares have equal claims to the profits of Shotts Ltd.

Shotts Ltd is the registered holder of only 70% of the share capital of Tarbet Ltd.

What is Risca plc's deemed holding in Tarbet Ltd for group relief purposes?

A   80%

B   70%

C   56%

D   49%

97 Rustic Ltd has the following results for the year ended 30 September 2004.

Trading loss	£15,000
Gift Aid	£2,000
Capital loss	£4,000

What is the maximum loss that could be surrendered for group relief?

A   £15,000

B   £17,000

C   £19,000

D   £21,000

98   The following is the group structure of the Herbs group. Each company in the group is shown together with its trading profit or loss for the year ended 31 December 2004.

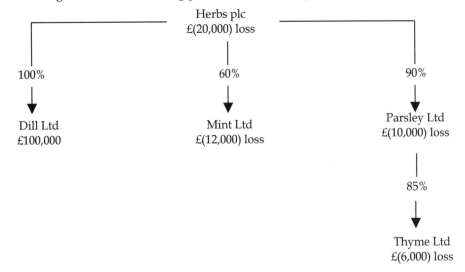

What is the maximum loss that may be surrendered to Dill Ltd for the year ended 31 December 2004?

A   £48,000

B   £36,000

C   £30,000

D   £20,000

99   Big plc, which makes up its accounts to 31 December, has a wholly-owned subsidiary, Small Ltd. Small Ltd incurred a loss of £8,000 in the year to 31 December 2004. In that year Big plc had profits chargeable to corporation tax of £6,000.

By what date must a claim for group relief be made and what is the maximum surrender?

A   31 December 2006   £8,000

B   31 December 2006   £6,000

C   31 December 2010   £8,000

D   31 December 2010   £6,000

100   Albion Ltd, a 75% subsidiary of Rovers Ltd, has the following results for the year ended 31 December 2004.

Schedule D Case I profit	£30,000
Gift Aid paid	£(2,000)

The company also has trading losses brought forward of £5,000.

What is the maximum loss which could be surrendered by Rovers Ltd to Albion Ltd?

A   £30,000

B   £28,000

C   £25,000

D   £23,000

101   Dingle Ltd has the following results.

	£
Trading loss brought forward at 1 April 2002	(5,000)
Year ended 31 March 2003	
Schedule D Case I	13,000
Year ended 31 March 2004	
Trading loss	(10,000)

The company will claim £6,000 group relief in the year ended 31 March 2003. It also wishes to utilise as much as possible of the loss sustained in the year ended 31 March 2004 under S393A ICTA88.

What is the maximum amount of the loss that can be carried back to the year ended 31 March 2003 after all other reliefs?

A   £10,000

B   £8,000

C   £2,000

D   £1,000

102   Rangers Ltd, a member of a 75% group, has the following results for the year ended 30 June 2004.

Schedule D Case I loss	£(20,000)
Schedule D Case III	£8,000
Gift Aid paid	£(1,000)

What is the maximum loss that Rangers Ltd can surrender to another company in the same group?

A   £12,000

B   £17,000

C   £20,000

D   £21,000

103   Martin Ltd is the 100% subsidiary of Aston Ltd. The following are results for the year ended 31 March 2004.

	Aston Ltd £	Martin Ltd £
Schedule D Case I losses	(100,000)	(5,000)
Non-trading income	20,000	27,000

Which of the following statements are correct?

(1)   Aston Ltd could surrender a maximum of £80,000 as group relief.
(2)   Aston Ltd could surrender a maximum of £100,000 as group relief.
(3)   Martin Ltd could claim maximum group relief of £22,000.
(4)   Martin Ltd could claim maximum group relief of £27,000.

A   (1) and (3)

B   (1) and (4)

C   (2) and (3)

D   (2) and (4)

104   Shutters plc, a member of a 75% group, has the following results for the year ended 31 December 2004.

Schedule D Case I profit	£14,000
Schedule D Case III income	£3,000
Gift Aid paid	£(2,000)

There are trading losses brought forward of £6,000.

What is the maximum amount of group relief that may be surrendered to Shutters plc from another group company in the year ended 31 December 2004?

A   £9,000

B   £11,000

C   £15,000

D   £17,000

105   Group relief is available between two companies which are members of the same group of companies. For this purpose one company must be the 75% subsidiary of the other or both must be 75% subsidiaries of a third company.

The 75% subsidiary relationship requires:

A   A holding of more than 75% of the ordinary share capital

B   A holding of not less than 75% of the issued share capital

C   A holding of not less than 75% of the ordinary share capital

D   A holding of more than 75% of the issued share capital

106 Walk Ltd and Run Ltd are members of the same gains group for corporation tax purposes.

Walk Ltd purchased a chargeable asset some years ago for £25,000. On 30 June 2004 it sells the asset to Run Ltd for £50,000.

The disposal by Walk Ltd will be treated as if made as 'no gain/no loss':

A Automatically, no claim being required

B Provided a claim is made within two years of the end of the accounting period in which the transfer takes place

C Provided a claim is made within six years of the end of the accounting period in which the transfer takes place

D Provided a claim is made within six years of the date of the transfer of the asset

107 Harrow plc acquired all the share capital of Seeds Ltd in 1982. In June 1990 Harrow plc purchased a freehold building for £60,000, and in February 1997 transferred it to Seeds Ltd. At the time of the transfer the market value of the building was £80,000.

In March 2004 Harrow plc sold Seeds Ltd to Milton plc, a non-group company. The market value of the building at the time of the transfer was £120,000.

Ignoring indexation, what is the chargeable gain that arises in respect of the building as a result of Harrow plc's disposal of Seeds Ltd?

A Nil

B £20,000

C £40,000

D £60,000

108 Consider the following group structure.

A Ltd

|

75%

|

B Ltd

|

80%

|

C Ltd

A chargeable asset was transferred from A Ltd to C Ltd on 15 December 2003. B Ltd sold its 80% shareholding in C Ltd on 30 June 2004.

All companies prepare accounts to 31 December annually.

When does the chargeable gain relating to the December 2003 transfer accrue, and in which company?

A On 15 December 2003 in A Ltd

B On 15 December 2003 in C Ltd

C On 30 June 2004 in A Ltd

D On 1 January 2004 in C Ltd

Objective Test Questions (Pilot Paper)

109 J Ltd, a manufacturing company which is registered for VAT, seconds a trainee accountant to an accounting firm, sending the firm an invoice for the exact cost of the trainee's salary.

For VAT purposes, the supply of the trainee's services to the accounting firm is:

A   exempt

B   zero-rated

C   standard-rated at 17.5%

D   outside the scope of VAT.

110 SD Ltd, a retail clothes shop, prepares accounts to 31 December each year. The accounts to 31 December 2003 show that a Jaguar car was sold for £13,000 and the following assets were bought:

		£
14 January 2003	New general lighting	1,200
18 January 2003	New shop front	900
4 July 2003	New computer	5,500

The tax written-down values at 1 January 2003 were:

	£
General pool	8,300
Jaguar car	27,000

The company's maximum capital allowances for the year ended 31 December 2003 are:

A   £10,575

B   £21,575

C   £22,055

D   £22,415

111 The entertainment account of S Ltd showed:

	£
Staff tennis outing for 30 employees	1,800
2,000 tee shirts with firm's logo given to race runners	4,500
Advertising and sponsorship of an athletic event	2,000
Entertaining customers	7,300
Staff Christmas party (30 employees)	2,400

The amount to be added back in arriving at the taxable profits is:

A   £7,300

B   £11,800

C   £16,300

D   £21,100

112 The form used to report the benefits of employees earning over £8,500 per annum under the PAYE system is:

A P9D

B P11D

C P45

D P60

113 BD Ltd is a building company which insists on being paid before starting a contract for a particular customer. It issued an invoice for the full amount on 1 September 2004, received half the amount on 9 September 2004 and the balance on 14 September. It started the work on 20 September 2004 and finished it on 1 October 2004.

The correct VAT tax point is:

A 1 September 2004

B 9 September 2004

C 14 September 2004

D 1 October 2004

114 M Ltd, a large company, has a corporation tax liability of £640,000 in respect of its accounting year to 31 March 2004.

On which date will the company be required to pay the final quarterly instalment of the liability?

A 14 April 2004

B 14 July 2004

C 31 April 2004

D 1 October 2004

115 A company with an accounting year to 30 September 2003 does not submit its CT600 corporation tax self-assessment return until 30 November 2004.

What is the latest date by which the Inland Revenue can normally open an enquiry into the return?

A 30 September 2005

B 30 November 2005

C 31 December 2005

D 31 January 2006

Objective Test Questions (May 2001)

116   When a company engages a new employee who is unable to produce a P45, the company must get the employee to complete which ONE of the following:

A   P35

B   P11D

C   P14

D   P46

117   On 1 September 2003 A Ltd places an order with B Ltd for a machine costing £12,000 exclusive of value added tax (VAT) for delivery before 30 September 2003. B Ltd completes the machine on 28 September but does not deliver it to A Ltd until 2 October 2003. A Ltd pays the full amount due (including VAT) into B Ltd's bank account by direct transfer on 7 October 2003 and B Ltd issues a VAT invoice on 18 October 2003.

The VAT tax point is:

A   1 September 2003

B   2 October 2003

C   7 October 2003

D   18 October 2003

118   CCD Ltd, a company which is liable to pay its corporation tax (CT) by quarterly instalments, has an estimated CT liability of £800,000 for its eight month chargeable accounting period ended 31 August 2003. Prior to this period, the company had made up accounts annually at 31 December.

The amount of the company's FINAL QUARTERLY instalment will be

A   £144,000

B   £200,000

C   £216,000

D   £300,000

119   A company, dealing only in standard rated goods for VAT purposes, started trading on 1 April 2003. Its MONTHLY turnover was as follows:

For first six months	£6,500
For second six months	£9,000
For third six months	£10,000

The company will require to be registered for VAT by

A   1 December 2003

B   1 January 2004

C   1 February 2004

D   2 March 2004

120   A company has been making up its accounts annually to 31 May for many years. For the year ended 31 May 2002 it did not submit its Corporation Tax Annual Return (CT600) until 30 November 2003.

What is the latest date by which the Inland Revenue can commence an enquiry into the company's Return?

A   31 May 2004

B   30 November 2004

C   31 December 2004

D   31 January 2005

121   An unmarried employee aged 35, who pays tax at the basic rate of 22% was provided with the following benefits at 6 April 2003:

1   The use of a one year old motor car which had a list price of £10,000 when new and a carbon dioxide emission rating of 199 gms/km. ALL of the private fuel was paid for by the employee.

2   The exclusive use of a TV system which cost the employer £3,000.

You establish that the employee pays an annual subscription of £300 to her professional body and that she has unpaid tax of £110 from the year 2002/2003 which will be collected through the PAYE system during 2003/2004.

Her code number for PAYE purposes for 2003/2004 will be

A   138L

B   K101

C   154L

D   151L

Note that the personal allowance for the tax year 2003/2004 is £4,615.

122   T Ltd, a company with no associated companies, had chargeable profits of £30,000 for its twelve month accounting period ended 31 December 2003.

Its corporation tax liability for the year will be:

A   £4,750

B   £4,938

C   £5,700

D   £5,775

Objective Test Questions (November 2001)

123   Class 1A National Insurance Contributions in respect of 2003/2004 must be paid by:

A   19 May 2004

B   5 July 2004

C   19 July 2004

D   31 July 2004

124   Shortly after the end of each income tax year, an employer must give every employee the Form

A   P14

B   P35

C   P45

D   P60

125   A company incurred the following legal fees during its year ended 31 March 2004 and these had all been charged in the Profit and Loss Account:

	£
Defending an action against the company for poor workmanship	2,800
Drawing up employees' service contracts	1,600
Making an appeal to the High Court against a CT assessment	6,500
Defending a charge of breach of the Health and Safety regulations (the company was found guilty)	800
Cost to obtain planning permission concerning an extension to a building	1,200

The amount which should be added back in arriving at the company's adjusted Schedule D Case I profit is

A   £4,800

B   £7,300

C   £8,500

D   £11,300

126   H Ltd, a UK company with no associated companies, has chargeable profits for its accounting period of twelve months ended 31 December 2003 amounting to £36,000.

It will be required to pay CT of

A   £4,500

B   £5,130

C   £6,175

D   £6,840

127   In relation to VAT, it is possible for companies in a group to make an election to have all of the companies in a single VAT registration.

Companies should be advised to exclude from the group registration companies making

A   wholly zero-rated supplies.

B   wholly standard-rated supplies.

C   wholly exempt supplies.

D   10% standard-rated supplies and 90% exempt supplies.

128   Q Ltd will be a large company for quarterly payment purposes and its total CT liability for its **nine-month** accounting period to 31 December 2003 was £240,000.

The company's **final** quarterly instalment will be payable on

A   14 July 2003

B   14 October 2003

C   14 January 2004

D   14 April 2004

129   IT Ltd is a UK company with no associates and it makes up accounts annually at 31 March. Its turnover has never exceeded £1,000,000 and it has twelve employees. It has the following balances for capital allowances purposes brought forward at 1 April 2003.

	£
Plant	90,000
Expensive car	18,000

During the year ended 31 March 2004, a motor car which had originally cost £8,000 was sold for £3,000 and a computer system was bought for £25,000.

The maximum capital allowances which the company may claim for the year ended 31 March 2004 are

A   £34,750

B   £48,500

C   £49,750

D   £51,250

Questions

Adjustment of profits

Question 1

C Ltd (May 2000)

You are the chief accountant of C Ltd, a company which owns a number of hotels, bars and restaurants.

You have been asked to attend a board meeting to advise the directors on the taxation implications of a number of transactions which have taken place during the recently-completed financial year.

Each of the costs and income items noted below have been reflected as revenue items in the company's profit and loss account for the year.

(a)   The company had been negotiating to buy a hotel in the north of England and had incurred valuation fees of £8,000 and solicitors' fees of £5,000. The proposed purchase was abandoned.

(b)   A major refurbishment of a number of hotels was undertaken and this was funded by means of a bank loan. To secure this loan, a full valuation of the company's assets was required, and this cost £60,000.

(c)   Legal fees to draw up the loan agreement were £15,000, and a finder's fee of £5,000 was paid to AB & Co.

(d)   A firm of accountants was engaged to prepare a report on a group of companies which C Ltd wishes to acquire. The firm's fees amounted to £45,000.

(e)   The purchase of the appropriate share capital of the companies in this group went ahead, and legal and accountancy fees of £38,000 were incurred.

(f)   The group taken over included two restaurants which were unsuitable. One was sold, incurring legal costs of £5,000, and the other was leased. The cost of setting up the lease was £3,000.

(g)   In order to build up cash to finance further future acquisitions, the company raised £5,000,000 by means of a rights issue, incurring professional fees of £380,000.

(h)   In the previous accounting period, a fire had seriously damaged a major hotel and the repairs cost £160,000. This had been charged in last year's accounts and had been allowed as a deduction in arriving at the trading profit. There was a protracted dispute with the insurers who finally paid during the current accounting period a sum of £140,000. This amount was credited to the profit and loss account.

Required

Write brief notes on EACH of the above transactions in preparation for the meeting. Your notes should explain, with reasons, how each item would be dealt with in arriving at the adjusted trading profit, bearing in mind that they are all already reflected in the net profit figure shown in the accounts. Where any of the transactions have additional taxation implications, these should be explained.

(Total : 20 marks)

Question 2

K Ltd (November 2001)

The following items appear in the Profit and Loss Account of K Ltd, a UK manufacturing company, for the year ended 31 March 2004.

EXPENDITURE

(1)   Loan interest of £20,000 was paid on money borrowed to acquire a controlling interest in a company engaged in the same trade as K Ltd.

(2)   £28,000 was spent on installing a roof on a recently-acquired warehouse which had been badly damaged in a fire prior to its acquisition by K Ltd.

(3)   Debenture interest of £50,000 gross was paid in respect of debentures issued during the year to raise funds to construct additional business premises. Legal fees of £18,000 were incurred in connection with the debenture issue.

(4)   Damages of £60,000 were paid to a potential customer who was injured during a visit to one of the company's factories. A metal beam fell from a roof and struck him.

(5)   A management charge of £55,000 was made by K Ltd's parent company in respect of the salary cost of a senior manager of the parent company who worked for nine months at K Ltd's premises engaged solely on contracts completed by K Ltd.

INCOME

(1)   K Ltd's premises suffered damage as a result of flooding during its year ended 31 March 2003. The company paid the repair costs during that year and these were allowed as a deduction in arriving at the Schedule D Case I profit figures. In May 2003, the company received £45,000 from its insurers comprising £40,000 in respect of damage to its business premises and £5,000 in respect of damages to property which it let to a supplier. The £45,000 was credited to the profit and loss account for the year ended 31 March 2004.

(2)   Interest of £8,000 (gross) was received in respect of a loan made to a supplier.

Required

State how each of the above items would be dealt with in arriving at the adjusted Schedule D Case I profit for the year ended 31 March 2004, explaining clearly your reasons for your treatment of each item. You must state whether the item would be **added** to the reported profit figure or **subtracted** from it, or whether **no action** is required.

In respect of those items on which action is required, you should indicate the subsequent taxation treatment of each item. **(20 marks)**

Capital allowances on plant and machinery

Question 3

Expenditure on a building (May 1996)

Your company is involved in the retail trade and is undertaking a feasibility study on proposals for a major rebuilding and refurbishing programme involving a number of locations.

Required

(a)   Discuss how the UK tax system provides relief for the various types of likely expenditure and mention the situations where no relief may be available.   **(6 marks)**

(b)   To help evaluate the extent to which the various elements of expenditure will qualify as plant for capital allowances purposes, identify FOUR leading cases explaining the basic principles these established and comment on Revenue practice.   **(14 marks)**

(Total : 20 marks)

Question 4

D Ltd (November 1998)

D Ltd commenced a trade of tool manufacturing on 1 October 2000. The company chose a 31 December accounting date preparing their first accounts to 31 December 2001.

The business was initially successful but faced increasing foreign competition as the pound sterling strengthened against the euro. Eventually the members decided to cease trading and passed a voluntary winding-up resolution on 30 April 2004. Trade ceased on that date.

The business has always been 'small' for capital allowance purposes.

The following purchases and sales of capital items took place.

Purchases		£
September 2000	Car for managing director	26,000
	General plant and equipment	160,000
August 2001	Two lorries (£25,000 each)	50,000
November 2001	Car for salesman	11,000
	Plant	20,000
July 2002	New car for MD	32,000
April 2003	Computer equipment	65,000
Sales		
January 2002	Plant (costing £16,000)	18,000
July 2002	MD's car	21,000
April 2004	Gift of car to salesman (MV £6,800)	-
July 2004	Net auction proceeds of:	
	MD's car	18,000
	Plant and lorries	46,000
	Computer	20,000

Required

Compute the maximum capital allowances for each accounting period.   **(Total : 20 marks)**

Industrial buildings allowance

Question 5 (November 1998)

R Ltd

R Ltd, a UK-resident manufacturing company, making up accounts each year to 31 March, provides the following information in respect of its various premises used in its trade.

Factory A

This was purchased new on 1 April 1978 for £80,000.

Factory B

This was acquired second-hand on 1 April 1994 for £60,000. The seller had bought it new on 1 April 1988 at a cost of £50,000.

Factory C

This was purchased new on 10 July 2003, the cost comprising:

	£
Land	25,000
Preparing site	10,000
Factory building	100,000
Office facilities	25,000

Factory D

This had been purchased on 1 April 2002 in an Enterprise Zone for £120,000. In the year to 31 March 2003, R Ltd had claimed allowances of £60,000: the company now wishes to claim the maximum possible in the year to 31 March 2004.

Factory E

On 31 March 2004, R Ltd sold this factory for £90,000. It had been bought on 1 April 1993 for £70,000. The factory had been used for non-qualifying purposes from 1 April 2000 to 31 March 2003 but reverted to industrial use on 1 April 2003.

Note: This is a building on which there was a 20% initial allowance available at the date of purchase.

Required

(a)   Compute the Industrial Buildings Allowance (IBA) available to R Ltd for its year ended 31 March 2004 (net of any balancing charges arising).   **(16 marks)**

(b)   Advise the directors of the IBA position in regard to factories which they are considering leasing rather than buying.   **(4 marks)**

(Total : 20 marks)

Question 6 (November 1999)

JAY Ltd

JAY Ltd is an unquoted UK company which runs a number of fast food outlets based in city centres.

JAY Ltd prepares and packages much of the food sold through the outlets. Until December 2002 this work had been carried out in a rented factory owned by Bee Ltd, a company in the same trade. During 2002, Bee Ltd had run into financial difficulties and ceased trading in November 2002. JAY Ltd was able to acquire the factory on 1 January 2003 for £100,000. It was established that it had been bought new by Bee Ltd for £80,000 on 1 January 1997 and has been used for manufacturing purposes ever since. JAY Ltd was able to acquire, also on 1 January 2003, at a cost of £24,000, wrapping and processing machinery which was already installed in the factory.

JAY Ltd had been making up accounts each year to 31 December but, during 2003, the directors decided that a March year ending would be more appropriate. They therefore made up accounts for the 15 months to 31 March 2004.

The following capital transactions, in addition to those mentioned above, took place during that period.

Purchases		*Cost*
		£
Meat slicers	28 June 2003	2,500
	15 January 2004	6,000
Wrapping machine	2 February 2004	12,000
Delivery vehicles	5 July 2003	28,000
	10 March 2004	32,000
New shop front for recently acquired retail unit		
	12 August 2003	14,000
Motor cars for newly-appointed managers:		
VW Polo	12 September 2003	11,600
Lexus	1 January 2004	24,000
Sandwich making plant		
	10 February 2003	14,000

Disposals		*Proceeds*
		£
30 March 2003	Plant (original cost £12,000)	8,000
3 July 2003	Motor car (original cost £11,000)	6,000
3 January 2004	Expensive car (1)	14,000
The sandwich machine bought in February 2003 proved unreliable and was sold in February 2003 for		3,000

The sandwich machine should be treated in the most advantageous manner.

The balances brought forward for capital allowances purposes at 1 January 2003 were:

General pool	*Expensive car (1)*
£48,000	£9,000

Required

Compute the maximum capital allowances, including industrial buildings allowance (IBA), which may be claimed by JAY Ltd for EACH of the above accounting periods.

(Total : 20 marks)

Question 7

W Ltd (Pilot Paper)

W Ltd, a company engaged in the manufacture of machine tools, prepares its accounts annually at 31 March.

The following information relates to transactions during the year ended 31 March 2004.

During 2001 and 2002 the company invested heavily in plant and machinery, mainly to take advantage of the first-year allowances (FYA) available to it under the capital allowances system. This had resulted in a low pool value brought forward and the company has decided to sell plant which is now surplus to its requirements.

The various values brought forward at 1 April 2003 are:

General pool	*Expensive car (1)*	*Expensive car (2)*	*Precision lathe (short-life asset)*
£64,000	£22,000	£30,000	£18,000

The following transactions took place during the year ended 31 March 2004:

Disposals:
- Two items in the general pool were sold for a total of £85,000. In each case the selling price was less than the original cost.
- Expensive car (2) was sold for £22,000.
- The precision lathe, which had been de-pooled under the short-life asset (SLA) rules, was sold for £20,000.

Purchases:
- A new lorry was bought for £18,000.
- A motor car costing £11,000 was bought.
- A computer system was bought for £20,000. This could, if wished, be treated as a SLA.

The factory in which the trade is carried on was bought new on 1 April 1992 for £120,000 and an extension costing £40,000 was added on 1 April 1994. Neither of these payments had qualified for initial allowance. On 1 April 2003 the factory was sold for £100,000 and, on the same day, the company took occupation of a second-hand factory for which they paid £210,000. This factory had been bought by the original owners for £180,000 on 1 April 1993 and first used by them on that date.

The company is one which qualifies for 100% FYA where appropriate and if claimed.

Required

(a)   Calculate the maximum capital allowances (including industrial buildings allowances) which could be claimed by W Ltd in respect of the year ended 31 March 2004.

(14 marks)

(b)   State clearly how you have treated the purchases of the lorry and the computer system.

(2 marks)

(Total : 16 marks)

Note: There was originally a third part to this question (for 4 marks) but this concerned a transitional relief which is now spent.

Question 8

P Ltd (May 2001)

P Ltd is a UK resident company which operates a chain of fast food outlets. Until 31 December 2002 most of the food sold in the outlets was processed and packaged in rented factory premises. On 1 January 2003 the company acquired and immediately brought into industrial use a factory which had been owned by one of its competitors, B Ltd, which had gone into liquidation. The price paid was £180,000 which included a payment of £30,000 for machinery already installed in this factory. B Ltd had bought the factory new for £220,000 (excluding any machinery) and brought it into use on 1 January 1993.

P Ltd had the following additional transactions in assets during its year ended 31 December 2003:

Purchases during the year ended 31 December 2003		*Cost*
		£
30 January	3 Ford cars for managers @ £9,000 each	27,000
3 March	3 delivery vans	42,000
20 May	2 new packaging machines	30,000
	New computer hardware and software to operate packaging machines	12,000
31 October	New shop fronts for two of the retail outlets	10,000
	3 food processing machines	9,000
	A second hand Lexus car for a director	28,000

Disposals during the year ended 31 December 2003		*Sold for*
		£
20 April	4 packaging machines which had cost £12,000	5,000
	Original computer system purchased in March 2000 for £7,000 (treated as short life asset)	2,000
	The Mercedes car purchased in 1999 for £25,000	9,000
31 December	**All** of the inexpensive cars were sold for	35,000
	These were not replaced, the directors having decided that all such cars should, in future, be leased.	

The capital allowances tax written down values brought forward at 1 January 2003 were:

General pool	*Mercedes*	*Computer (SLA)*
£70,000	£13,000	£2,362

You establish that P Ltd's turnover has not exceeded £1.5 million; that its assets are valued at £750,000 and that its average number of employees is forty.

Required

(a) Compute the maximum capital allowances which may be claimed by P Ltd in respect of its year ended 31 December 2003. Explain clearly your treatment of the computer systems and the inexpensive cars. **(17 marks)**

(b) Describe the circumstances in which it may be more tax efficient to include in the general pool an asset which had been purchased and could otherwise be treated as a short life asset. **(3 marks)**

(Total : 20 marks)

Introduction to corporation tax – the computation of the CT liability

Question 9

PGD Ltd (November 1997)

PGD Ltd, a manufacturing company in the United Kingdom, which controls 70% of another UK company, CCD Ltd, produces a profit and loss account for its accounting year ended 30 September 2003 showing a net profit before taxation of £226,300, AFTER accounting for the following items:

	£	
Expenditure		
Debenture interest (gross)	12,000	Note 1
Loan interest (gross)	8,000	Note 2
Patent royalties (gross)	10,000	Note 3
Depreciation	11,000	
Income		
Loan interest receivable (gross)	6,000	Note 4
Rents receivable	7,000	Note 5
Insurance recovery	6,800	Note 6
Patent royalties received during year	30,000	Note 7
Franked investment income (FII) (including tax credits)	8,000	

Notes

1   This represents interest on debentures issued by PGD Ltd to several individuals in 2002 to provide funds to build a factory extension. The figure of £12,000 includes accrued interest of £3,000 (gross). Note that the interest is paid net.

2   This represents interest paid on a 10 year loan raised by PGD Ltd to purchase property which is currently let to another company. The interest is paid gross.

3   The figure for patent royalties includes an accrued amount of £2,000 (gross). The use of the patent commenced during the year so there was no opening accrual. The other £8,000 (gross) was paid in May 2003. The patent royalties are paid net and relate to a trading activity.

4   The loan interest receivable is in respect of a loan made by PGD Ltd to a supplier, and the figure of £6,000 includes an accrued amount of £1,500.

5   The rents receivable relate to the property let by PGD Ltd.

6   This represents an amount recovered from the company's insurers during the year in respect of goods destroyed in a fire last year. The cost of these goods was written off and allowed as an expense last year.

7   The patent royalties were paid to PGD Ltd by a partnership of individuals and were therefore paid net. The figure shown is the gross equivalent and is equal to the amount accrued for the period. The rights are held as an investment.

PGD Ltd had surplus ACT of £14,700 brought forward at 1 October 2002 and paid a dividend of £140,000 on 10 August 2003.

PGD Ltd had the following balances for capital allowances purposes brought forward at 1 October 2002:

	£
General pool	67,500
SLA (computer)	12,000
Expensive car	11,200

During the year the company sold plant for £9,400 (inclusive of VAT) which had cost £8,500 (exclusive of VAT). It also sold the computer for £4,700 (inclusive of VAT). Purchases during the year comprised electrical machinery costing £18,800 (inclusive of VAT) and a motor car costing £10,500.

Required

(a) Compute the maximum capital allowances which may be claimed by PGD Ltd for its chargeable accounting period to 30 September 2003. **(6 marks)**

(b) Using your answer at (a), compute the adjusted Schedule D Case I profit stating CLEARLY your treatment of any interest paid or received and the patent royalties paid. **(8 marks)**

(c) Compute the mainstream corporation tax (MCT) payable by PGD Ltd in respect of the above accounting period, showing CLEARLY your treatment of income tax and advance corporation tax (ACT). **(14 marks)**

(Total : 28 marks)

Question 10

K Ltd (May 1998)

K Ltd is a UK resident manufacturing company with a 100% subsidiary company, L Ltd. During its chargeable accounting period of 12 months to 31 March 2004, K Ltd had trading profits chargeable to corporation tax amounting to £80,000.

This figure had been arrived at after adding back £50,000 in respect of a loan to a supplier which had gone into liquidation, as it was unable to pay any of its debts. Interest of £2,000 had been received on this loan during the early part of the above period, and this is included in the figure of £80,000.

During the same period, L Ltd had chargeable profits of £220,000.

Required

(a) Describe the taxation treatment of the above items under the Loan Relationship rules. **(11 marks)**

(b) Advise the directors of K Ltd what action should be taken in this case. **(4 marks)**

(Total : 15 marks)

Further aspects of corporation tax

Question 11

WJ Ltd (May 1998)

WJ Ltd is a trading and manufacturing company in the United Kingdom with no associated companies. For many years, it has been making up accounts annually at 31 October. Shortly before October 2003, the directors decided to change the accounting date to the end of February and consequently made up one set of accounts for the period from 1 November 2002 to 29 February 2004.

The following information refers to this period.

		£
Income		
Trading profit (before capital allowances)		602,000
Capital gains:	31 August 2003	40,000
	20 December 2003	360,000
Rents receivable (annually in advance):	1 November 2002	17,000
	1 November 2003	21,000
Debenture interest received (gross) - 30 June 2003		10,000
Patent royalties received (gross) - 31 October 2003		24,000
Franked investment income (FII) (including tax credit) (received 15 Feb 2003)		20,000
Payments		
Gift Aid (gross) - 31 October 2003		8,000
Loan interest paid (gross) - 30 September 2003		15,000
Dividends paid:	31 January 2003	160,000
	31 January 2004	350,000

The debenture was issued by a UK company, has been held for several years, pays interest annually, and is still held at 30 June 2004.

The patent royalties were received net of basic rate income tax. The patent rights were acquired on 1 April 2003 as an investment costing £180,000 and is to be written off evenly over its 12 year life. The royalties accrual at 29 February 2004 is £10,000 (gross).

The loan interest was paid on a loan raised to buy an investment property which was let to another company. £15,000 is paid each year at the same date without deduction of income tax.

In addition, you establish that there were capital losses brought forward at 1 November 2002 of £30,000 and surplus ACT of £63,000.

The written down values at 1 November 2002, for capital allowances purposes, were as follows:

	£
General pool	168,000
Expensive car	20,000
Computer (short-life asset)	8,000

The following transactions in assets took place during the above accounting period:

Purchases		£	*Disposals*		£
10 March 2003	Plant	10,000	8 July 2003	Lorry sold for	6,000
10 July 2003	Lorry	24,000	26 September 2003	Expensive car	12,000
10 July 2003	Car	14,000	20 November 2003	Computer	2,000

The company is one which qualifies for 40% First Year Allowance (FYA) where appropriate.

Required

(a) Compute the maximum amount of capital allowances which can be claimed by WJ Ltd in respect of each of the two chargeable accounting periods involved. **(8 marks)**

(b) Compute the mainstream corporation tax (MCT) payable in respect of each of the two periods, showing CLEARLY your treatment of advance corporation tax (ACT) and income tax. **(22 marks)**

(Total : 30 marks)

Question 12

EIS Funding (November 1999)

Your unquoted UK trading company is about to embark on a major expansion programme and is seeking to raise funding for this.

Required

Draft a report to your board of directors covering the following matters:

♦ The tax implications of raising funds by means of a share issue.

♦ The income taxation implications for potential investors willing to take up shares in your company through an Enterprise Investment Scheme (EIS).

♦ The conditions which will be placed on the company for an EIS arrangement to be appropriate.

♦ The conditions which must be satisfied by potential shareholders in order to enjoy the income tax advantages of any EIS investment. **(Total : 15 marks)**

Corporation tax losses

Question 13

STD Ltd ceasing (May 1997)

After two years (1999 and 2000) in which trading losses were incurred, STD Ltd made profits for the following three years. However, because of a collapse in the demand for the company's products, it sustained a substantial loss in the year to 31 March 2004, at which date it ceased trading. The losses in 1999 and 2000 were fully relieved by being carried back, extinguishing all of the taxable income for all years back to 1998.

The following information relates to the last four years of trading.

	31 March 2001 £	31 March 2002 £	31 March 2003 £	31 March 2004 £
Trading profits	140,000	180,000	45,000	-
Trading loss	-	-	-	(320,000)
Schedule A	20,000	11,000	5,000	-
FII (gross)	30,000	20,000	10,000	6,000
Capital gains	10,000	-	15,000	-
Capital losses	-	(30,000)	-	(50,000)
Charges paid (gross)				
Patent royalties	15,000	15,000	-	-
Gift Aid	11,000	-	8,000	-
Dividends paid (in August)	-	100,000	80,000	-

Required

(a)   Compute the mainstream corporation tax (MCT) liability for EACH of the THREE years ended 31 March 2001, 31 March 2002 and 31 March 2003 BEFORE taking into account any loss relief.

You should assume that ALL possible claims are made in these years.   **(10 marks)**

(b)   Compute the amount of MCT which will be repaid for the above years as a result of making the appropriate claims for relief of the loss in the year ended 31 March 2004.

(8 marks)

(Total : 18 marks)

Question 14

L Ltd (losses) (May 1999)

L Ltd, a UK company with no associated companies, commenced trading on 1 February 2001. It made up accounts to 31 January 2002 but decided that 30 September would be a more appropriate accounting date. It therefore made up its second set of accounts to 30 September 2002.

The following information refers to the first THREE periods of trading:

	12 months to 31 January 2002 £	8 months to 30 September 2002 £	12 months to 30 September 2003 £
Income			
Schedule D Case I profit	17,000	24,000	-
Schedule D Case I loss	-	-	(62,000)
Schedule A	3,000	2,000	4,000
Patent royalties received (gross figures)	6,000	4,000	2,000
Chargeable capital gains	7,000		4,000
Allowable capital losses		(8,000)	
Payments (gross figures)			
Patent royalties	4,000	3,000	5,000
Gift Aid (paid gross)	-	2,000	-

The profit for the eight month period and the trading loss figure is before taking any account of patent royalties paid.

The company had deducted income tax on all payments of patent royalties.

The patent royalties received had suffered income tax deduction at source. The patent rights had been acquired as an investment. The company has no plans to write off any of the original cost of the patent rights.

The patent royalties were paid and received on the last day of each accounting period, and there were no accrued amounts.

Required

(a) Compute the mainstream corporation tax (MCT) payable for each of the first TWO accounting periods, without taking account of the trading loss for the year ended 30 September 2003. **(6 marks)**

(b) On the assumption that relief for the trading loss for the year ended 30 September 2003 is claimed at the earliest opportunity, show the effect of such a claim on ALL of the accounting periods, identifying the amount of tax which will be refunded as a result of the claim. **(11 marks)**

(c) Show the amounts which will be available for carry forward at 30 September 2003. **(3 marks)**

(Total : 20 marks)

Employee's taxation - benefits

Question 15

Mr K (May 2000)

Mr K is the managing director of Q Ltd. The company provides him with a number of benefits in addition to his salary of £60,000 per annum.

For 2003/04 these benefits comprise:

(i) *Motor cars*

Mr K was given the use of a Mercedes car which had cost the company £24,000 in August 2002 and had a carbon dioxide emission rating of 237 gms/km. On 5 August 2003, Mr K was involved in a serious accident in which the Mercedes was totally destroyed. Mr K was injured and did not drive or return to work until 5 October 2003.

Up to 5 August 2003, Mr K had covered 7,200 miles for business purposes.

On his return to work on 5 October 2003, he was provided with a Lexus motor car which cost the company £36,000 and, in the period from 5 October 2003 to 5 April 2004, he covered 8,000 miles for business purposes. The car's carbon dioxide emission rating was 267 gms/km.

As a result of the car crash, Mr K was found guilty of dangerous driving and the company paid his legal costs and fine amounting to £1,200 with Mr K making a contribution of £300.

Mr K was provided with all fuel by the company, including that used for private mileage.

(ii) *Suits*

Mr K was provided, for the whole of the tax year, with two suits of clothes, each costing £800.

(iii) *Housing*

Mr K lived in a house owned by the company which bought it last year for £125,000. The annual rental value was £8,000 and Mr K paid rent of £5,000 to the company.

In addition to the above, the company provided other benefits to various members of staff, the total cost to the company in 2003/04 being agreed with the Inland Revenue at £9,600 (including the tax) for the purpose of a PAYE Settlement Arrangement.

Required

(a)   Compute the total value of the benefits assessable on Mr K for the year 2003/04.

(12 marks)

(b)   Compute any additional cost to be met by the company as a result of providing the above benefits.   **(3 marks)**

Notes:

1   The fuel benefit basis figure for 2003/04 is £14,400.

2   You may assume an official rate of interest of 5%.   **(Total : 15 marks)**

Employees' taxation – remuneration and compliance

Question 16

Reporting benefits (May 1999)

Jay and Co is a successful firm which had been run for many years as a partnership. Most of the work has been done by the three partners, helped by a small number of part-time employees.

A company has now been formed to take over the business, with the three partners becoming directors. They have informed you that over the next 12 months they will be taking on 20 full-time employees who will be paid salaries ranging from £7,000 to £20,000 per annum. Most of these employees will be given various benefits, with some of them, like the directors, being supplied with motor cars.

The directors are aware that this will impose new fiscal responsibilities on them, and seek your advice.

Required

Draft a report to the directors setting out their duties in relation to reporting benefits provided to members of staff. Your report should identify the forms used, their broad content and the relevant time limits for submission.   **(Total : 16 marks)**

Question 17

F Ltd (May 2000)

F Ltd is a UK resident company whose two full-time working directors, Mr and Mrs F, each own 50% of the voting shares of the company. F Ltd owns 57% of the share capital of N Ltd, another UK resident company.

In February 2004, the projected draft accounts of F Ltd for the year to 31 March 2004 showed a trading profit for tax purposes of £280,000.

The two directors of F Ltd, who each have an annual salary of £45,000, had decided to extract from these profits £20,000 each and were considering two alternative methods:

(a)   to take £20,000 each as a bonus to be added to their salary at the end of March 2004; or

(b)   to take a dividend in cash of £20,000 each payable on 31 March 2004.

Required

Prepare a report for the directors, setting out all of the taxation and NIC implications arising from each of the alternative methods, both from the directors' point of view and from that of the company.

Note: The rates of income tax are given in the Tax Tables at the front of this book.   **(Total : 15 marks)**

Question 18

Advertising Company (Pilot Paper)

The advertising company of which you are the chief accountant is about to reorganise the method of remunerating certain members of staff. Until recently, a number of individuals had been acting as freelance agents. They were not on the company's payroll, and had been paid gross.

As a result of a major investigation by the Inland Revenue the company has been advised that these individuals should now become employees, subject to the employment income rules.

It is the intention that each of these individuals will be given the use of a company-owned motor car and provided with fuel to cover both business and private mileage. A number of them will need to move house and the company has undertaken to give each person affected an amount of £5,000 towards their relocation costs. In addition, some of them will be give interest-free loans in order to enable them to refurnish their new homes.

This will be the first time your company has provided this range of benefits (apart from motor cars, which are provided to the directors). The board in anxious to ensure that it will be complying with the rules for both quantifying and reporting the benefits. It also wishes to be in a position to explain to these new staff members the effect of the benefits on their monthly PAYE deductions.

Required

(a)   Prepare a report to the head of payroll, briefly setting out the rules for quantifying each of the above benefits. Your report must also deal with:

♦   the compliance rules for returning details of the benefits to the Inland Revenue, and

♦   the company's responsibilities under income tax self-assessment rules, making reference to the documentation, deadlines and penalties.   **(15 marks)**

(b)   Prepare a brief information sheet for staff members, explaining the method by which they will be taxed on their employment benefits and the effect of this on their PAYE code numbers.   **(5 marks)**

(Total : 20 marks)

You should assume that the rules for 2003/04 continue to apply.

Question 19

Mr K (May 2001)

Mr K, a married man aged 45, is managing director of CD Ltd, a company in the entertainment industry.

During 2002, the company provided for his use a new Jaguar car with a list price of £32,000, including accessories. During the tax year 2003/2004 he used this car for both business and private purposes until 5 September 2003 when he fell ill and was unable to work until 5 November 2003. During this period the car was not available for his use. The car had a carbon dioxide emission rating of 278 gms/km.

On returning to work on 6 November 2003, he was provided with a two year old Mercedes car, with a list price of £40,000, as a replacement car for the Jaguar. This car has a carbon dioxide emission rating of 229 gms/km. The cost of all private fuel used was paid for by him to the company.

On 6 November 2003 the company provided for his use two suits costing £600 each.

For the past two years he has lived, with his family, in a house owned by the company which had cost £240,000. The agreed annual rental was £12,000 to which he contributed £5,000 each year. He does not require to live in the house to perform his duties.

The company also met the following expenses related to the house:

(1)   Heating and lighting   £2,800
(2)   Maintenance   £1,500

On 6 April 2001 Mr K was given the use of an integrated TV and audio system which had cost the company £4,000. On 6 April 2003 he bought it from the company for £1,200 when its market value was £1,500.

Required

(a)   Calculate the total amount of benefits assessable on Mr K for the tax year 2003/2004.
                                                                                            (12 marks)

(b)   Calculate the additional cost incurred by the company as a result of providing the above benefits and state when this amount will be payable.   **(4 marks)**

(c)   On the assumption that the benefits which were in place at 5 April 2004 continue during 2004/2005, provide Mr K with an estimate of his PAYE code number for 2004/2005.   **(4 marks)**

Note: You may assume that the employment benefit rules and the personal allowance of £4,615 applicable to 2003/2004 remain the same for 2004/2005. Assume an official rate of interest of 5%.   **(Total : 20 marks)**

Capital gains – principles and computation

Question 20

L Ltd (rents) (November 1996)

L Ltd, a UK-resident trading company, owns six properties in the UK which it lets during its 12 month accounting period to 31 October 2003.

Details of the various leases are as follows:

Property	Type of lease	Period of lease and date of commencement	Annual rent	Agreed allowable expenditure for the year to 31.10.2003
A	A landlord's repairing lease	10 years, commencing in 1998	£5,000	£3,000
B	A tenant's repairing lease	Let for the first time on 1 April 2003 for a term of 8 years	£12,000	£3,100
C	A landlord's repairing lease	Let for the first time on 1 July 2003 for a term of 6 years	£6,000	£7,400
D	A landlord's repairing lease	10 years, commencing in 1997	£7,200	£2,800
E	A tenant's repairing lease	10 years, commencing in 1999	£16,000	£4,800
F	A tenant's repairing lease	Let for the first time on 1 October 2003 for a term of 6 years	£20,000	£9,000

All rents are due quarterly in advance on 1 January, 1 April, 1 July and 1 October each year. All rents were collected.

Required

(a)   Compute the amount to be included in the company's corporation tax computation for the above period in respect of Schedule A income.   **(7 marks)**

(b)   Advise the board of L Ltd of the method of assessing the company on any premiums it may receive on granting a short lease out of a freehold property.   **(8 marks)**

(Total : 15 marks)

Capital gains – shares and securities

Question 21

B Ltd and Z Ltd (November 1996)

(a)   B Ltd, a UK-resident company with no associated companies, trades from several retail stores.

During its year ended 31 March 2004 it made the following disposals:

(i)   *30 September 2003*
A painting which had been hanging in the dining room was sold for £4,200. It had originally cost £7,100 in January 1990.

(ii)   *31 October 2003*
A lease for a retail unit was sold for £100,000. B Ltd had acquired this lease, which had a term of 35 years, in October 1999 at a cost of £45,000.

In addition, you are informed that a warehouse, which had cost £12,000 in October 1977 and which had a market value at 31 March 1982 of £7,000, was destroyed in a fire in December 2003. Unfortunately, the building had been under-insured and the insurers paid only £5,000.

In January 1992, the company had made an election under section 35 of the Taxation of Chargeable Gains Act 1992 (TCGA).

Required

Compute the amount to be included in respect of chargeable gains in the company's corporation tax computation for the above chargeable accounting period.   **(11 marks)**

(b)   Z Ltd acquired 10,000 shares in X Ltd in June 1993 for £110,000. In January 2004, X Ltd made a rights issue of one share for every five held at £10 per share. Z Ltd did not take up the rights issue and instead sold the rights for £9,800. The market value of each X Ltd share on the first dealing day after the rights issue was £16. After the rights issue X Ltd had an issued share capital of 600,000 shares.

Required

(i)   Compute the chargeable gain arising as a result of the sale of the rights.

(4 marks)

(ii)   Show the capital gains tax treatment had the rights been sold for £8,000 rather than for £9,800.   **(5 marks)**

Indexation factors relevant to this question: *Lease table extract:*

January 1990 - September 2003	0.518		31 years	88.371%
October 1999 - October 2003	0.091		35 years	91.981%
June 1993 - January 2004	0.300			

(Total : 20 marks)

Question 22

BD Ltd (May 1998)

BD Ltd is a UK resident company owning 100% of the shares of a French company, Mince SA. During its accounting period of 12 months to 31 March 2004, it made the following disposals, all during July 2003:

(i)   In July 1995, BD Ltd acquired a 35 year lease at a cost of £48,000. In July 2003, it granted a sub-lease of six years to E Ltd for a premium of £12,000.

In using this information in your answer, you should show the effect of any Schedule A assessment on the amount of any chargeable gain.

(ii)   An office was sold in July 2003 for £42,000. This has been acquired in October 1989 as part of a block of six offices which had cost, at that date, a total amount of £100,000. The market value (MV) of the five remaining offices was agreed at £190,000.

(iii)   In May 1980, BD Ltd purchased 20,000 ordinary shares in X Ltd at a cost of £15,000. In July 1992, following a reorganisation of the share capital of X Ltd, BD Ltd received for each ordinary share then held, one 50p ordinary share and one 50p 6% preference share. The value of these shares on the day following the reorganisation were:

50p ordinary share	£1.80
50p preference share	£0.80

The MV of the original shares at 31 March 1982 can be taken as £1.00 per share.

In July 2003, BD Ltd sold all of the ordinary shares for £75,000. BD Ltd's holding represents less than 4% of the shares of X Ltd in issue.

Required

(a)   In each of the above situations, compute the chargeable gain or allowable loss arising.

(16 marks)

(b)   Assuming that BD Ltd had other chargeable income of £160,000 (but NO FII) for the above period, compute the amount of corporation tax (CT) payable on the above gains.

(4 marks)

Note that in part (b) you are NOT required to compute the total CT payable, only the CT on the chargeable gains.

The relevant indexation factors are:

July 1995 - July 2003	0.213
October 1989 - July 2003	0.540
March 1982 - July 2003	1.277

The relevant percentage values applicable to short leases for taxation of capital gains purposes are:

35 years	91.981
27 years	83.816
21 years	74.635

(Total : 20 marks)

Capital gains – rollover and holdover reliefs

Question 23

P Ltd, G Ltd and R Ltd (May 1999)

(a)   On 25 July 2003, P Ltd sold 25,000 ordinary shares in T Ltd for £150,000. These shares were part of a holding of 27,000 shares which had been acquired as follows:

Date	*Shares*	*Cost*
		£
January 1980	3,000	3,000
February 1982	4,000	6,000
January 1984	5,000	10,000
March 1990	10,000	50,000
April 1996	5,000	20,000

You are advised that a global election is in place to have all assets owned at 31 March 1982 dealt with at their market value at that date. The market value of each share in T Ltd at 31 March 1982 was £1.20. P Ltd's holding in T Ltd has never exceeded 3% of the total issued share capital.

Required

Compute the chargeable gain arising as a result of this disposal. **(9 marks)**

(b)   The managing director of G Ltd has decided that his company should acquire 80% of the share capital of H Ltd, a company in the same trade. On examining the latest balance sheet of H Ltd, he noted that its premises were valued at £60,000. He considers that this property will be surplus to the company's requirements and that it could be sold for £150,000 once his company has acquired H Ltd, thus providing valuable working capital. On making further enquiries he establishes that the property had cost H Ltd £40,000 in March 1993 and that H Ltd had rolled over a previous gain of £10,000 against the cost.

Required

On the assumption that H Ltd is acquired in April 2003 and that the property is sold in July 2003, advise the managing director of the amount of additional funds that will be generated, after paying any corporation tax on the resulting gain. H Ltd's other taxable profits will be approximately £350,000 for the year ended 31 March 2004.

(6 marks)

(c)   R Ltd is about to make its first disposals for capital gains tax purposes. In July 2003, it sells two factories as follows:

	Date purchased	Cost	Market value at 31 March 1982	Sold for
		£	£	£
Factory A	October 1979	80,000	100,000	70,000
Factory B	March 1978	27,000	40,000	125,000

Required

Advise the board of R Ltd whether a global election for market value (MV) at 31 March 1982 should be made, supporting your advice with detailed computations.   **(6 marks)**

Indexation factors which may be used in answering this question are:

March 1982 - July 2003	1.277
January 1984 - April 1985	0.091
April 1985 - March 1990	0.281
March 1990 - April 1996	0.257
April 1996 - July 2003	0.185
March 1993 - July 2003	0.299

(Total : 21 marks)

Question 24

V Ltd (May 2000)

The following information relates to transactions carried out by V Ltd, a UK resident company, during its accounting year ended 31 March 2004.

(A)   In March 1995, the company sold for £250,000 a building which had cost £120,000 in May 1986. Of the proceeds, £210,000 was used to purchase fixed plant and machinery and the maximum possible holdover relief was claimed. In July 2003 a fire completely destroyed all of this plant and compensation was received from the company's insurers.

(B)   A new office block was constructed during the year and the directors decided to dispose of, during July 2003, some of the contents of the previous boardroom as follows:

(i)   A painting, which had cost £2,000 in January 1980 and which had a market value (MV) at 31 March 1982 of £1,000, was sold at auction for £8,000 on which fees of £200 were paid. A global election for MV at 31 March 1982 had been made by V Ltd on the occasion of a previous disposal in 1991.

(ii)   A pair of matching sculptures were gifted, one to the general manager and the other to his wife who was also an employee. The market value of the pair of sculptures at July 2003 was agreed at £10,000 and they had been bought by the company for £4,000 in May 1993.

(iii)   Three tables were sold in July 2003 to individual employees for £1,000 each, having cost the company £2,000 each in June 1990.

(C)   In July 2003, V Ltd sold 10,000 75p ordinary shares in X Ltd for £60,000. These had been acquired as part of a reorganisation of the share capital of X Ltd in March 1991. In March 1989, V Ltd had purchased 20,000 ordinary £1 shares in X Ltd for £30,000, and in March 1991 these were converted into the following holdings:

	Market value immediately after reorganisation
15,000 75p ordinary shares	£1.40 per share
8,000 7% £1 preference shares	£1.25 per share
£5,000 debentures	at par, ie £5,000

Required

(a)   Compute the chargeable capital gains or allowable losses which will arise as a result of the above transactions.   **(16 marks)**

(b)   Advise the board of any other tax implications arising from the transactions involving staff members, and suggest how these might be dealt with.   **(4 marks)**

Indexation factors which may be used in answering this question are:

May 1986 - March 1995	0.507
March 1982 - July 2003	1.277
May 1993 - July 2003	0.282
June 1990 - July 2003	0.428
March 1989 - July 2003	0.611 **(Total : 20 marks)**

Question 25

S Ltd (May 2001)

S Ltd is an unlisted UK resident trading company with no associated companies. During its twelve month accounting period ended 31 March 2004 it made the following disposals:

(1)   *April 2003*

A warehouse was sold for £120,000. This had been purchased in June 1994 for £80,000 as an investment property. It was immediately rented to a major supplier and was never used for the purpose of S Ltd's trade.

(2)   *May 2003*

Two offices were sold for £40,000. These offices were part of a group of six offices purchased by the company for £50,000 in June 1990. All of the offices had been used for the purpose of S Ltd's trade up to May 2003. At the time of sale, the agreed value of the four offices retained by the company was £60,000.

(3)   *June 2003*

Sold 10,000 £1 ordinary shares in T Ltd for £10 each. These shares were part of a holding of 14,000 shares acquired as follows:

May 1979   5,000 shares purchased at £2 each (market value (MV) at 31 March 1982 was £1.60 per share - adjusted for the bonus issue).

May 1983   5,000 shares were purchased at £1.90 each.

June 1985   A bonus issue of one share for every five held was made.

August 1998   2,000 shares were purchased at £7 each.

There are 200,000 £1 ordinary shares of T Ltd in issue.

Note: On the occasion of a disposal of another asset made by the company in 1996 a global election for Market Value at 31 March 1982 was made.

Required

(a)   Compute the chargeable gains arising as a result of each of the above disposals.

(12 marks)

(b)   Prepare a report to the directors of S Ltd setting out **all** of the opportunities of deferring the corporation tax payable on each of the above gains.   **(8 marks)**

Indexation factors which should be used in answering this question:

March 1982	-	June 2003	1.272
May 1983	-	April 1985	0.120
April 1985	-	August 1998	0.727
June 1990	-	May 2003	0.425
June 1994	-	April 2003	0.245
August 1998	-	June 2003	0.103

(Total: 20 marks)

Value added tax

Question 26

Partial exemption (November 1997)

Your company has, up to the present time, dealt only with goods which are standard-rated for VAT purposes.

In the near future it will begin to make, for the first time, supplies which are exempt from VAT. This will account for about one-quarter of the total turnover in a full year.

The directors wish to be advised of the effect this decision will have on the company's ability to claim a deduction for input VAT.

Required

Draft a brief report for the board on the VAT and any other implications of this change in the sales mix.   **(Total : 15 marks)**

Question 27

Export sales (November 1998)

Your company is about, for the first time, to engage in exporting its products. Some of the customers will be situated in European Union (EU) countries and others will be in North America.

Your directors are aware that the VAT regulations governing export sales are somewhat different from those applying to UK sales.

Required

Write a brief report to the board setting out the main regulations covering export sales, distinguishing clearly between exports to the EU and those to non-EU countries.

(Total : 15 marks)

Question 28

Tax points and entertainment (November 1999)

As a result of a recent inspection carried out by value added tax (VAT) officers, your company has incurred a number of penalties resulting from persistent and serious errors in recording systems and the completion of the VAT returns. Two areas singled out by the VAT authorities for particular criticism were failure to recognise the correct tax point for both outputs and inputs, and errors in the treatment of VAT on specific entertainment expenditure.

Required

Draft an instruction sheet to the members of staff dealing with the VAT records, showing clearly the rules for identifying the correct tax point (for both outputs and inputs). Your instruction sheet should also indicate the extent to which VAT on entertainment expenditure may be claimed as a deduction in the VAT return.

(Total : 15 marks)

Question 29

TC Ltd and D Ltd (November 2001)

(a)   TC Ltd is a rapidly-growing UK company in the highly competitive computer software industry. In recent times, it has had a high turnover of technical staff who have left to join competitor companies. The board is keen to introduce new methods of rewarding staff in an effort to retain them and asks you, as the company accountant, to prepare notes to form the basis for discussion on this matter at the next board meeting.

Required

Prepare **brief notes** identifying **three** methods of rewarding staff (apart from salary and bonuses), in each case providing a brief description of the benefit and how it is quantified and indicating the tax and NIC implications for both the company and the employee.   **(10 marks)**

(b)   In your capacity as Chief Accountant of D Ltd, you receive the following memorandum from your Managing Director.

MEMORANDUM

To: Chief Accountant   From: Managing Director

Subject: VAT   Date: 19 November 2004

As you are aware from previous discussions, the company intends to commence making VAT-exempt supplies relating to insurance products in the forthcoming financial year. It is anticipated that these exempt supplies will account for around 25% of the company's total turnover in the first year and could increase in later years.

Please advise me of the likely VAT implications of this change in the sales mix.

Required

Prepare a response to the above Memorandum from the Managing Director.   **(10 marks)**

(Total : 20 marks)

Groups of companies

Question 30

A Ltd and B Ltd (November 1998)

On 1 April 2003 A Ltd, a manufacturing company resident in the United Kingdom, acquired 100% of the share capital of B Ltd, also a manufacturing company. B Ltd makes up accounts each year to 31 March. For its year ended 31 March 2004, it sustained a trading loss of £130,000 and had no other chargeable income. A Ltd produced the following information in relation to its NINE month period of accounts to 30 September 2003:

Income	£
Adjusted trading profits	36,000
Rents receivable	20,000
Local Authority Stock interest receivable (gross) [including £2,000 accrued at 30 September 2003]	8,000
Bank interest receivable	15,000
Patent royalties receivable (gross) [including £6,000 accrued: £12,000 received 1 April 2003]	18,000
Franked Investment Income (FII) [including tax credit]	8,000
Payments (gross figures)	
Patent royalties payable (£6,000 paid March 2003)	8,000
Gift aid payment	5,000

All payments and receipts of patent royalties were subject to deduction of tax at source and were paid or received in respect of the companies trading activities. The adjusted trading profit figure does not include any patent royalties received or paid.

A dividend of £12,000 was paid during the period. You establish that there was surplus ACT brought forward at 1 January 2003 of £22,000.

Required

(a)   Compute the final taxation position of A Ltd for the above accounting period, assuming maximum group relief is claimed by A Ltd in respect of B Ltd's trading loss.

(22 marks)

(b)   The directors of A Ltd have advised you that, in the next accounting period, they will dispose of an asset which is likely to give rise to a capital gain and that B Ltd will also dispose of an asset giving rise to a capital loss.

Advise the directors on the procedures which should be adopted in order to minimise the taxation liability of the group.   **(6 marks)**

(Total : 28 marks)

Question 31

S Ltd and T Ltd (November 1998)

The following information relates to the accounting year ended 31 March 2004 of S Ltd, a company whose whole share capital had been acquired by T Ltd during 1998. In addition, you establish that on 31 October 2003, T Ltd disposed of 40% of the shares in S Ltd to a third party.

(i)   In April 1991, S Ltd had acquired 20,000 ordinary shares in X Ltd (being 4% of the total share capital) at a cost of £120,000. During November 2003, X Ltd made a rights issue of one share for every four shares held, which S Ltd chose not to take, and the rights were sold for £18,000. The value of the shares in X Ltd at November 2003, immediately after the rights issue, was agreed with the Inland Revenue at £9 per share.

(ii)   On 1 March 1994, S Ltd sold for £175,000 a business property which had cost £80,000 in January 1980. The MV of the property at 31 March 1982 was agreed at £90,000. The proceeds received in 1994 had been immediately wholly invested in new plant and machinery, all of which was still in use at 31 March 2004. Holdover relief was claimed in respect of the gain arising in March 1994.

(iii)   In May 1999, T Ltd had transferred a factory building to S Ltd under the group arrangements for capital gains tax purposes. The factory had cost T Ltd £80,000 in May 1993 and its agreed market value at May 1999 was £105,000. As stated above, T Ltd sold 40% of the shares in S Ltd during the year.

Required

(a)   Compute the chargeable gains or allowable losses for S Ltd arising during the accounting period to 31 March 2004 as a result of the above information.   **(16 marks)**

(b)   Assuming that S Ltd had other chargeable income for the above period of £140,000 (but no FII), compute the corporation tax (CT) which will be attracted by any gains in your answer to part (a) above.

You are NOT required to calculate the total corporation tax liability - ONLY the tax on the gains.   **(4 marks)**

Indexation factors which may be used in answering this question are:

April 1991 - November 2003	0.371
March 1982 - March 1994	0.794
May 1993 - May 1999	0.174

(Total : 20 marks)

Question 32

M Ltd and B Ltd (May 1999)

(a)   The share capital of M Ltd, a UK company, is held as follows:

A Ltd	15%
B Ltd	60%
C Ltd	5%
D Ltd	4%
Individuals	16%

All of the shares in A Ltd, B Ltd, C Ltd and D Ltd are owned by individuals and none of these companies owns shares in any other company.

All of the companies make up accounts to 31 March. The trading results for the year ended 31 March 2004 were as follows:

		£
A Ltd	Loss	(60,000)
B Ltd	Profit	160,000
C Ltd	Loss	(20,000)
D Ltd	Loss	(40,000)
M Ltd	Profit	220,000

None of the companies had any other income.

Required

On the assumption that all possible claims for relief are made, compute the MCT payable by B Ltd and M Ltd.   **(14 marks)**

(b)   K Ltd has been making up its accounts to 30 September for many years. During 2003, it decided to change its accounting date to 31 December. It made up accounts for the period from 1 October 2002 to 31 December 2003. K Ltd is not a large company for quarterly instalment payment purposes.

Required

Advise the directors of K Ltd of their responsibilities under the corporation tax self assessment rules in terms of the filing requirements on this occasion, and of the payment dates involved.   **(6 marks)**

(Total : 20 marks)

Question 33

Group disposals (May 1999)

A diversified group of companies comprises a parent and several subsidiaries which had been acquired over a period from 1990 until 1998. The group is about to reorganise its business activities by focusing on one main trading activity which it hopes to expand over the next few years.

This will involve the disposal of a number of assets held by various companies in the group and the sale of some of the subsidiary companies themselves.

Required

Draft a report to the board on the potential taxation implications of this course of action. Your report should concentrate mainly on the capital gains aspects.   **(Total : 15 marks)**

Question 34

Acquiring shares or assets (May 1999)

When a limited company wishes to acquire control of another company, there are two methods of achieving this commercial objective:

1   To acquire a majority holding of the voting shares in the other company.

2   To purchase the assets, trade and contracts of the other company, and offer continuing employment to its workforce. This company would then be wound up.

Required

Identify and discuss the taxation implications of EACH of the above alternative course of action.   **(Total : 15 marks)**

Question 35

H Ltd Group (May 2000)

The following information relates to a UK-resident group of companies, the parent company being H Ltd, the shares of which are all held by individuals.

H Ltd has the following holdings of shares:

    68% of G Ltd   80% of J Ltd   90% of L Ltd

J Ltd owns 80% of K Ltd, the other 20% of K Ltd being owned by G Ltd.

L Ltd owns 80% of M Ltd and X Ltd holds 24% of G Ltd.

All of the other shares in these companies are owned by individuals.

All of the companies make up accounts to 31 March each year and the results for the year ended 31 March 2004 are as follows:

	H Ltd £	G Ltd £	J Ltd £	L Ltd £	K Ltd £	M Ltd £	X Ltd £
Trading losses			(64,000)			(42,000)	(24,000)
Trading profits	48,000	60,000		30,000	90,000		
Schedule D Case III	4,000	5,000	6,000		10,000	1,000	
Gift Aid (PAID)	2,000	4,000	3,000			3,000	

Required

(a)   Draw a diagram illustrating the above structure.   **(3 marks)**

(b)   Identify all of the associated companies and any groups and/or consortia present in the structure.   **(5 marks)**

(c)   Compute the MCT payable by each company, assuming all possible reliefs are claimed in the most tax-efficient manner, with taxable profits after the deduction of reliefs.
                                                                                          (12 marks)

                                                                                          (Total : 20 marks)

Question 36

D Ltd (Pilot Paper)

The following information relates to events and transactions involving D Ltd, a UK resident company, 90% of whose share capital is owned by T Ltd, another UK resident company. D Ltd made up accounts for the year ended 31 December 2003.

1   In May 1994, D Ltd had sold a building for £280,000 which had cost £120,000 in May 1980 and which had a market value (MV) of £130,000 at 31 March 1982. On the occasion of this disposal D Ltd had made a global election to use MV at 31 March 1982 for all sales of assets held at that date.

       Of the proceeds, £270,000 was used to purchase new plant and machinery and the maximum possible holdover relief was claimed. This plant and machinery was scrapped in May 2003 and £10,000 was recovered for its scrap value.

2   In June 1998 the ownership of a factory was transferred to D Ltd from its parent company, T Ltd, at the agreed market value of £260,000. The factory had cost T Ltd £180,000 in June 1989. In May 2003, T Ltd sold a block of its shares in D Ltd, reducing its holding to 70%.

3   In June 2003, D Ltd sold, for £300,000, an office block which had been held as an investment property and let. It had cost £180,000 in June 1978 and its MV at 31 March 1982 was £150,0000.

4   In September 2003, D Ltd sold for £180,000 two plots of land which had been used for the purpose of the trade. These were part of a block of nine plots which had been bought by D Ltd in June 1992 for a total amount of £500,000. The market value of the seven unsold plots at 30 September 2003 was £1,200,000.

Required

(a)   Compute any chargeable gain or allowance loss arising from each of the above events.

                                                                   (16 marks)

(b)   Explain briefly whether any of the above gains could be deferred.   **(4 marks)**

                                                               (Total : 20 marks)

Indexation factors which may be used:

March 1982 – May 1994	0.822
June 1989 – June 1998	0.416
June 1998 – May 2003	0.105
March 1982 – June 2003	1.272
June 1992 – September 2003	0.302

Question 37

Reliefs for groups and consortia (May 2001

The careful use of tax reliefs within a group or consortium can produce significant savings in corporation tax.

Required

(a)   Discuss the role which may be played by non-UK resident companies in group and consortium structures for UK corporation tax purposes.

Your answer should include at least two relevant illustrations of group/consortium structures.   **(10 marks)**

(b)   Describe the strategy which should be adopted to maximise the effect of loss claims in a group.   **(4 marks)**

(c)   In the following situation, identify any consortia, and state how much loss can be claimed by which companies. All companies have an accounting year to 31 March 2004. Apart from H Inc, all of the companies are UK resident. H Inc does not operate a permanent establishment in the UK.

E Ltd owns 65% of G Ltd. The remainder of G Ltd's shares are held: 8% by F Ltd and 27% by H Inc.

E Ltd has a loss of £54,000; H Inc has a loss of £6,000; G Ltd has a profit of £30,000 and F Ltd a loss of £60,000.   **(6 marks)**

(Total : 20 marks)

Question 38

S Ltd (November 2001)

All of the ordinary share capital of S Ltd, a UK-resident company, had, until 30 September 2003, been owned by H Ltd, also a UK-resident company. On that date, H Ltd sold 40% of the shares to a number of private individuals.

You established that in June 1998, H Ltd had transferred a building to S Ltd under group arrangements on a no gain/no loss basis. At the date of transfer, the building had a market value of £220,000. It had cost H Ltd £90,000 in August 1985 and an extension was added in June 1991 at a cost of £30,000.

S Ltd had the following disposals during its accounting year to 31 March 2004:

1   *June 2003*

Sold rights to shares for £15,000. This arose from a holding of 50,000 ordinary shares in C Ltd which S Ltd had purchased in October 1991 for £160,000. When C Ltd made the rights issue, S Ltd did not wish to exercise its rights and these were sold for £15,000. The market value of the 50,000 shares still held by S Ltd on the day following the rights issue was £270,000. S Ltd's holding before the rights issue represented 6% of the share of C Ltd then in issue.

2   *September 2003*

An office building held by S Ltd as an investment and not used for its trade was sold for £230,000. This building had originally been purchased in June 1978 for £50,000 and since then the following capital expenditure had been incurred on the building:

December 1981	£10,000
October 1991	£20,000
June 2003	£30,000

A global election was not in place and the agreed market value of the building at 31 March 1982 was £70,000.

Required

(a)   Compute the chargeable gains on S Ltd for the year ended 31 March 2003, arising from each of the above transactions.   **(16 marks)**

(b)   Compute the **total** CT payable by S Ltd and state when this will be payable, assuming S Ltd had other chargeable income for the year amounting to £13,500.   **(4 marks)**

Indexation factors which should be used in answering this question

March 1982	–	September 2003	1.283
August 1985	–	June 1998	0.711
June 1991	–	June 1998	0.218
October 1991	–	June 2003	0.336
October 1991	–	September 2003	0.343
June 2003	–	September 2003	0.005

(Total : 20 marks)

International aspects

Question 39 (November 1998)

Z Ltd

Z Ltd, a UK-resident company with two wholly-owned UK subsidiaries, also owns 8% of Q SA, a non-resident company.

For its year to 31 March 2004, Z Ltd had the following income:

	£
UK trading profits	500,000
Overseas dividend - GROSS figure:	
Q SA (withholding tax £17,000)	90,000

During the year to 31 March 2004, Z Ltd paid Gift Aid of £10,000 and paid a dividend of £408,000. There was surplus ACT of £56,000 brought forward at 1 April 2003.

Required

Compute the mainstream corporation tax payable (MCT) by Z Ltd for the above year, showing CLEARLY your treatment of surplus advance corporation tax (ACT) brought forward and double tax credits, and bringing out any surplus ACT remaining.

(Total : 15 marks)

Question 40

X Ltd (May 1999)

X Ltd, a company resident in the United Kingdom, makes up accounts each year to 31 March. It acquired a 55% interest in Z Ltd on 30 December 2003 and sold its 60% interest in Y Ltd on 30 November 2003.

During its year ended 31 March 2004, X Ltd had an adjusted trading profit (before capital allowances) of £226,000 after adding back £10,000 in respect of a loan to a customer which proved irrecoverable.

The company let various properties to other businesses and, during the year to 31 March 2004 this activity resulted in a loss of £22,000 (before any interest paid on loans used to purchase one of these properties).

On 31 March 2004 the company received patent royalties of £12,000 (gross figure) and paid patent royalties of £6,000 (gross figure).

The patent royalties (received and paid) had been subject to deduction of tax at source and had been received or paid as part of the company's trading activities. The royalties paid and received have not been included in trading profits.

The other income and payments during the year ended 31 March 2004 were:

	£
Income	
(Gross figures - including tax credits where relevant)	
Loan Stock interest (including an accrual of £2,000) [Note 1]	14,000
Chargeable gain arising on the sale of shares in Y Ltd	28,000
Loan interest (on loan to customer) [received gross]	1,000
Dividend from foreign company (withholding tax was 35%)	4,000
Franked Investment Income (FII)	15,000
Payments	
(Gross figures)	
Debenture interest paid in year (purchase of let property) [Note 2]	6,000
Gift Aid payment to charity	2,000

Notes:

1. The loan stock interest received was in respect of a holding of Local Authority Stock and had been received net on 31 July 2003.

2. The interest paid was on debenture stock held by several individuals and had been paid net.

A dividend of £120,000 was paid on 31 May 2003.

In addition, you establish that there is surplus advance corporation tax (ACT) of £24,000 brought forward at 1 April 2003.

The balances for capital allowances purposes at 1 April 2003 were:

General pool	£108,000
Expensive car	£18,000

During the year there were two items bought - plant, costing £12,000 on 30 May 2003, and a computer system costing £23,750 on 31 July 2003. An inexpensive motor car was sold for £6,000 on 31 January 2004.

Note: This is a 'small' company for the purpose of qualifying for first-year allowances (FYA).

Required

(a)   Compute the capital allowances claimable for the year ended 31 March 2004. **(6 marks)**

(b)   Compute the mainstream corporation tax (MCT) payable for the year ended 31 March 2004, showing clearly your treatment of ACT, income tax and interest paid and received under the loan relationship rules.   **(17 marks)**

(c)   State briefly how the surplus ACT remaining at 31 March 2004 may be relieved in the future.   **(5 marks)**

(Total : 28 marks)

Question 41

A Ltd (May 2000)

A Ltd, a company resident in the United Kingdom, owns 80% of the voting shares of L Inc, a company resident in and managed in a Caribbean country where the rate of corporation tax is 5%. The following information relates to A Ltd's NINE MONTH accounting period ended 31 December 2003.

	£
Income	
Adjusted trading profit (before capital allowances)	475,250
Patent royalties (gross figure but received on 10 August 2003 net of basic rate income tax - an accrual of £4,000 is included)	20,000
Capital gains	122,000
Local Authority Stock interest receivable (an accrual of £3,000 is included)	12,000
Dividend from UK company received 14 July 2003 (cash amount)	9,000
Payments	
Loan interest payable (the gross figure is shown, but the amount paid was net of income tax of 20% and it was paid on 31 August 2003)	15,000
Gift Aid payment to charity	8,000

Additional information:

♦   The patent rights were acquired as an investment on 1 April 2003 for £80,000. The company has decided to write off the cost evenly over its 10 year life but no adjustment has yet been made.

♦   A dividend of £360,000 was paid on 31 July 2003.

♦   The loan interest payable related to a debenture issued to private individuals to purchase property which is let. The letting gave rise to a loss of £24,000 during the above accounting period.

♦   There was a surplus ACT of £40,000 brought forward to 1 April 2003.

♦   L Inc's profits for the nine months to 31 December 2003, computed in accordance with UK tax rules, amounted to £60,000. L Inc paid no dividends.

♦   For capital allowances purposes, there was a balance of £84,000 in the general pool brought forward at 1 April 2002. Two delivery vehicles were purchased in August 2003 for a total cost of £40,000. The company had previously rented its factory premises, but on 1 April 2002 it purchased a second-hand factory for £150,000 from B Ltd. B Ltd had purchased the factory new for £96,000 on 1 April 1994 and used it continuously for qualifying purposes.

Required

(a) Compute the maximum capital allowances which can be claimed by A Ltd for the above nine month accounting period. **(5 marks)**

(b) Compute the corporation tax payable before any surplus ACT has been deducted. This figure should include any tax payable as a result of A Ltd's ownership of L Inc. **(14 marks)**

(c) Compute, using the shadow ACT rules, the maximum amount of surplus ACT brought forward at 1 April 2002 which may be relieved against the corporation tax liability computed at (b) above. (You may ignore the effect that the ownership of L Inc has on this situation). **(7 marks)**

(d) Advise the directors on the effect of their future dividend policy on the utilisation of surplus ACT. **(4 marks)**

(Total : 30 marks)

Question 42

M Ltd (Pilot Paper)

M Ltd is a UK resident company which owns controlling interests in two other UK resident companies and in two non-resident companies.

It also has the following interests in three non-resident companies:

Company	Shareholding %	Rate of withholding tax %	Post-tax profits Y/E 31/03/03 £	Foreign tax paid £
A Inc	6	15	400,000	80,000
B PG	8	25	900,000	300,000
C SA	30	20	800,000	200,000

M Ltd has experienced a prolonged period of poor trading and, as a result of losses brought forward from earlier years, its chargeable Schedule D I income for the year ended 31 March 2004 is only £20,000.

During the year, M Ltd commenced a new separate trade which has considerable potential but has generated a loss of £75,000 due to start-up costs. The company wishes to set the loss off under S393A – against current year total profits.

The only other income received by M Ltd during the year consisted of dividends from the above three companies, each of which had substantial undistributed profits. The figures (net of withholding tax) were:

	£
A Inc	170,000
B PG	150,000
C SA	120,000

Required

(a) Compute the MCT payable in M Ltd in respect of the year ended 31 March 2004. Your answer should show clearly your treatment of the current year loss of the new trade and of the foreign taxes suffered. You should explain why you are dealing with items in a particular way and use a columnar layout. **(16 marks)**

(b) Explain briefly what the taxation implications would be if C SA were deemed to be a controlled foreign company. **(4 marks)**

(Total : 20 marks)

Note: *The on-shore pooling provisions for foreign dividends and tax credits are excluded from the syllabus as being too complicated. You should therefore deal with each foreign dividend and its associated tax credits in isolation and ignore the 'on-shore' pooling facility to pool foreign tax credits from different sources.*

Question 43

BG Ltd (November 2001)

BG Ltd is a UK-resident company with two 100%-owned UK-resident subsidiaries. All of the ordinary shares in BG Ltd are held by a corporation resident in the United States of America.

In addition, BG Ltd holds 8% of the voting rights in P Inc and 15% of those of Q SA, both of which are non-UK resident. FG Ltd, another UK-resident company, owns 45% of the voting rights of P Inc, which is wholly managed in its country of residence.

The following information is provided in respect of P Inc and Q SA in respect of the year ended 31 March 2004 – the date to which BG Ltd also makes up its accounts annually:

	Rate of withholding tax	Post-tax profits	Tax actually paid for year
P Inc	10%	£700,000	£140,000
Q SA	20%	£1,000,000	£350,000

The above profits are the figures calculated under UK tax rules.

Both P Inc and Q SA have paid only modest dividends in recent years and have substantial undistributed profits. During the year ended 31 March 2004, large dividends were paid.

For the year ended 31 March 2004, BG Ltd had chargeable Schedule D Case I profits of £30,000, arrived at after adding back a Charitable Covenant of £50,000, under an agreement it had entered into three years ago when its UK profits were much higher.

BG Ltd's only other chargeable income for the year comprised overseas dividends, as follows:

P Inc £144,000
Q SA £160,000

Both figures are net of the relevant withholding tax shown above.

Required

(a) Compute the CT payable by BG Ltd in respect of the year ended 31 March 2004 and state when this will be payable. You should use a columnar layout showing clearly your treatment of the charitable Covenant and the foreign tax credits. **(15 marks)**

(b) Your Chairman has sent you, in your capacity as company accountant, the following note:

"As you are aware, our company is currently considering acquiring a further 10% interest in Q SA, bringing our holding up to 25%. On discussing this with a business colleague, she mentioned that this action could have important taxation implications for our company but she was uncertain of the details. I would be grateful if you could report back to me on the possible taxation implications of our proposed investment."

Required

Respond briefly to this note. **(5 marks)**

(Total : 20 marks)

Scenario questions

Question 44

X Ltd (Pilot Paper)

(a) X Ltd is a UK-resident company which manufactures household appliances. Until 1998 its shares were wholly owned by the members of the Smith family. During 1998, 80% of the shares were acquired by Z Ltd, a UK company which owns a chain of retail outlets selling household appliances. The remaining 20% of the shares continue to be held by Mr J Smith, aged 43, who is employed as general manager of X Ltd.

The directors of X Ltd are also directors of Z Ltd.

For the purpose of this scenario you are the chief accountant of X Ltd.

At a meeting arranged by you with the directors of X Ltd held in April 2004, you are provided with their estimates of the results for the year to 31 March 2005, together with additional information which may have a bearing on the taxation liability of the company.

It is fairly obvious that the directors have very little grasp of how the CT self assessment rules work and were surprised to be asked for their estimates at such an early stage (and were similarly surprised in past years!).

The estimates are as follows:

INCOME	£
Trading profit	820,000
Loan interest receivable (Note 1)	5,000 (gross)
Patent royalties received (Note 2)	15,000 (gross)
Rental income	10,000
PAYMENTS	
Loan interest payable (Note 3)	12,000 (gross)
Gift Aid	4,000

Notes

1   The loan interest receivable is in respect of a loan of £50,000 made by X Ltd to a major supplier, S Ltd, two years ago.

2   Patent royalties are received net of basic rate income tax on 31 March each year being the amount accrued to date. The company registered the patent several years ago as part of its trading activities but the income is not included in the trading profit figure above.

3   The loan interest payable is on a debenture issued to several private individuals to finance the purchase of equipment and is paid net.

In addition to the above, you establish that the company has a corporation tax (CT) liability of £270,000 for the year ended 31 March 2004, based on chargeable income of £900,000. This is similar to the results of the previous year.

It has surplus advance corporation tax (ACT), generated in the year to 31 March 1999, brought forward at 31 March 2004, of £30,000. The directors have decided to pay a dividend of £624,000 during May 2004 in respect of the year ended 31 March 2004 having last paid a dividend in May 1998. There was no FII received in any year.

Required

Prepare a report to the directors of X Ltd

(i)   producing your calculation of the estimated corporation tax liability of the company for the year ended 31 March 2005;   **(8 marks)**

(ii)   illustrating, by means of a schedule, how and when this liability will be settled;   **(6 marks)**

(iii)   advising them of the effect of paying the divided in May 2004;   **(3 marks)**

(iv)   explaining why it is necessary to have reliable estimates of the chargeable income;   **(2 marks)**

(v)   advising them of their statutory obligations under the Corporation Tax Self Assessment (CTSA) system.   **(3 marks)**

       Presentation and style   **(5 marks)**

(Total : 27 marks)

Note that your calculations, in arriving at the corporation tax liability and the schedule of payments, should be shown in appendices attached to your report and you should assume that FY2003 rates continue to apply for FY2004.

The schedule of payments should cover the period from April 2004 to January 2006.

(b)   During the year to 31 March 2005 X Ltd's parent company, Z Ltd, experienced cash-flow problems. On 31 December 2004 Z Ltd sold its holding in X Ltd to B Ltd, a UK company which already owned two UK subsidiaries. You are aware that X Ltd owned an asset which had been transferred to it by Z Ltd under group arrangements in August 2000. The gain on this transaction at the time of the transfer was £30,000.

In May 2005 you have a meeting with the directors of B Ltd, who have been provided with a copy of your report made to X Ltd in April 2004, and they provide you with the following information:

♦ apart from the trading profit, which was £810,000, all of the other estimates shown in Part (a) were accurate;

♦ the supplier, S Ltd, to whom the loan of £50,000 was made, became insolvent on 31 January 2005 and nothing was recoverable;

♦ during January 2005, the directors of B Ltd considered that Mr Smith, the general manager of X Ltd, was unsatisfactory and dismissed him, making him a gratuitous payment of £24,000. This has not been treated as a deduction in the reported profits of X Ltd. Mr Smith later sold his 20% holding in X Ltd to B Ltd.

Required

Prepare a report for the directors of B Ltd:

(i) producing your calculation of the corrected corporation tax liability for the year ended 31 March 2005, and indicating whether there has been an over or under payment of corporation tax to date; **(6 marks)**

(ii) explaining the reasons for the difference between the projected and actual liability for the year ended 31 March 2005; **(4 marks)**

(iii) explaining how the over/under payment will affect the quarterly payment position by producing a revised schedule of payments. **(5 marks)**

Presentation and style **(4 marks)**

(19 marks)

(Total : 46 marks)

Any detailed calculations should be shown in appendices attached to your report.

Question 45

W Ltd (May 2001)

For the purposes of this scenario you are the chief accountant of W Ltd, a successful trading company resident in the United Kingdom. It is engaged in the manufacture and installation of kitchen equipment in domestic dwelling houses. The directors of the company are Mr W who owns 52% of the shares, his wife who owns 23% and their son who owns 25%. Neither W Ltd nor any of the directors owns shares in any other company.

For the year ended 31 December 2002 (the company's normal accounting date), the company had profits chargeable to corporation tax (CT) of £1,600,000 resulting in a CT liability of £372,000. For the year ended 31 December 2003 your staff had estimated that the chargeable profits, excluding any capital gains, would be £900,000. The company has surplus advance corporation tax (ACT) brought forward at 1 January 2003 amounting to £30,000.

During the month of May 2003, the directors asked you to attend a meeting at which they outlined their plans to expand the business. They proposed to acquire, on 1 July 2003, control of two companies, details of which are as follows:

(1)   B Ltd, an unlisted UK resident company engaged in the manufacture and installation of bedroom furniture in hotels. This company had formerly been profitable but, as a result of losing some major contracts, it has recently incurred trading losses. The directors of this company are Mr B and his wife who own all of the shares in equal holdings. This company also makes up accounts annually at 31 December. At 1 January 2003 it had trading losses brought forward of £35,000 and surplus ACT of £12,000. The directors estimated, at May 2003, that there would be a trading loss of £28,000 for the year ended 31 December 2003. The directors of W Ltd have decided that B Ltd has excellent future prospects and are keen to acquire control of it.

(2)   L Ltd is a small newly established company which manufactures luxury bathroom fittings. As a result of advertising on the Internet, it has secured a growing number of orders from residents of other countries including some in countries in the European Union (EU). For its year ended 31 December 2003 its directors have estimated that 80% of the company's turnover will be export supplies. As a result of substantial start up costs, they have estimated that the chargeable profit for the year to 31 December 2003 will be £30,000. The only shareholders and directors of this company are also a married couple, Mr and Mrs L, who hold equal amounts of shares.

The directors of W Ltd have advised you that they intend that the company will acquire all of the share capital of B Ltd and L Ltd from the existing shareholders, who will be retained as managers in their existing companies on long term contracts. They ask you to consider the tax implications of this approach and advise them of any alternative approach.

At the meeting, the directors advise you that the funds required to acquire control of B Ltd and L Ltd will amount to approximately £250,000. They propose to raise this partly by borrowing and partly by selling the following assets of W Ltd in June 2003:

♦   A plot of land which had been used for parking the company's trucks. This had been acquired in March 1989 for £35,000 and was to be sold for £60,000.

♦   A building bought in May 1987 for £70,000 was to be sold for £140,000. This building had been purchased using the full proceeds of the sale, in May 1987, of another building which had been bought in June 1978 for £30,000 and which had a market value at 31 March 1982 of £28,000. As both buildings had been used in the trade, full rollover relief was claimed on the occasion of the sale in May 1987.

These are the company's first disposals since March 1987.

The directors wish to establish how much of the acquisition price of £250,000 will require to be borrowed.

All of the companies are registered for value added tax (VAT) and your directors have asked you to advise them of any VAT implications there will be as a result of a group coming into existence.

The directors of W Ltd are in dispute amongst themselves concerning the level of dividend which should be paid - Mr W and his wife wish to keep the dividend at a modest figure of £20,000 because they wish to ensure that the surplus ACT brought forward at 1 January 2003 is utilised. Their son wishes the dividend to be £100,000.

Required [at June 2003]

(a)   Prepare a report for your board of directors, based on the information and estimates made available to you at May 2003 on the following matters:

    (i)   The amount of funds generated by W Ltd's sale of the assets in June 2003 **after** any corporation tax payable on the gains. This will enable the directors to arrange to borrow the balance of the acquisition price.   **(8 marks)**

    (ii)   The estimated corporation tax liabilities of W Ltd and L Ltd for the year ended 31 December 2003 on the assumptions that the share acquisitions take place on 1 July and that all possible loss reliefs are claimed. The effect of the alternative dividends should be shown and the dates of paying the corporation tax liabilities are required.   **(12 marks)**

    (iii)   The matters to be considered in deciding how to organise the VAT arrangements for the group.   **(6 marks)**

Note that any detailed calculations should be shown in appendices attached to your report.

(Presentation and style : 6 marks)

(Total for (a) : 32 marks)

On completion of the accounts, the following figures for the year ended 31 December 2003 are finalised and agreed:

    W Ltd - a chargeable profit of £860,000 (including the chargeable gains)
    B Ltd - a trading loss of £24,000
    L Ltd - a trading profit of £18,000

Required [post December 2003]

(b)   Prepare a brief report for the board of directors on the following matters:

    (i)   the correct corporation tax liabilities of W Ltd and L Ltd with taxable profits.

(7 marks)

    (ii)   the tax implications of any alternative method of gaining control of future target companies.   **(5 marks)**

(Presentation and style : 2 marks)

(Total for (b) : 14 marks)

Total marks for Question 2 : 46 marks)

Note: You may use the following indexation factors in answering the capital gains aspects of this question:

    March 1989 - June 2003   0.607
    March 1982 - May 1987   0.283
    May 1987 - June 2003   0.771

Question 46

L plc group (November 2001)

For the purpose of this scenario you are the chief accountant of L plc, a company resident in the United Kingdom with a number of interests in UK and overseas companies.

Your assistant has prepared the following diagram of the structure of the group together with some explanatory notes. The figures represent the percentages of the voting shares held in each case. Apart from T SA's acquisition of 20% of P Ltd on 1 October 2003, all of the holdings were acquired several years ago.

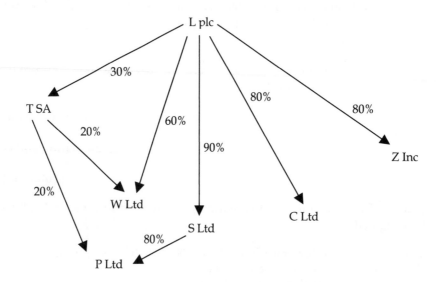

Notes:

1   Apart from T SA and Z Inc, all of the companies were incorporated in the UK.

2   Z Inc is a company which is incorporated abroad but which is centrally managed and controlled from the UK. It operates in a country where the only rate of corporation tax (CT) is 10%. Z Inc has no financial interest in any other company, resident either in the UK or overseas. The remaining 20% of Z Inc is owned by individuals.

3   T SA is incorporated abroad and is wholly managed abroad in a country where the rate of CT is 15%. Another 40% of its shares are owned equally by two other UK-resident companies.

Shortly after 31 March 2004, the date to which all of the companies make up accounts for twelve months, your assistant collates the results which are shown in the following table:

	L plc £000	S Ltd £000	C Ltd £000	P Ltd £000	Z Inc £000	W Ltd £000	T SA £000
Schedule DI profit	200	160	450				120
Schedule DI loss				(280)	(200)	(100)	
Other income	100		50	20		30	
Capital gain		80					
Capital loss			(90)				

Notes:

1   The capital gain arising in S Ltd was on an asset sold on 30 June 2003 and the capital loss in C Ltd arose from a sale in September 2003. Both sales were to third parties.

2   The profit in T SA has been computed in accordance with UK tax law.

3   None of the companies paid any dividends.

4   For the year ended 31 March 2003, C Ltd had chargeable profits of £600,000 and L plc and S Ltd both had profits of less than £200,000.

Required

(a)   Prepare a report for the Board of Directors showing the final corporation tax liabilities for the profit-making companies in the group, indicating in each case when the liabilities have been or will be paid. You may assume that any companies which were large companies this year were also large companies last year. Your report should explain:

   ♦   the application of the associated companies rules in the case of your group

   ♦   the nature of the reliefs which have been claimed, indicating why you chose to claim the reliefs in the manner in which you did;

   ♦   the nature of any elections which were required to be made to minimise the liabilities of group companies;

   ♦   the effect of the presence of T SA on the CT liability of L plc.

Your calculations of the liabilities of the various group companies should be included in an Appendix to your report and references to the figures in the Appendix should be shown in the body of your report.

(Your report (including presentation marks of 6) : 22 marks)

(Your Appendix : 14 marks)

(Total for section (a) : 36 marks)

During discussions with your Managing Director, he raised the following points:

♦   He indicated that L plc was considering operating a number of new profitable businesses in overseas countries and wished to know about the taxation implications of running them as branches of L plc or as separate subsidiaries, incorporated and managed overseas.

♦   He advised you that the Board of L plc was considering transferring the management of Z Inc to its country of operation and he wished to know the taxation consequences of this decision. It is anticipated that Z Inc will sustain trading losses for at least the next accounting year, but will become profitable thereafter.

Required

(b)   Prepare a memorandum to the Managing Director, responding to the points raised.

(10 marks)

(Total marks : 46 marks)

May 2002 Exam Questions

SECTION A - 14 MARKS

ANSWER *ALL* SEVEN SUB-QUESTIONS - 2 MARKS EACH

Each of the sub-questions numbered from 47.1 to 47.7 inclusive, given below, has only ONE correct answer.

Question 47 (1 of Exam Paper)

47.1   At the end of each income tax year, an employer is required to submit a return to the Inland Revenue showing the amount of income tax and NIC deducted from each employee during the tax year. This information is submitted on:

      A   Form P60

      B   Form P11D

      C   Form P35

      D   Form P45

47.2   X Ltd had been making up accounts annually to 31 May for several years. Early in 2003 the directors decided to make up accounts to 31 August 2003 (instead of 31 May 2003) and annually thereafter at 31 August. The two chargeable accounting periods for CT purposes will be:

A	1 June 2002 – 31 March 2003	and	1 April 2003 – 31 August 2003
B	1 June 2002 – 31 May 2003	and	1 June 2003 – 31 August 2003
C	1 June 2002 – 31 December 2002	and	1 January 2003 – 31 August 2003
D	1 June 2002 – 31 August 2002	and	1 September 2002 – 31 August 2003

47.3   G Ltd, a company resident in the United Kingdom with no associated companies, made up accounts for the nine month period to 30 September 2003. The total profits for this period were £35,000 including £5,000 of FII. The CT liability for the period will be:

      A   £5,598

      B   £5,700

      C   £5,714

      D   £6,000

47.4   A customer of J Ltd ordered a machine on 1 October 2003. J Ltd delivered it on 10 October 2003 and sent out an invoice on 20 October 2003. The customer paid in full on 1 November 2003.

The tax point for VAT purposes will be:

A   1 October 2003

B   10 October 2003

C   20 October 2003

D   1 November 2003

47.5   B Ltd, a large company for CT quarterly payment purposes, made up accounts for the eight month period to 31 August 2003.

The final payment under the quarterly system will be payable by:

A   14 July 2003

B   14 October 2003

C   14 December 2003

D   14 January 2004

47.6   During its accounting year ended 31 March 2004, K Ltd sold an antique table that had been in the boardroom for several years. The selling price was £6,600 and the cost plus indexation allowance amounted to £3,800.

The chargeable gain will be:

A   £2,800

B   £2,200

C   £360

D   £1,000

47.7   Q Ltd, a UK-resident company with no associated companies, had for its year ended 31 March 2004 turnover of £3.4 million and at no time during the year did the number of employees drop below 60.

At 1 April 2003 the balances brought forward for capital allowance purposes were:

General pool	£360,000
Expensive motor car	£24,000

During the year, £90,000 was spent on new computer equipment and the car was sold for £12,000.

The maximum capital allowances that the company can claim for the above year are:

A   £138,000

B   £168,000

C   £183,000

D   £192,000

(Total : 14 marks)

SECTION B - 46 MARKS

ANSWER THIS QUESTION

Question 48 (2 of Exam Paper)

A Ltd and B Ltd

The date at which this scenario takes place is September 2003.

You are chief accountant for A Ltd, a manufacturing company resident in the United Kingdom that has been making up accounts annually at 31 December. Up to September 2003 the company had no associated companies.

During September 2003, the directors decided that, instead of making up accounts for the 12 months to December 2003, accounts would be prepared for the 15 months ending 31 March 2004.

At a meeting with the board during September 2003, you were advised that between September 2003 and March 2004 the following transactions would occur:

1 An 80% holding of the ordinary shares of B Ltd would be acquired. B Ltd is an unquoted company engaged in the same trade as A Ltd and makes up its accounts to 31 December each year. Until 31 December 2002, it was making annual profits of £50,000 on average, although its estimated profit for the year ended 31 December 2003 is £70,000. The directors of A Ltd see B Ltd as having the potential, with better management, to earn much higher profits in the future. At present around 85% of B Ltd's products are exported. The price to be paid for the shares is approximately £100,000.

2 £90,000 would be invested by A Ltd in a new computer system.

3 An office block that had until recently been used for A Ltd's trade and which is now surplus to its requirements would be sold for £600,000. The building had cost £120,000 in March 1987.

The directors are aware that there are taxation implications concerning the precise timing of the above transactions and seek your guidance on this. They are concerned to ensure that the timings produce the smallest possible corporation tax (CT) liabilities.

The appendix below shows the actual (up to September 2003) and estimated income and expenditure of A Ltd for the 15 month period ending 31 March 2004 together with other relevant information.

Required

Prepare a report for the directors, based on the information available at September 2003, showing the estimated corporation tax (CT) liabilities of A Ltd for each of the two chargeable accounting periods [(i) 12 months to 31 December 2003; (ii) three months to 31 March 2004], in each case stating when the amounts should be paid.

Your report should explain **clearly** why you have chosen the dates on which the transactions (1) to (3) above should take place and should show approximately how much CT will be saved as a result of following your advice. You should also report on any other general taxation implications of A Ltd acquiring the above interest in B Ltd.

All of your calculations should be shown in appendices to your report.

Allocation of marks for reporting on and completing appendices for the relevant corporation tax, capital allowances and capital gains transactions:

(Transaction (1) = 13 marks)
(Transaction (2) = 9 marks)
(Transaction (3) = 8 marks)
(Other tax issues = 8 marks)
(Presentation = 8 marks)

(Total : 46 marks)

APPENDIX

(i)   These figures, estimated where necessary, relate to the 15 month period ending 31 March 2004 in respect of A Ltd:

	£	£
Income		
Estimated trading profits **before** capital allowances and patent royalties paid or received		1,500,000
Patent royalties received from UK companies:		
30 June 2003 (actual)	15,000	
31 December 2003 (estimated)	10,000	
		25,000
Patent royalties accrued at:		
31 March 2004 (estimated)		5,000

The patent royalties are received as part of A Ltd's trading activities and any amounts due are paid 6 monthly in arrears.

Dividends from foreign company receivable:	
28 February 2004 (estimated) [net of withholding tax @ 15%]	17,000

Expenditure

Patent royalties to UK company paid:	
30 September 2003 (actual)	30,000
31 March 2004 (estimated)	40,000

The use of the patent (for trade purposes) commenced on 1 April 2003 and the royalties are paid 6 monthly in arrears.

A Gift Aid payment of £10,000 will be paid some time between September 2003 and 31 March 2004.

(ii)   **Capital allowances**

At 1 January 2003 the balance brought forward on the general pool was £320,000 and, up to September 2003, no purchases or disposals were made.

(iii)   A Ltd's turnover for the 15 month period ended March 2004 is estimated at £10 million and the number of employees fluctuated between 120 and 150.

(iv)   The total profits of A Ltd for corporation tax purposes for the year ended 31 December 2002 amounted to £1,250,000.

(v)   As a result of additional costs to improve the performance of B Ltd, it is estimated that for the year ending 31 December 2004 a trading loss of approximately £80,000 is likely to occur and thereafter the company will start to earn substantial profits.

(vi)   The indexation factors that may be used in dealing with the sale of the office block purchased in March 1987 are:

For a sale in December 2003	0.818
For a sale in March 2004	0.835

SECTION C - 40 MARKS

ANSWER TWO QUESTIONS ONLY

Question 49 (3 of Exam Paper)

P Ltd and T Ltd

(a)   For the quarter ended 30 September 2003, P Ltd, a company registered for VAT, had turnover comprising £90,000 of supplies which were standard rated and £30,000 which were exempt. There were no zero-rated supplies made.

The input VAT on expenditure during the quarter was allocated as follows:

	£
Attributable to standard rate sales	4,000
Attributable to exempt sales	2,200
Unattributable	2,000

Required

Compute the amount of input VAT that P Ltd may recover in respect of the quarter ended 30 September 2003, explaining clearly how you arrived at your answer.

State what adjustment may be required at the end of the company's normal accounting year.   **(8 marks)**

(b)   You are the chief accountant of T Ltd, a rapidly growing successful company engaged in software engineering. The company employs a number of highly skilled workers whom the directors are anxious to retain. The managing director has read that employee share schemes introduced in the FA 2000 and as extended by the FA 2001 were designed to achieve this objective.

Required

Prepare a report for the directors describing the operation of:

(i)   the Share Incentive Plan (SIP); and   **(7 marks)**

(ii)   the Enterprise Management Incentive (EMI)   **(5 marks)**

Your answer should describe briefly the conditions that must be satisfied by both the company and the employees.   **(Total : 20 marks)**

Question 50 (4 of Exam Paper)

IB Ltd

IB Ltd, a UK manufacturing company making up accounts at 31 March each year, had the following industrial buildings in use at 1 April 2003.

Building 1　　This building had been purchased new on 1 April 1978 at a total cost of £80,000.

Building 2　　This building had been purchased new on 1 April 1999 at a cost of £140,000 including £20,000 for the cost of the land and £35,000 in respect of administration offices.

Building 3　　This building had been purchased second-hand from X Ltd on 1 April 1990 for £160,000. It had originally cost X Ltd £110,000 new on 1 April 1982.

All of the above buildings had been brought into use immediately on purchase and had been used at all times for qualifying purposes for Industrial Buildings Allowance.

Building 4　　This building, situated in an Enterprise Zone, had been purchased by B Ltd on 1 April 2001 for £100,000 and the company had claimed total allowances of 60% in the year ended 31 March 2002 and thereafter had claimed the maximum allowances available.

During the year ended 31 March 2003, the directors of IB Ltd were considering the purchase, on 1 April 2003, of one more second-hand qualifying building on which they were prepared to spend £120,000. They had narrowed the choice down to the following three buildings, each of which would be suitable for the business and each of which would cost £120,000 exclusive of the cost of land.

Building (a)　　Originally purchased by the previous owner for £150,000 on 1 April 1977.
Building (b)　　Originally purchased by the previous owner for £100,000 on 1 April 1980.
Building (c)　　Originally purchased by the previous owner for £120,000 on 1 April 2001.

All of the above prices are exclusive of the cost of the land.

All three of these buildings were brought into use by the original owners on the date of purchase and have always been used for industrial purposes.

Required

Compute the maximum Industrial Buildings Allowances that may be claimed by IB Ltd for the year ended 31 March 2004, assuming the most tax efficient choice was made concerning the building which was purchased on 1 April 2003. **(20 marks)**

Question 51 (5 of Exam Paper)

L Ltd and E Ltd

(a)   L Ltd, a UK-resident company, controls 78% of the ordinary shares of S Ltd, also UK-resident. Both companies make up accounts to 31 March 2004.

In May 2003, W Ltd, a major supplier of raw materials to both L Ltd and S Ltd, was experiencing serious cash flow problems. Had this company ceased to trade it would have created serious problems for L Ltd. After careful consideration and after having a valuation report on W Ltd prepared by a firm of accountants at a cost of £6,000, L Ltd made a loan to W Ltd of £50,000.

In December 2003, W Ltd paid L Ltd interest of £3,000 on the loan. This interest was credited to L Ltd's profit and loss account. In February 2004, one of W Ltd's major customers became insolvent and, as a result, W Ltd was unable to pay back any of the loan from L Ltd which wrote it off in its profit and loss account.

The results for the year ended 31 March 2004 were:

L Ltd   Profit of £60,000 – after writing off the above loan and costs and crediting the interest received from W Ltd.

S Ltd   Profit of £220,000.

Required

Explain how the above transactions would be dealt with by L Ltd for taxation purposes and indicate how the group of L Ltd and S Ltd can gain maximum relief under the loan relationship rules. You should show how much CT has been saved by your treatment.

(10 marks)

(b)   You are the financial controller of E Ltd, a small UK-resident manufacturing company engaged in the electronics industry.

Your chairman calls you to a meeting, at which he informs you that 80% of the company's share capital is about to be acquired by a company resident in the USA which already has 35 European subsidiaries including 4 which are resident in the UK.

Required

Draft a brief report to the chairman setting out the UK tax implications for E Ltd as a result of the takeover.   **(10 marks)**

(Total : 20 marks)

Question 52 (6 of Exam Paper)

G Ltd

G Ltd, a UK-resident company with two associated companies, had the following disposals during its year ended 31 March 2004.

1   G Ltd granted a 5 year lease to Z Ltd in May 2003 for a premium of £36,000. This sub-lease was out of a 40 year lease acquired by G Ltd for £50,000 in May 1998. G Ltd was able to charge this premium because of changes in market conditions.

2   In June 2003 a plot of land was sold for £80,000. G Ltd had originally purchased a larger plot of land in April 1985 for £15,000 and in May 1988 had sold a part of it for £12,000 when the value of the remainder of the land was agreed at £58,000. The land sold in 2003 represented the remainder of the original plot. In May 1988, G Ltd chose to apply the rules for small part-disposals of land.

3   In August 2003, a factory was sold for £180,000. This had originally been purchased in May 1976 for £30,000 and over the years the following qualifying expenditure had been incurred:

	£
June 1978	8,000
May 1981	12,000
August 1990	8,000
September 1998	15,000

The market value at 31 March 1982 was agreed at £40,000. On the occasion of previous disposals, G Ltd has failed to make a global election.

In addition to the above, you establish that in August 1995 G Ltd had sold a building for £200,000 giving rise to a chargeable gain of £50,000. £180,000 of the proceeds were immediately invested in plant and machinery and the maximum holdover relief claimed. In September 2003 the items of plant and machinery bought in 1995 were scrapped.

Required

Compute the capital gains or losses arising from the above transactions and, on the assumption that G Ltd had other taxable income of £200,000, calculate the additional CT arising as a result of the above.

(20 marks)

Indexation factors which may be used in answering this question:

March 1982	-	August 2003	1.281
April 1985	-	May 1988	0.120
April 1985	-	June 2003	0.904
May 1988	-	June 2003	0.700
May 1998	-	May 2003	0.105
August 1990	-	August 2003	0.415
September 1998	-	August 2003	0.102

The following percentages represent value of a short lease at the number of years remaining on the lease:

Number of years to run	% value remaining
40	95.457
35	91.981
30	87.330

November 2002 Exam Questions

SECTION A - 14 MARKS

ANSWER *ALL* SEVEN SUB-QUESTIONS - 2 MARKS EACH

Each of the sub-questions numbered from 53.1 to 53.7 inclusive, given below, has only ONE correct answer.

Question 53 (1 of Exam Paper)

53.1   On 1 October 2003, A Ltd places an order with B Ltd for a machine costing £12,000 exclusive of VAT. In order to obtain a discount of 10%, A Ltd pays £10,800 plus VAT on 10 October 2003 and the machine is delivered on 15 October 2003. B Ltd issues a VAT invoice for £10,800 plus VAT three days later.

The VAT tax point is:

A   1 October 2003

B   10 October 2003

C   15 October 2003

D   18 October 2003

53.2   When a company dismisses an employee, it must provide the employee with a:

A   Form P45

B   Form P35

C   Form P14

D   Form P46

53.3   CCD Ltd is a company which is liable to pay its corporation tax by quarterly instalments. It prepares accounts for the seven month accounting period ended on 31 July 2003. Prior to this period, the company had made up accounts annually at 31 December.

The due date for the **final quarterly payment** is:

A   14 July 2003

B   14 October 2003

C   14 November 2003

D   31 January 2004

53.4   An employee aged 45 has an annual salary of £20,000 and is provided with a motor car on which the assessable benefit is £2,400. The employee has underpaid tax for the year 2002/2003 of £110. Note that the personal allowance for 2003/2004 was £4,615.

The correct code number for 2003/2004 is:

A   171L

B   204L

C   221L

D   461L

53.5   A company has been making up its accounts annually to 30 June for many years. For the year ended 30 June 2002, it did not submit its annual return (CT600) until 31 August 2003.

What is the latest date by which the Inland Revenue can commence an investigation into the company's annual return?

A   30 June 2003

B   30 June 2004

C   31 August 2004

D   31 October 2004

53.6   L Ltd is a UK company whose annual turnover has not fallen below £20 million in recent years. The number of employees has fluctuated between 400 and 500 in the last three years and, in the year to 31 December 2003, the average number was 465. During the year, the company has spent £150,000 on new computer equipment.

It will be able to claim a first year allowance for this expenditure at which of the following rates?

A   100%

B   50%

C   40%

D   0%

53.7   T Ltd incurred legal fees during its 12 month accounting period ended 31 December 2003 on the following:

	£
Directors' service contracts	12,000
On a loan to be used to acquire a subsidiary company	9,000
Defending an action for faulty workmanship	6,000
Bringing a tax appeal to the High Court	16,000
Obtaining planning permission to extend a factory	8,000

In arriving at the company's Schedule D Case I profit, the amount to be added back will be:

A   £25,000

B   £31,000

C   £33,000

D   £39,000   **(Total : 14 marks)**

SECTION B - 46 MARKS

ANSWER THIS QUESTION

Question 54 (2 of Exam Paper)

TD Ltd

You are the Chief Accountant of TD Ltd, a company resident in the United Kingdom which owns two foreign subsidiaries, one resident in Germany and one in France. The latter was acquired during the year ended 31 December 2003. For the purpose of this question, today's date is 6 April 2004.

You are presently engaged in computing the company's final Corporation Tax (CT) liability in respect of its year ended 31 December 2003. For that year, the company had a turnover of £15 million and had employed, on average, 350 employees throughout the year.

You establish that the company had chargeable profits of £850,000 for the year ended 31 December 2002 and that, in January 2003, the estimate of the chargeable profits for the year ended 31 December 2003 had been £1 million. A significant increase in orders for the company's products in the final quarter of the year ended 31 December 2003 had increased the profits to the actual level achieved (see below).

You have asked your assistant, who is a trainee, to prepare a schedule of items of expenditure and income which have been reflected in the draft profit figure for the year and about which she is uncertain as to the taxation treatment. She has already made a number of standard adjustments, which you have approved, such as depreciation. The provisional adjusted profit she has arrived at, **before** any of the items in her schedule have been dealt with, is £1,320,000. A copy of this schedule is shown in Appendix 1.

You have also asked her to prepare a capital allowances computation for the year ended 31 December 2003 and a copy of her computation is shown in Appendix 2. She has deducted her capital allowances figure of £275,000 in arriving at her provisional adjusted profit figure of £1,320,000.

Required

(a)   Prepare a report for the directors of TD Ltd in respect of the year ended 31 December 2003, dealing with each of the following matters:

      (i)   the final adjusted Schedule D Case I profit figure (including the revised capital allowance figure). The report should give a full explanation of **four** of the items you have adjusted (apart from those involving loans).   **(16 marks)**

      (ii)   the company's final CT liability, indicating when and how this is payable. This should include the revised capital allowances computation.   **(16 marks)**

(Presentation marks : 4)

    Note: The calculations of the adjusted profit, the CT computation and the corrected capital allowances computation should all be shown in separate Appendices.

(Total marks for (a) : 36)

(b)   Prepare a separate report for the directors explaining the taxation treatment of those items of expenditure and income involving transactions associated with loans.

(8 marks)

(Presentation marks : 2)

(Total marks for (b) : 10)

Note: In **both** reports it is necessary to give any required explanations **only** in the actual reports. It is not necessary to repeat the explanations in your Appendices.

(Total : 46 marks)

APPENDIX 1 FOR QUESTION 54

Schedule of items included in the profit and loss account for the year ended 31 December 2003 to be considered in adjusting profits

Expenditure

(A)   A senior manager was seconded to work abroad for Oxfam for six months of the year. The manager's salary of £20,000 was paid by TD Ltd although he did no work for the company during that period.

(B)   The figure for repairs included £40,000 spent on bringing a recently purchased second-hand printing press into working order.

(C)   Loan interest of £15,000 was paid to a UK finance company in respect of a loan used to buy new plant and machinery.

(D)   The company paid legal fees in respect of the following:

Costs of a share issue	£12,500
Costs of raising the loan in (C) above	£8,000

(E)   A senior employee, who is also a shareholder, was found to have misappropriated goods valued at £35,000. This amount has been charged as an expense in the accounts. No conviction has yet been obtained in the Courts.

(F)   A loan of £40,000 made to a supplier who was experiencing financial difficulties proved irrecoverable and was written off in the accounts.

(G)   A severance payment of £40,000 was made to a manager who was dismissed because of his disruptive behaviour. The trade did not cease and no other person was made redundant at this time. The statutory amount was £18,000.

(H)   The company spent £30,000 acquiring a 10% interest in the share capital of an unquoted UK company which satisfied the conditions to be an Enterprise Investment Scheme (EIS) company.

(I)   The company paid loan interest of £28,000 to a UK bank in respect of a loan obtained to purchase a controlling interest in a company resident in France.

Income

(J)   The company received a sum of £22,000 from an insurance company. This represented the cost value of bales of paper which had been destroyed as a result of flooding in the previous accounting period. The figure of £22,000 had been written off in the accounts for the previous year.

(K)   Loan interest of £5,000 was received in respect of the loan made to the supplier referred to in (F) above.

(L)   Dividends of £60,000 (net) were received from UK companies.

(M)   The company made a gain of £130,000 on the sale of a property in June 2003 and this amount was credited to the profit and loss account. This represented the gain arising by comparing the proceeds of £340,000 with the book value. The property had cost £220,000 in June 1997. The company reinvested £300,000 of the proceeds in a replacement business property and claimed the maximum possible rollover relief. The Indexation Factor for the period June 1997 to June 2003 is 0.146.

(N)   The company received rents of £24,000 from letting part of its premises to sub-contractors.

APPENDIX 2 FOR QUESTION 54

Capital allowances computation prepared by assistant

Year ended 31 December 2003

Balances brought forward at 1 January 2003

	£
General pool	650,000
Expensive car	28,000
Short-life asset (SLA)	20,000

Transactions during the year:

Acquisitions

Two cars costing	£32,000 and £24,000
New computer costing	£250,000

Disposals

Original expensive car – sold for	£12,000
SLA sold for	£25,000

Assistant's computation

		General pool £	Expensive cars £	SLA £	Allowances £
Brought forward		650,000	28,000	20,000	
Disposals			(12,000)	(25,000)	
Additions			56,000		
			72,000		
Balancing charge				5,000	(5,000)
WDA		162,500	18,000		180,500
		487,500	54,000		
	FYA £				
Computer	250,000				
FYA 40%	100,000	150,000	-		100,000
Carried forward 31 December 2003		637,500	54,000	Total allowances	275,500

SECTION C - 40 MARKS

ANSWER TWO QUESTIONS ONLY

Question 55 (3 of Exam Paper)

Hols Ltd

Hols Ltd owns a large luxury hotel in the English Lake District. Its profits have been declining in recent years and, in an attempt to revive its fortunes, it decided to employ a number of high-calibre staff, including a new Manager and a Senior and Assistant Chef, all of whom commenced employment on 6 April 2003. In order to attract staff of the required quality, certain inducements had been offered to them. You are provided with the following information:

1   The new Manager was provided with an apartment within the hotel that had been occupied by the previous Manager and £8,000 was spent on refurbishing it. The new Manager was paid relocation expenses of £12,000 to meet the costs of moving from the south of England.

2   The Senior Chef was provided with a house owned by the company which is situated a mile from the hotel. It was not a condition of his employment that he should live in the hotel although accommodation was available for him. The house had cost the company £140,000 two years ago and, in the year ended 5 April 2004, the company paid heating and maintenance costs of £5,000. The Senior Chef's annual salary was £35,000 and he was paid relocation expenses of £10,000. He paid no rent for the house which had a gross annual value of £12,000. In order to allow him to furnish the house to his taste, on 6 April 2003 the company made him an interest-free loan of £8,000, all of which remained outstanding at 5 April 2004.

3   The Assistant Chef was required under his contract of service to live in the hotel so that he was available at all times. The cost of his accommodation to Hols Ltd was £7,000 per annum. He has two children of school age and the company undertook to pay their school fees amounting, in the year to 5 April 2004, to £6,000 in total. He received relocation expenses of £5,000.

4   All members of staff were provided with free meals in a staff dining room, the annual estimated cost being £20,000.

Note: All of the relocation costs were paid on 6 April 2003.

Required

In respect of the income tax year 2003/2004:

(a)   compute the total amount of Class 1A National Insurance Contributions (NIC) the company will be required to pay in respect of the above arrangements, explaining in each case how you arrived at the assessable benefit.   **(16 marks)**

(b)   state how and when these benefits will be reported to the Inland Revenue and indicate the date by which the Class 1A NIC must be paid.   **(4 marks)**

Note: Assume an official rate of interest of 5%.   **(Total : 20 marks)**

Question 56 (4 of Exam Paper)

New Ltd

New Ltd, a UK trading company with no associated companies, started trading on 1 July 2001. The directors decided, during the month of June 2002, to choose 30 September as the accounting date and made up the first accounts for the period to 30 September 2002. Thereafter, accounts were made up annually to 30 September. Initially the company made good profits, but in May 2002 a major customer went into liquidation causing a large reduction in New Ltd's turnover which remained at a much lower level throughout the year ended 30 September 2003. This resulted in a substantial trading loss for that year. Early in October 2003, a number of new profitable contracts were obtained, resulting in the company returning to profitability. The results for the first three trading periods were:

	Period ended 30 Sept 2002 £	*Year ended 30 Sept 2003* £	*Year ended 30 Sept 2004* £
Trading profit	900,000		860,000
Trading loss		1,100,000	
Patent royalties received (gross figures):			
31 May 2002	60,000		
30 September 2002	5,000		
30 September 2003		12,000	
30 September 2004			40,000
Payments			
Patent royalties paid (gross figures):			
30 April 2002	20,000		
30 September 2003	10,000		
30 September 2003		30,000	
30 September 2004			30,000
Gift Aid payments (gross figures):			
December 2001	20,000		
December 2003			15,000

The patent royalties (both paid and received) relate to the company's trading activities and are paid/received as they accrue. No account has been taken of patent royalties or Gift Aid in arriving at the above figures of trading profits and loss.

Notes: **IGNORE** any income tax on interest and patent royalties. Simply use the gross figures. Assume the FY 2003 CT rates and thresholds apply throughout.

Required

Compute the amounts of corporation tax that will be payable and recoverable in respect of each of the above accounting periods, assuming the maximum possible relief for trading losses is claimed at the earliest opportunity. In the case of payments, indicate the dates on which these payments are due. **(20 marks)**

Question 57 (5 of Exam Paper)

H Ltd and S Ltd

(a)   On 1 October 2001, H Ltd, a trading company making up accounts to 30 September each year, granted a 20 year lease of a freehold property to S Ltd, also a trading company, at an annual rental of £20,000. In addition, S Ltd was required to pay a premium to H Ltd of £60,000.

On 1 October 2003, S Ltd, which also makes up its accounts to 30 September each year, granted a 5 year sub-lease of the above property to W Ltd at an annual rental of £12,000 and required W Ltd to pay a premium of £15,000.

Required

(i)   Compute the total amount assessable on S Ltd under Schedule A in respect of the year ended 30 September 2004. Show clearly all your workings.   **(8 marks)**

(ii)   Explain briefly the interaction between Schedule A and capital gains in the context of the taxation of leases. You are **not** required to compute any capital gains.   **(4 marks)**

(b)   A very successful UK trading company has generated a large amount of surplus funds and has decided to expand by acquiring a controlling interest in a number of other UK companies which are engaged in a wide variety of diverse activities.

Some of these companies supply, for VAT purposes, only standard-rated goods and services, others make only zero-rated supplies, one makes only exempt supplies and one exports all of its output.

Required

Draft a brief report to the directors explaining the most efficient method of organising the VAT registration structure.   **(8 marks)**

(Total : 20 marks)

Question 58 (6 of Exam Paper)

E Ltd

E Ltd, a UK resident company engaged in the electronics industry, is the wholly-owned subsidiary of a French company which also owns all of the share capital of four other UK companies.

During the year ended 31 March 2004, the French parent company disposed of 30% of its holding in E Ltd to an American company.

You establish that E Ltd owns a property which was transferred to it by one of the other UK subsidiaries, F Ltd, in March 1999 on a no gain/no loss basis. This property had cost F Ltd £200,000 in March 1992 and its market value at the date of transfer was agreed at £350,000.

In addition you are advised that the following disposals were made by E Ltd during its year ended 31 March 2004.

1   **31 July 2003**

30,000 ordinary shares in K Ltd were sold for £120,000. These were part of a holding of 50,000 shares which had been acquired as follows:

Date		Number of shares	Cost £
January 1980		5,000	6,000
January 1982		10,000	15,000
May 1990		15,000	40,000
June 1990	A bonus issue of one share for every two held	15,000	-
June 1996		5,000	15,000

The market value (MV) of each share at 31 March 1982 was £1.40 (adjusted for the bonus issue). K Ltd has an issued share capital of 800,000 ordinary shares.

2   **30 September 2003**

A warehouse, which had been used for the purpose of the trade, was sold for £180,000. This had been acquired using the full proceeds of the sale of a building for £60,000 in March 1986. This original building had cost £30,000 in March 1981 and, on the occasion of its disposal, E Ltd had claimed the maximum rollover relief.

The MV of the warehouse at 31 March 1982 was £28,000.

3   **25 December 2003**

The company gifted a painting which was valued at £20,000 to a local art gallery which is open to the public. The painting had originally cost the company £1,500 in March 1987.

You are advised that another of the French company's 100% UK subsidiaries, H Ltd, had, in October 2002, sold a property to a third party, giving rise to an allowable loss of £30,000. H Ltd had no chargeable gains in its year ended 31 March 2004.

Required

(a)   Compute the amount of capital gains which would be included in E Ltd's corporation tax (CT) computation for the year ended 31 March 2004, assuming all possible reliefs are claimed and that no global election for MV at 31 March 1982 had been made.

(16 marks)

(b)   Compute the **additional** CT arising on the gains you have calculated in your answer to requirement (a) above, assuming that E Ltd had other income chargeable to CT for the year ended 31 March 2004 amounting to £120,000.   **(4 marks)**

(Total : 20 marks)

Indexation factors may be used in answering this question.

March 1982	-	July 2003	1.277
March 1982	-	March 1986	0.218
March 1986	-	September 2003	0.875
March 1987	-	December 2003	0.818
May 1990	-	June 1996	0.212
March 1992	-	March 1999	0.200
June 1996	-	July 2003	0.182

May 2003 Exam Questions

SECTION A – 20 MARKS

ANSWER *ALL* TEN SUB-QUESTIONS – 2 MARKS EACH

Question 59 (1 of Exam Paper)

59.1 In order to attract a high-calibre sales director, R Ltd agreed to provide her from 6 April 2003 with a new house which had cost the company £200,000. The annual value of the house was £15,000 and the director is to pay rent of £500 per month to the company. The company will pay the Council Tax of £2,500 and all other running costs will be paid by the director. You may assume an official rate of interest of 5%.

Her assessable benefit for 2003/04 will be:

A   £17,750

B   £21,250

C   £22,250

D   £23,750

59.2 A customer of X Ltd, a machine manufacturer, orders a machine on 31 October 2003. On 5 November 2003, the customer sends a cheque for the full amount and this is credited to X Ltd's bank account on 8 November 2003. The machine is delivered by X Ltd on 15 November 2003 together with an invoice dated the same date.

For VAT purposes the tax point is:

A   31 October 2003

B   5 November 2003

C   8 November 2003

D   15 November 2003

59.3   MG Ltd provided its sales manager with the use of a motor car throughout 2003/04. The car was a diesel car with CO_2 emissions of 205 grams per kilometre. The list price of the car was £25,000 and the company spent a further £3,000 on extras before providing it to the manager. During 2003/04 his total mileage was 30,000, of which 24,000 was business mileage.

The taxable benefit for 2003/04 is:

A   £6,250

B   £6,272

C   £7,000

D   £7,840

59.4   An employee paying higher rate tax is provided with a motor car throughout 2003/04 and the assessable benefit is agreed at £3,300. The employee has underpaid tax for the year 2002/03 of £80, which is to be collected via his PAYE code number for 2003/04.

The correct code number for 2003/04 is:

A   461L

B   131L

C   123L

D   111L

Note that the personal allowance for 2003/04 is £4,615.

59.5   A company has been making up its accounts annually to 31 March for many years. During 2003 it decided to change its accounting date and made up accounts for the nine months ended 31 December 2003. The company failed to submit its Corporation Tax Annual Return (CT600) for this period until 24 April 2005.

What is the latest date by which the Inland Revenue can commence an investigation into the company's annual return?

A   31 December 2005

B   24 April 2006

C   30 April 2006

D   31 July 2006

59.6   K Ltd is a UK company which made up accounts for the twelve month period to 31 March 2004.

In its profit and loss account, it had listed the following amounts under an expense heading 'Charges'.

			£
(i)	Patent royalties paid to an individual (gross amount)		7,800
(ii)	Patent royalties paid to a UK company (including an accrued amount of £5,000)		20,000
(iii)	Debenture interest paid (debenture used to acquire business premises)		30,000
(iv)	Loan interest payable (including £5,000 accrued) Loan used to finance acquisition of a subsidiary company		25,000

The amount to be added back in arriving at the company's adjusted Schedule D Case I profit is:

A   £25,000

B   £52,800

C   £55,000

D   £82,500

59.7   STD Ltd is a company which is liable to pay its corporation tax by quarterly instalments. It prepared accounts for the eight month chargeable accounting period ended on 31 August 2003 and the agreed CT liability for this period is £240,000.

The final instalment will be:

A   £80,000 due on 14 January 2003.

B   £60,000 due on 14 December 2003.

C   £80,000 due on 14 December 2003.

D   £60,000 due on 14 January 2004.

59.8 S Ltd is a company which is partially exempt for VAT purposes. For its quarter ended 30 June 2003, its unattributable input VAT for the quarter which cannot be linked directly to its chargeable supplies or exempt supplies is £6,000. Its sales for the quarter comprised:

	£
Zero rated	20,000
Standard rated	10,000 (excluding VAT)
Exempt	6,000

The amount of the **unattributable** input VAT of £6,000 it may recover for the quarter is:

A £1,000

B £1,200

C £1,667

D £5,000

59.9 B Ltd is a UK-resident company with a turnover of £20 million for its year ended 31 March 2004. It never had fewer than six hundred employees during that year.

The balances brought forward at 1 April 2003 for capital allowances purposes were:

	£
General pool	840,000
Jaguar car	11,000 (cost £24,000)
Bentley car	48,000

During the year to 31 March 2004, the Bentley car was sold for £24,000 and three new cars conforming to the new low CO_2 emissions regulations were purchased on 24 April 2003 at a cost of £15,000 **each**.

The company may claim maximum capital allowances for the year to 31 March 2004 of:

A £230,750

B £231,000

C £251,750

D £281,750

59.10 W Ltd, a UK company with one associate, had chargeable profits of £9,000 for its chargeable accounting period of **nine months** ended 30 September 2003.

Its CT liability is:

A Nil

B £356

C £1,247

D £1,710

SECTION B – 40 MARKS

ANSWER THIS QUESTION

Question 60 (2 of Exam Paper)

BJD Ltd

For the purpose of this question you are the chief accountant of BJD Ltd and the report you will produce is required early in 2004.

BJD Ltd is a company resident in the United Kingdom. It is involved in the manufacture and supply of telecommunications equipment to both UK and overseas customers. Mr D formed the company in 1998 and he holds 60% of the ordinary shares in the company. His wife, Mrs D, holds 30% and both are full-time directors. The other 10% is held by his son, SD, who also works full-time in the business as the sales manager.

Mr D also holds 75% of the shares of TEC Ltd, a UK-resident company that supplies components to BJD Ltd. It is currently sustaining substantial trading losses and Mr D hopes to claim relief for these against BJD Ltd's CT liability.

Mr D calls you to a meeting early in January 2004 and asks you to produce a report by the end of January 2004 dealing with the following matters:

(1)   The CT liability of BJD Ltd for its chargeable accounting period of 12 months ended 31 December 2003. The required information is shown in the Appendix.

(2)   The taxation implications of his son receiving from the company a short-term interest-free loan of £40,000 which will be repaid sometime during 2004.

(3)   The tax advantages which will be available to the company if it spends £50,000 on research and development during 2004.

(4)   The tax implications of operating a proposed overseas manufacturing unit based in a country where the rate of corporation tax is currently slightly higher than the UK rate but could fall in the near future. Mr D seeks advice on the tax differences between running this operation as a branch or as a subsidiary. The unit is likely to break even in its first year and Mr D asks whether he should set it up before 31 December 2004.

(5)   He also wishes BJD Ltd to acquire a 40% interest in an existing foreign company resident in a country where the rate of CT is 12%. If this proceeds, 40% of the shares in the foreign company will be held by BJD Ltd, 40% by Z Ltd (a non-UK resident company) and the other 20% will be held by individuals resident in the foreign country. He seeks your advice on the CT implications of this plan.

Required

Prepare a suitable report for Mr D, in professional style, dealing with each of the above matters. Any calculations should be included in an appendix and referred to in your report.

The allocation of the marks for this question is as follows:

Content	*Item (1) (including computation)*	*12 marks*
	Item (2)	*6 marks*
	Item (3)	*4 marks*
	Item (4)	*7 marks*
	Item (5)	*5 marks*
	Presentation	*5 marks*
		(Total – 40 marks)

APPENDIX FOR QUESTION 60

The following information relates to BJD Ltd's accounting period of 12 months ended 31 December 2003:

Turnover	£2.1 million
Number of employees	30

Income

		£
Draft adjusted Schedule D Case I profit	*(Note (i) below)*	254,000
Rents receivable		18,000
Interest receivable	*(Note (ii) below)*	6,000
Dividends from UK companies (gross FII figure)		20,000
Capital gain	*(Note (iii) below)*	80,000

Expenditure

Dividends paid	30,000
Gift Aid payments	12,000

Notes:

(i)   The adjusted profit figure includes patent royalties of £20,000 (gross) received net from individuals during the year.

(ii)   The interest was receivable in respect of a loan of £30,000 to a supplier company. During the year, this company went into liquidation and BJD Ltd wrote off the £30,000. The adjusted profit of £254,000 is after adding back this £30,000.

(iii)   There were capital losses of £95,000 brought forward at 1 January 2003.

(iv)   TEC Ltd had trading losses of £100,000 for the year ended 31 December 2003.

(v)   You may assume an official rate of interest of 5%.

SECTION C – 40 MARKS

ANSWER TWO QUESTIONS ONLY

Question 61 (3 of Exam Paper)

G Ltd

G Ltd has engaged a new sales manager who will take up his appointment from 6 April 2003 but has yet to decide whether to provide him with a company car paying for both business and private running costs or pay him to use his own car.

The company is aware that new rules on CO_2 emissions and new approved mileage allowance payments (AMAP) have been introduced. AMAPs are tax-free amounts which can be paid to employees who use their own car for an employer's business (see below). As a result of these new rules, the company considered it appropriate to offer the new sales manager the alternative of taking a higher salary instead of taking a company car.

As company accountant, you have been asked to prepare statements for both the manager and the directors of the company showing the implications of this suggested approach for both the employee and the company. You should assume that you are doing this work prior to 6 April 2003 and trying to make the correct decisions.

The following details are relevant to the question:

♦ The manager is a higher rate taxpayer (40%).

♦ The car chosen by the manager is a VW Passat (petrol) – list price £18,000 – with an engine capacity of 1,800 cc.

♦ The fuel benefit base figure for 2003/04 is £14,400.

♦ Based on the CO_2 emissions, the taxable percentage of the car's list price is 24%.

♦ The AMAP tax-free rates are 40p per mile for the first 10,000 business miles and 25p per mile for any additional business miles. The company will pay the manager 20p for each business mile travelled.

♦ You may assume the following:

(1) The manager's total mileage for the year 2003/04 will be 24,000 miles including 4,000 private miles.

(2) The car will do, on average, 35 miles per gallon and the price of petrol will, on average, be £3.50 per gallon.

(3) The manager will, if providing his own car, be able to lease it for £3,600 per annum. Insurance and repairs will cost him about £1,200 in a year.

(4) Instead of providing a car, the company will increase the manager's salary by £300 per month (gross).

(5) The company will be paying its CT at 19%.

(6) The rate of Class 1A NIC is 12.8%.

Required

(a) Prepare a computation for the manager showing him the differences between the cash position which will arise in respect of 2003/04:

♦ if he provides the car himself and claims the AMAP rates; and
♦ if the employer provides him with a car and applies a car and fuel benefit.

(12 marks)

(b) Prepare a computation for the directors showing the effect on the company's cash position under each of the above alternatives advising them as to which alternative should be chosen. **(8 marks)**

(Total – 20 marks)

Question 62 (4 of Exam Paper)

CCD Ltd

CCD Ltd, a UK-resident manufacturing company with no subsidiaries, made up its accounts for the **ten month** period to 31 October 2003. Its turnover for this period was £8 million and it had, on average, 100 employees.

On 30 June 2003, the company sold a factory for £180,000 which it had bought new in January 1999 for £210,000 and used for qualifying purposes until 31 December 2000. Thereafter, up to 31 December 2002, the building did not qualify for Industrial Buildings Allowance (IBA) but did qualify from 1 January 2003 until it was sold. The company replaced this building on 1 July 2003 with a second-hand qualifying factory that cost £220,000. This had cost the original owner £140,000 new on 1 January 1990.

In May 2003, the company converted the area above one of its storage facilities, at a cost of £120,000 into two apartments which were then residentially let.

The following balances for capital allowances purposes were brought forward at 1 January 2003:

	£
General pool	740,000
Jaguar car	18,000
BMW car	34,000
Short-life asset (SLA) – computer	25,000

During the ten month period to 31 October 2003, the following transactions took place:

Disposals		**Sold for** £
10 April 2003	Jaguar car	12,000
12 April 2003	BMW car	28,000
30 June 2003	Plant (original cost £14,000)	6,000
30 September 2003	SLA (computer)	4,000
10 October 2003	Low emissions car (A)	15,000

Purchases		**Cost** £
8 January 2003	Energy-saving heating system	45,000
11 April 2003	Low emissions car (A)	16,000
24 April 2003	Low emissions car (B)	18,000
26 September 2003	New computer system	60,000

Required

(a)   Compute the maximum capital allowances (including Industrial Buildings Allowances) which can be claimed by CCD Ltd for the **ten month** period ended 31 October 2003.   **(16 marks)**

(b)   Explain your treatment of the low emissions cars and the new computer.   **(4 marks)**

(Total - 20 marks)

Question 63 (5 of Exam Paper)

PGD Ltd

Until 30 September 2003, 80% of the shares of PGD Ltd, a UK-resident company, were held by MD Ltd, another UK company. On that date, MD Ltd disposed of half of its shares in PGD Ltd. In October 1999, MD Ltd had transferred a building to PGD Ltd on a no gain no loss basis. The building had originally cost MD Ltd £140,000 in May 1995 and its market value at October 1999 was agreed at £200,000.

In March 2004, PGD Ltd purchased a further building for £210,000.

During its 12-month accounting period to 31 March 2004, PGD Ltd made the following disposals:

August 2003

(1)   Sold 10,000 ordinary shares of 50p each in TD Ltd for £36,000 (a 1% holding).

These shares had been acquired in May 1997 as a result of a reorganisation of the share capital of TD Ltd.

PGD Ltd had originally bought 2,000 ordinary shares in TD Ltd in April 1987 at £1.20 each.

In May 1997, these were converted and PGD Ltd received the following holdings:

Holding	*Value on first day of trading*
12,000 ordinary shares of 50p each	£2.20 per share
5,000 preference shares of 25p each	60p per share
£1,000 5% debentures – total value	£2,000

November 2003

(2)   Sold for £4,800 a marble statue which had been standing in the entrance to PGD Ltd's premises.

This had cost £8,000 in May 1986.

December 2003

(3)   Sold part of the landscaped gardens surrounding the business premises to a house builder for £280,000.

The whole of this land had an original cost of £60,000 allocated to it when the site was purchased in May 1985 and the agreed value of the gardens retained is £160,000.

Required

(a)   Compute the total gains which will be included in the CT computation of PGD Ltd for the year ended 31 March 2004.   **(16 marks)**

(b)   Explain the extent to which the CT on any of the above gains may be deferred.

(4 marks)

(Total : 20 marks)

Indexation Factors which may be used in answering this question:

May 1986	-	November 2003	0.865
April 1987	-	August 2003	0.780
May 1995	-	October 1999	0.113
May 1985	-	December 2003	0.921

Question 64 (6 of Exam Paper)

O Ltd

O Ltd, a UK-resident company, had four wholly-owned subsidiaries, two of which were resident in the UK and the other two resident overseas. It made up accounts for the twelve months ended 31 March 2004.

It also had interests in three other non-UK resident companies, details of which for the year ended 31 March 2004 were as follows:

Company	Shareholding	Rate of withholding tax	Post-tax profits	Foreign tax paid
	%	%	£	£
X SA	7	10	480,000	50,000
Y Inc	9	28	800,000	200,000
Z PG	15	20	960,000	240,000

O Ltd is in a period of poor trading and, for the year ended 31 March 2004, it made a trading loss of £150,000. Its other taxable UK income in that year comprised rental income of £25,000 and a chargeable gain of £30,000. During the year, the company made a Gift Aid payment of £5,000.

During the year, O Ltd received dividends from its overseas holdings shown above. None of the companies had made any distributions for several years and they were able to make the following payments to O Ltd from undistributed profits:

Company	£
X SA	162,000
Y Inc	144,000
Z PG	120,000

It is assumed that O Ltd will make the most efficient claim for loss relief at the earliest opportunity.

Required

(a)   Compute the CT payable by O Ltd for the year ended 31 March 2004. Your answer should show clearly, in *columnar* layout (treating each item of overseas income in a separate column), your treatment of the trading losses and the Gift Aid payment. You should explain why you have chosen to make any deductions from particular items of income. **(15 marks)**

(b)   State briefly the circumstances in which any of the three identified foreign companies above would be treated as a controlled foreign company. **(5 marks)**

(Total - 20 marks)

Note: The syllabus excludes 'on-shore' pooling of foreign tax credits and you should NOT include the effect of these provisions in your answer.

November 2003 Exam Questions

SECTION A - 20 MARKS

Answer ALL ten sub-questions – 2 marks each.

Question 65 (1 of Exam Paper)

65.1   N Ltd, a manufacturing company, started trading on 1 October 2003. Its turnover was:

	£
For each of the first four months	7,000
Monthly turnover thereafter	10,000

The company must be registered for VAT no later than:

A   1 May 2004

B   1 June 2004

C   1 July 2004

D   1 August 2004

65.2   A basic rate taxpayer, aged 45, is employed by a UK company. He has unpaid tax of £220 in respect of 2002/03 and he has asked for this to be collected through his code number for 2003/04. During each year he pays an allowable professional subscription of £200. The personal allowance for 2003/04 is £4,615.

His code number, for PAYE purposes, for 2003/04 is:

A   61L

B   261L

C   381L

D   379L

65.3   D Ltd is a large company that pays its corporation tax (CT) quarterly. For the year ended 31 March 2004, the directors had estimated the total CT at £600,000 and, by 14 January 2004, £300,000 had been paid. During February 2004, the company lost a major customer and the directors revised the estimated CT to £500,000.

How much should the company pay on 14 April 2004?

A   £75,000

B   £125,000

C   £150,000

D   £175,000

65.4   During its accounting period of 12 months ended 31 December 2003, L Ltd had the following transactions:

(i)   It paid debenture interest of £20,000 (gross). The debentures had been issued last year to fund the building of business premises.

(ii)   It paid loan interest of £15,000 (gross) on a loan raised during 2003 to fund the purchase of a French subsidiary. Costs of securing the loan were £2,000.

(iii)   Received loan interest of £8,000 (gross) on a loan made to a supplier company.

(iv)   Suffered a bad debt of £50,000 as a result of the above loan in (iii) proving irrecoverable. Costs of unsuccessfully pursuing the loan were £3,000.

The non-trade loan deficit available to L Ltd will be:

A   £12,000

B   £62,000

C   £70,000

D   £82,000

65.5   A Ltd, a UK resident company with one associated company, had chargeable profits for its year ended 31 March 2004 of £160,000. In addition, it had FII of £10,000.

Its CT liability for the above period is:

A   £14,500

B   £30,400

C   £32,000

D   £32,988

65.6   M Ltd, a very small company, made up accounts for the period of 12 months ended 31 December 2003.

During this period, it bought machinery costing £16,000 and a computer system costing £12,000. In June 2003, it purchased a new low emissions car costing £14,000 and sold the expensive car for £8,000.

The balances brought forward for capital allowances purposes at 1 January 2003 were:

Pool	£36,000
Expensive car	£13,000

The maximum capital allowances claimable for the above period are:

A   £32,600

B   £43,400

C   £46,400

D   £53,000

65.7   During its year ended 31 March 2004, V Ltd, a VAT registered company, paid a fire insurance premium of £10,000.

For VAT purposes this payment is:

A   Exempt

B   Standard rated

C   Zero rated

D   Outside the scope

65.8   On 1 January 2004, G Ltd made interest free loans of £4,000 to EACH of its ten employees.

The amount of Class 1A National Insurance Contributions the company will be required to pay for 2003/04 in respect of these loans will be:

A   Nil

B   £75

C   £175

D   £283

65.9   T Ltd makes up its accounts to 30 June each year. It submitted its CT 600 Corporation Tax return for the year to 30 June 2003 on 10 October 2004.

The company will be required to pay a penalty of:

A   £100

B   £200

C   £500

D   £1,000

65.10   An employer pays 15p per mile to an employee who does 20,000 business miles in his own car during 2003/04.

How much can the employee claim as a deduction against his taxable income for the tax year 2003/04?

A   £3,000

B   £3,400

C   £3,500

D   £6,500

(Total : 20 marks)

SECTION B – 40 MARKS

Answer this question.

Question 66 (2 of Exam Paper)

R Ltd

R Ltd is a UK resident company, engaged in manufacturing and distributing optical equipment, whose turnover has ranged between £6 million and £8 million in recent years. Its workforce has never exceeded 150. The turnover of R Ltd's group has never exceeded £15 million and the number of group employees has not exceeded 200.

The directors of R Ltd had estimated that, at September 2003, its total chargeable profits for the year ended 31 March 2004 would be £600,000 and based its quarterly payments on this amount. During the quarter to December 2003, the directors revised this figure to £800,000. Your computations, based on other information contained in the attached appendix, will enable you to establish the actual chargeable profits and the final CT liability for the year ended 31 March 2004. You may assume that the figures were finalised and agreed in May 2004.

The Inland Revenue has written to the company enquiring into its operation of the quarterly payment system. R Ltd was required to pay its CT liability for the year ended 31 March 2003 on a quarterly basis.

R Ltd is considering paying a substantial dividend in the near future. You establish that the company has been carrying forward surplus ACT of £60,000 since 1999.

At 1 April 2003, R Ltd had the following percentage holdings of voting shares in other UK resident companies:

S Ltd – 80%

These shares had been acquired in 1995 and were held throughout the year ended 31 March 2004. For that year, S Ltd had chargeable profits of £300,000 and it had capital losses of £50,000 brought forward from earlier (post-acquisition) years.

T SA – 80%

These shares were acquired in 1997 and were also held throughout the year ended 31 March 2004. This company was incorporated in Switzerland, but was *wholly* managed in the UK. The directors of R Ltd are currently considering moving the management to Switzerland. T SA had total chargeable income for the year ended 31 March 2004 of £200,000. Most of its profits were earned in mainland Europe.

V Ltd – 90%

These shares had been acquired in March 1998 for £240,000 and, on 30 September 2003, R Ltd sold one third of its holding for £120,000. You establish that V Ltd had transferred a property to R Ltd in December 2001 when its market value (MV) was agreed at £300,000 and which had cost V Ltd £220,000 in May 1996. V Ltd had chargeable income of less than £1,000 for the year ended 31 March 2004, and is an investment company.

Assume an indexation factor from March 1998 to September 2003 of 0.128.

Required

Prepare a report for the directors of R Ltd dealing with each of the following matters:

(i)   The final Corporation Tax (CT) liability of R Ltd for the year ended 31 March 2004, explaining your treatment of:

♦   any capital gains (including any reliefs claimed, where beneficial);
♦   and Research and Development (R&D) expenditure.

Your CT computation should appear in an appendix.   **(13 marks)**

(ii)   An explanation of the operation of the quarterly payment system in the case of R Ltd. Note that a generalised answer is *not* acceptable – you must refer to the **actual** liability of R Ltd and the due dates of payment. Your answer must include a schedule of payments actually made based on the estimates and final liability (arrived at in (i) above).

The schedule of payments computation should appear in an appendix.   **(10 marks)**

(iii)   The effect of the proposal to move the management of T SA to Switzerland.   **(6 marks)**

(iv)   An explanation of the operation of surplus ACT and its impact on the decision to pay dividends.   **(6 marks)**

Presentation marks for clarity, layout and logic.   **(5 marks)**

(Total : 40 marks)

Appendix for question 66 – information relating to R Ltd

The total profits chargeable to corporation tax (PCTCT) for the year ended 31 March 2004 were £730,000 before taking the following matters into account:

1   Any chargeable gains arising as a result of the information given above.

2   During the year, R Ltd spent £40,000 on qualifying revenue expenditure on R&D. The above figure does not reflect **any** deduction for R&D.

3   R Ltd received Franked Investment Income (FII) of £10,000 during the year.

4   Patent fees paid during the year of £8,000 have been shown in R Ltd's balance sheet as an intangible asset and had NOT been deducted in arriving at the above profit.

5   A loan of £20,000 to a major supplier proved irrecoverable and was written off. This is not yet reflected in the above profit.

SECTION C – 40 MARKS

Answer two questions only.

Question 67 (3 of Exam Paper)

CCD Ltd

CCD Ltd, a UK resident manufacturing company, made up accounts for its year ended 31 March 2004. All of the following items of expenditure and income have been included, where appropriate, in the company's operating profit and loss account in arriving at the net profit.

Expenditure items

(a) £45,000 was spent on installing a roof on a second-hand factory purchased during the year. This factory had its roof destroyed in a fire when it was being used by the previous owner.

(b) Costs, amounting to £3,000, of raising a loan to provide funds to acquire an investment property which will be let.

(c) Gross interest of £8,000 paid on the above loan.

(d) Costs of leasing motor cars used by directors:

Car	List price £	Annual lease cost £
(i) Lexus 300	32,000	7,200
(ii) Audi A2 – low emissions	15,000	4,800

(e) Ten employees were made redundant on the closure of a trade run by the company. Each employee was paid £10,000 compared to their statutory redundancy entitlement of £2,000 each.

(f) £4,000 was charged in the profit and loss account in respect of the annual instalment of a premium of £20,000 paid last year to secure a five-year lease of office premises at an annual rental of £10,000 per year.

Income items

(g) As a result of a fire which occurred last year, repair costs were recovered from the insurers during the year ended 31 March 2003 as follows:

(i) In respect of factory premises owned and used by CCD Ltd	£9,600
(ii) In respect of damages to property let out by CCD Ltd	£5,400

These repair costs were paid and allowed as deductions, where appropriate, last year.

(h) Gross interest of £6,000 was received on a loan made to a major supplier company.

Required

State how each of the above items would be dealt with in arriving at the adjusted Schedule D Case I profit or loss of CCD Ltd for its year ended 31 March 2004. In each case, you should give reasons for your treatment of **each** item. You are reminded that, for expenditure items, you must either add them back or leave them (explaining clearly why you have not adjusted an item) and, for income items, you must either subtract them or leave them.

For each of those items you have adjusted for, you must explain how they will **finally** be treated in the company's CT computation. You are **not** required to compute an adjusted profit figure.

(Total : 20 marks)

Question 68 (4 of Exam Paper)

H Ltd

The diagram below shows the structure of a number of connected companies with a UK parent company H Ltd:

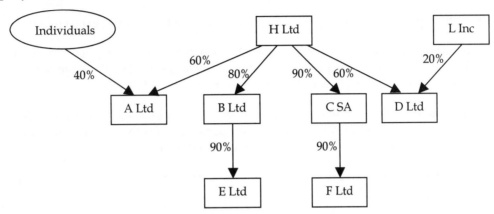

All of the companies, apart from L Inc and C SA, are UK resident for tax purposes. All of the holdings were owned at 1 April 2003, apart from the holding in F Ltd which C SA acquired on 1 October 2003. The group has experienced poor trading results in recent years, with the parent company, H Ltd, sustaining substantial losses as have some of the UK subsidiaries.

All of the companies make up accounts to 31 March each year and the trading results for the year ended 31 March 2004 were as follows:

		£	
H Ltd	Trading losses	(480,000)	
L Inc	Trading profits	120,000	(Sterling)
A Ltd	Trading losses	(60,000)	
B Ltd	Trading profits	420,000	
C SA	Trading profits	260,000	(Sterling)
D Ltd	Trading profits	140,000	
E Ltd	Trading losses	(90,000)	
F Ltd	Trading profits	110,000	

Required

(a) Interpret the above structure identifying:

    (i)   the associated companies and revised thresholds for CT purposes.
    (ii)   groups that exist for group relief purposes.
    (iii)   any consortia that exist.

    Explain which company may surrender losses to which other company and describe the role played by the non-UK resident companies. **(12 marks)**

(b) Using the above trading results, compute **the income chargeable to CT** for each UK resident profit-making company, assuming the most efficient group reliefs are claimed.
    (8 marks)

(Total : 20 marks)

Question 69 (5 of Exam Paper)

MD Ltd

Mr D, aged 45, is a director of MD Ltd, an advertising company, and receives a salary of £54,000 for the tax year 2003/04.

In addition, he is provided with an attractive package of benefits for this year as follows:

1   He is provided with a Mercedes car (petrol version) with a list price of £45,000. The CO_2 emissions of the car produce a benefit percentage of 32%. The company pays for all of the fuel. Car fuel benefit basis figure for 2003/04 is £14,400.

2   His wife, who does not work for the company, is provided with a Ford Mondeo diesel car with a list price of £17,000. The benefit percentage for the petrol version of this car is 25%. She personally pays for all of the fuel used by this car.

3   Mr D is provided with the use of two business suits during 2003/04. One suit cost the company £700 and the other £500.

4   The company pays Mr D's annual subscription of £350 to the Institute of Sales and Marketing.

5   On 6 April 2001, Mr D was given the use of a home cinema system, for his private use, which cost the company £3,600. On 6 April 2003, Mr D took this into his personal ownership when its market value was agreed at £1,500. He paid nothing to the company.

6   The company paid the school fees of £2,100 for each of his two children.

7   The company purchased garden furniture for £2,800, which it gave to Mr D for no cost.

8   Mr D, accompanied by his wife, attended a professional conference in Australia at a cost to the company of £6,000. Included in this figure was the agreed cost of his wife's travel and accommodation of £2,200.

Required

(a)   Compute the total benefits assessable on Mr D for the year 2003/04, explaining how you arrived at the assessable benefit in each case.   **(12 marks)**

(b)   On the assumption that all the above information was known before 6 April 2003, what would Mr D's correct Code Number be for the tax year 2003/04? How will this affect Mr D's monthly PAYE deduction?   **(5 marks)**

(c)   Calculate any additional costs which the company will bear as a result of the above benefits and state when this will be paid.   **(3 marks)**

Note: For 2003/04, the rate of Class 1A National Insurance Contributions is 12.8%.

(Total : 20 marks)

Question 70 (6 of Exam Paper)

J Ltd

Until 30 September 2003, all of the share capital of J Ltd, a UK resident company, had been owned by a UK holding company, HC Ltd. On that date, HC Ltd sold 30% of the shares of J Ltd to private UK individuals. HC Ltd continued to have two other wholly-owned UK resident subsidiaries, one of which had capital losses brought forward of £100,000.

You establish that, in May 1999, HC Ltd transferred a property to J Ltd under group arrangements on a no gain/no loss basis. At the date of transfer, the property had a market value (MV) of £180,000 and it had cost HC Ltd £75,000 in July 1993. The legal fees arising on the transfer were £3,000.

During its year ended 31 March 2004, J Ltd had two other disposals for capital gains purposes.

Transaction 1 – December 2003

Sold rights to shares for £20,000. This arose from a holding of 30,000 ordinary shares in G plc (out of total share capital of 500,000 shares) which J Ltd had purchased in September 1993 for £180,000. When the rights issue was announced, J Ltd did not wish to take up the rights and these were sold for £20,000. The MV of the 30,000 shares still owned by J Ltd, on the day following the rights issue, was £280,000. These were the only shares in any company held by J Ltd.

Transaction 2 – January 2004

Sold an office building for £200,000. This has been purchased in May 1976 for £40,000 and, since then, the following additional capital expenditure was incurred on the building:

May 1980	£8,000
September 1993	£20,000
July 2002	£24,000

No global election is in place and the MV at 31 March 1982 was agreed at £60,000.

Required

(a)   Calculate the gain arising when J Ltd ceased to be a group member. Explain the relief which is now available for such gains on de-grouping. **(8 marks)**

(b)   Compute the gains arising as a result of transactions 1 and 2 above and, assuming J Ltd had *other* chargeable income for the year ended 31 March 2004 of £200,000, compute the CT which arises as a result of the **chargeable gains** arising. You are **not** asked to calculate the total CT payable. **(12 marks)**

Indexation Factors which may be used in answering this question:

July 1993	–	May 1999	0.177
September 1993	–	December 2003	0.289
March 1982	–	January 2004	1.307
September 1993	–	January 2004	0.292
July 2002	–	January 2004	0.042

(Total : 20 marks)

Objective test answers

1   C

$$\frac{12{,}000 + \frac{1}{2}\,(16{,}000 - 12{,}000)}{16{,}000} \times 5{,}000 = \pounds 4{,}375$$

2   C

		£
Annual rental		3,600
Less: Allowed $\dfrac{12{,}000 + \frac{1}{2}\,(14{,}000 - 12{,}000)}{14{,}000} \times 3{,}600$		(3,343)
Disallowed		257

3   C

	£
Increase in general provision	250
Loan to former employee w/o	400
Disallowed	650

4   D

Gifts costing less than £50 each bearing conspicuous advertising not being food, drink, tobacco or vouchers exchangeable for cash are allowable. Entertaining of staff is allowable (400 + 300) = £700.

5   B

Gift of food not allowable. Remainder (2,450) allowed.

6   D

		£	£
Profits per accounts			142,350
Add:	Depreciation	4,850	
	Legal re new lease	250	
	Loss on sale of van	835	
			5,935
			148,285

7   D

Legal expenses for renewal of 19 year lease.

8 A

	£
Annual rental	6,000
Less: Allowed $\dfrac{12{,}000 + \frac{1}{2}\,(16{,}000 - 12{,}000)}{16{,}000} \times 6{,}000 =$	(5,250)
Disallowed	750

9 B

The abortive work is related to a capital purchase and so is disallowed even though the purchase did not go through. Remainder (1,750) allowed.

10 D

Renewal of short lease allowed, remainder (14,800) disallowed.

11 A

Injunction costs against competitor £2,000.

12 C

	£
Debtors in liquidation	600
Specific debtors	200
	800

13 A

These sums will be allowable to Cheer Ltd but may of course be assessed as benefits on the employees to some extent.

14 B

Costs of registering a patent are specifically allowable. Defalcations by staff are generally allowable although for persons in positions of responsibility, eg directors, the loss would not be allowable. Loan to ex-employee (250) written off is not allowed for DI but would be allowable for DIII.

15 A

Allowable expenses	£
Trade samples	820
Staff party	570
Diaries (less than £50 per customer)	650
	2,040

16 D

Any round-sum allowance will be allowed (as earnings of an employee) against the company's Schedule D Case I, ie £2,750. (The employee, however, will not be able to deduct the entertaining expenses as an employment expense).

17 B

The costs of tax appeals, even if successful, are not allowed.
Costs of maintaining trading rights and assets (1,830) allowable.

18   C

Specific (Williams Ltd) trade debt only allowable.
Disallowed (1,742 + 1,200) = £2,942.

19   A

Disallowed	£
Donation to charity	1,000
Legal cost of new lease	300
	1,300

20   B

No VAT is recoverable on the initial purchase of the car as there is some private use. VAT can, however, be recovered on accessories subsequently purchased and there is no restriction for private use $(1,175 \times \frac{7}{47}) = £175$.

21   B

A set of books is plant.
False ceiling not plant.

22   B

	General pool £	Expensive car £	Total £
Costs	6,000	14,000	
WDA $(25\% \times \frac{9}{12})$	1,125		1,125
$(3,000 \times \frac{9}{12})$		2,250	2,250
			3,375

23   B

Under hire purchase arrangements the company is entitled to capital allowances on the vehicle's cost and charges the interest to profit and loss account. Therefore:

	£
Capital allowances 24,000 × 25% restricted to	3,000
Interest/finance charges	3,200
	6,200

24   B

The correct answer is (3,800 + 8,400) = £12,200.
Canopy not allowed.

25   C

Expenditure on general lighting is treated as part of the cost of a building, ie the setting, and not as plant and machinery with which the trade is carried on.

Lighting provided for the purposes of a trade which involves the creation of 'atmosphere', eg pubs, hotels, restaurant etc, is said to have a functional part to play and may be treated as plant and machinery.

26   D

	£	General pool £	£
Balance b/f		2,800	
Sale proceeds (restricted to cost)		(2,300)	
		500	
WDA 25%		(125)	125
		375	
Addition with FYA	1,500		
FYA 40%	(600)		600
		900	
WDA c/f		1,275	
Total allowances			725

27   C

	£	CAs £
Plant WDV b/f (40,000 – 16,000)	24,000	
WDA – 25%	(6,000)	6,000
WDV c/f	18,000	

28   C

(A)   Motor car does not qualify
(B)   Outside time limit
(D)   Not beneficial
(C)   Nil proceeds, so accelerated BA beneficial

29   C

	£
Dockside crane is plant	18,000
Portacabin not plant	-
Grain silos are plant	260,000
	278,000

30   D

	Pool £	Expensive car £	Allowances £
(AP 1 Aug 2002 to 31 Jul 2003)			
Acquisitions (1,500 + 2,400)	3,900	15,000	
FYA 40%/100%/WDA 25% restricted	(3,000)	(3,000)	6,000
WDV c/f	900	12,000	

31   C

	£
(1.6.03 – 31.1.04) Purchase $14,100 \times {}^{40}/_{47}$	12,000
FYA 40%	(4,800)
C/f	7,200

(The FYA is not reduced for a short AP.)

32   C

			£
Melton (375,000 × 4%)			15,000
Stilton			
Residue	=	<u>255,000</u>	
Balance of tax life	=	(25 – 15)	25,500
			40,500

33   B

Residue of expenditure	=	42,000		
Balance of life	=	21 years	Hence	£2,000

34   C

	£
12 m/e 31 December 1986	
IA 25% + WDA 4% of 200,000	58,000
y/e 31 December 1987 to 31 December 2002	
4% × 16 years	128,000
Balancing charge = IBAs given	186,000

35   D

(25% × 180,000) = 45,000

∴ Offices qualify for IBA, so total cost of 180,000 qualifies.

36   B

	£
Clearing land	5,000
Factory	30,000
Drawing office	15,000
Canteen	10,000
(General office excluded as cost exceeds 25% limit)	
	60,000

37 C

	£
y/e 31.12.01	
Cost	10,000,000
Less: IA 40%	(4,000,000)
WDA 25%	(2,500,000)
	3,500,000
y/e 31.12.02	
WDA 25% of cost	(2,500,000)
y/e 31.12.03 WDA	1,000,000

38 A

$210,000 \times 25\% = 52,500$. Therefore, no allowances for non-industrial parts.
Qualifying cost is $(210,000 - 60,000) = £150,000$.

39 A

In order to claim a WDA, the building must be in industrial use at the end of the period.

40 C

	£
Building 1 $(280,000 \times 4\%)$	11,200
Building 2 $(350,000 \times 4\%)$	14,000
	25,200

41 B

	£
Rent accrued	
First tenants ($\frac{9}{12} \times 4,000$)	3,000
Second tenants	-
	3,000
Less: Allowable expenses	(1,000)
Schedule A	2,000

42 A

All of the company's income from UK property is pooled and all profits/losses are set-off against each other, ie $(5,500 + 10,000 - 8,600 - 2,000) = £4,900$.

43 A

	£
Goodwill written off is allowable under the FA 2002 rules on intangible fixed assets	-
The stock write down is specific and is allowable in the same way as specific bad debts charges	-
Interest on overdue tax is an allowable expense for DIII purposes	1,000
	1,000

44   A

The donation is not an allowable trading expense. The repayment interest is not trading income.
Amount disallowed (100 – 85) = £15.

45   B

Costs of raising loan finance (1,050) allowable.
Other costs are treated as capital expenditure.

46   C

	£
9 months 1.1.04 – 30.9.04	
Additions	9,200
WDA (9,200 × 25% × $\frac{9}{12}$)	(1,725)
WDV c/f	7,475

There is no restriction of the WDA in respect of an employee's use as this is subject to a car benefit on the employee.

47   C

First AP must run for 12 months from commencement of trading, ie 1.12.02 – 30.11.03. Balance of four months to 31.3.04 is separate AP.

48   C

10,000 × 62% = 6,200

$$\frac{6,200}{20} = £310$$

49   B

(A)   This is 'profits' for SCR purposes

(C)
and } Income could include non-taxable FII.
(D)

50   C

(A)   This is relief for surplus ACT b/f
(B)   There is no payment of ACT after 5.4.99
(C)   Correct
(D)   Nonsense

51 C

	£	£
PCTCT	238,600	
ACT capacity @ 20%		47,720
Shadow ACT =		
Dividends paid	75,000	
Dividends received	(18,000)	
	57,000	
@ 25%		(14,250)
Maximum ACT set-off		33,470
Surplus ACT b/f		34,000
Utilised (ie set-off in y/e 30.6.04)		(33,470)
Surplus ACT c/f		530

52 D

	£
12m AP ended 30.9.04	
Schedule D Case I	1,502,000
Schedule D Case III (gross)	128,000
Charges	(20,000)
PCTCT	1,610,000
CT payable FY03 and FY04 1,610,000 × 30%	483,000

53 B

CT61s are to be submitted for return periods not exceeding three months in length, ie quarterly.

54 C

		£
(i)	IT suffered (25.3.03) $(15,600 \times {}^{22}\!/_{78})$	4,400
(ii)	IT payable (30.11.03) $(100,000 \times 5\% \times 20\%)$	(1,000)
		3,400

55 C

	£
Schedule D Case I	720,000
Schedule D Case III	6,000
Chargeable gain	8,900
	734,900
Less: Gift Aid	(20,000)
PCTCT	714,900
Add: Franked Investment Income $(32,040 \times {}^{10}\!/_{9})$	35,600
'Profits'	750,500

56   B

	£
Schedule D Case I	209,000
Local Authority interest (Schedule D Case III)	3,000
Charges	(300)
PCTCT	211,700
FII $(42,129 \times {}^{100}\!/_{90})$	46,810
Profits	258,510

FY 2003 small company limits (for six months period)

Upper	750,000
Lower	150,000

FY 2003 $(211,700 \times 30\%)$	63,510
Less: ${}^{11}\!/_{400}$ $(750,000 - 258,510) \times \dfrac{211,700}{258,510}$	(11,069)
	52,441

57   C

	Assessments £	Losses £
7 m/e 31.12.03		(36,000)
Schedule D Case III	6,000	
S393A relief	(6,000)	6,000
Available to c/b	-	(30,000)
Relief for Gift Aid lost		
12 m/e 31.5.03		
Schedule D Case I	39,000	
Schedule D Case III	6,000	
	45,000	
S393A loss relief (preceding 12m)	(30,000)	30,000
	15,000	
Less: Gift Aid payment	(500)	
PCTCT	14,500	

58   B

As the time limit is two years from the end of the AP in which the loss arose, the claim must be lodged by 31.12.2005.

59 C

	£	Loss £
12 m/e 30.09.03		(73,000)
Schedule D Case III	4,000	
S393A relief, same AP	(4,000)	4,000
Available to c/b to preceding 12m		(69,000)
9 m/e 30.09.02		
Profits after charges	6,250	
S393A relief	(6,250)	6,250
		(62,750)
12 m/e 31.12.01		
Profits after charges	26,000	
S393A relief ($\frac{3}{12}$)	(6,500)	6,500
Profits after charges	19,500	
Total c/f		(56,250)

60 A

	£	Loss £
6 m/e 30.6.03		(150,000)
Schedule D Case III	10,000	
S393A relief	(10,000)	10,000
	-	
Excess non-trading charges wasted	-	
		(140,000)
12 m/e 31.12.02		
Schedule D Case I	100,000	
Schedule D Case III	20,000	
	120,000	
Less: S393A relief (preceding 12m)	120,000	120,000
Carried forward	(20,000)	

Excess non-trading charges wasted.

61 A

Two years from the end of the loss making AP, ie by 31.12.2005.

62 C

	£
Loss 9 m/e 30.6.04	(250,000)
Relief in same AP	10,000
	(240,000)
Carried back	
30.9.03 (leaving profit to cover trading charges)	80,000
C/f	(160,000)

Excess non-trade charges are wasted.

63   C

	£
Loss in y/e 31.12.02	(116,000)
Less: S393A same AP before charges	2,000
Available to c/b	(114,000)
Preceding 12 m/e 31.12.01 (54,000 + 2,000 – 3,000)	53,000
	(61,000)
Excess trade charges 12 m/e 31.12.02	(3,000)
c/f	(64,000)
y/e 31.12.2003	
(59,000 – 59,000 + 4,000)	4,000

64   C

	£
Loss in y/e 30.6.04	59,000
Less: S393A – current year before charges	(14,000)
30.6.03 (16,000 + 7,000)	(23,000)
	22,000

65   C

A loss arising may be carried back into the preceding 12 months using S393A. Therefore 1.1.03 is the earliest date.

66   A

	£	£
Loss y/e 31.12.02		(10,000)
S393A same AP		2,000
Available to c/b		(8,000)
Preceding 12 m/e 31.12.01		
DI	3,000	
DIII	1,500	
	4,500	
S393A relief	(4,500)	4,500
12 m/e 31.12.2003		(3,500)
DI	500	
S393(1) relief	(500)	500
	-	
DIII	1,000	
PCTCT	1,000	
Unrelieved loss c/f		3,000

67   C

The losses brought forward are set against Schedule D Case I profits of £14,000 only.

68 D

Losses b/f under S393(1) are available for set-off against trading profits only, ie 110,000 – 90,000 = £20,000 c/f.

69 B

Two years from end of loss making AP, ie by 31.12.2005.

70 D

Six years after the end of the accounting period.

71 C

	£
CT liability 2,200,000 × 30%	660,000
Less: Income tax suffered (22% × 400,000)	(88,000)
CT payable	572,000
Last quarter instalment payable on 14 April 2004	143,000

72 D

Company not allowed to deduct specific expenses of entertaining. This includes an entertaining allowance paid to an employee or reimbursed entertainment expenses.

(A company can deduct a round sum expenses allowance as part of the gross labour cost).

Employee not assessed on entertaining expenses reimbursed or paid from a specific allowance (follows from company treatment).

The correct answer is therefore D.

73 A

	£
Basic car benefit (19,000 × 35%) (over 255 gms/km)	6,650
Fuel charge (14,400 x 35%)	5,040
	11,690

74 A

	£
Luncheon vouchers [240 – (240 × 15p)]	204
Credit token – goods only	272
	476

75 A

	£
Salary	11,640
Car benefit	2,140
Employment income	13,780

76 B

Albert will be considered to be earning more than £8,500, as the benefits must be included in determining whether earnings are in excess of £8,500.

	£
Car benefit (6,160 × 18% - (15% + (170 – 155) × $\frac{1}{5}$))	1,109
Expense allowance	960
	2,069
Less: Allowable expenses	(750)
	1,319

77 A

First 15p per day tax free for employees.

78 C

An annual earnings period applies to directors.

Annual Class I primary limits

Upper limit	£30,940
Earnings threshold	£4,615
Lower limit	£4,004

	30,940 - 4,615 =	£26,325 × 9.4%	2,474.55
	33,000 - 30,940 =	£2,060 × 1%	20.60
Less:	4,615 - 4,004 =	£611 × 1.6% (rebate)	(9.78)
			2,485.37

79 A

NICs payable by the employee are not generally payable on assessable benefits. Only salary counts as earnings, ie £23,000.

80 A

	£
Deemed sale proceeds (as sold for <6,000)	6,000
Costs of sale	(150)
Cost	(8,200)
Unindexed loss	(2,350)

Indexation cannot increase a loss.

81 A

Kruggerrand. Not a specifically exempt asset.

82 B

Chattels which are also wasting assets (useful life less than 50 years) are exempt from capital gains tax, ie racehorse.

83 C

Indexation runs from the month the expenditure is incurred, ie June 2003.

84   C

With acquisitions in the previous 9 days, ie acquisition on 23 July 2003.

85   B

(1)

and   }   Chargeable instead under Schedule D Case III

(2)

(3)   Shares in company chargeable (unless 10% + holding).

86   C

	£	£
Indexed gain		50,000
Proceeds	200,000	
Replacement already bought (land)	(10,000)	
Replacement bought before CT due (weighbridge)	(160,000)	
Not reinvested, ie chargeable	30,000	30,000
Rolled-over		20,000

Note that when the weighbridge is acquired in 2004 the total reinvested becomes £170,000. As this occurs before the normal due date, it is assumed that PCTCT is reduced to reflect this. £30,000 will be chargeable and £20,000 rolled over. (Earth mover does not qualify as it is presumably not 'fixed' plant).

87   B

	£
Indexed gain	44,300
Less: Amount not reinvested and chargeable	(8,000)
Gain rolled over	36,300

88   D

12 months before to 36 months after date of sale (1 September 2002 to 31 August 2006).

89   C

(A)   Too early
(B)   Does not qualify
(D)   Too late
(C)   Leasehold (over 60 years) within time limit qualifies

90   B

Tax point is earlier of:

(i)   Adoption of goods   30 September 2003
(ii)   12 months after despatch   1 July 2004

However, invoice issued within 14 days after (i) on 3 October 2003 which becomes the tax point.

91   B

Deposit is a payment (albeit in advance) and creates a tax point; this overrides the issue of the invoice. Tax point 16 May 2003.

92   C

Tax point is date invoice issued for balance, ie 13 June 2003 being within 14 days after the goods were made available on 31 May 2003.

93   C

The rate of VAT must be shown; the other items must only be shown on a full tax invoice.

94   C

	£
Retail price	10,500.00
Less: Cash discount at 2½%	(262.50)
Amount on which VAT charged	10,237.50
VAT at 17½% thereon	1,791.56

95   B

The consortium group relief claim is limited to the percentage of the consortium companies loss equal to the percentage held.

96   D

Holdings of ordinary share capital determine group structure.
Holdings in Shotts 140 out of 200 shares – 70%
Shotts holding in Tarbet – 70%
Holding of Risca in Tarbet 70% × 70% = 49%

97   B

Gift Aid may be surrendered as it is an excess charge. Capital loss cannot be surrendered.
(15,000 + 2,000) = 17,000 maximum surrender.

98   B

	£
Herbs plc (100%) can surrender	20,000
Parsley Ltd (90%) can surrender	10,000
Thyme Ltd (76.5%) can surrender	6,000
	36,000

99   B

Group relief claim must be lodged within two years from end of claimant company's AP, ie by 31 December 2006. The maximum surrender is the lower of the loss available and the PCTCT of the recipient company - £6,000.

100   D

	£
Available profits	
Schedule D Case I	30,000
Less: Loss b/f	(5,000)
Charges	(2,000)
	23,000

101   C

	£
12 months ended 31 March 2003	
Schedule D Case I	13,000
Less: Loss b/f	(5,000)
	8,000
Group relief	(6,000)
Available to relieve loss carried back under S393A	2,000

102   C

Any amount can be surrendered up to the profit available in the claimant company. Rangers need make no claims itself as a pre-requisite. (Charges will be set against the Schedule D Case III – ie no excess charges). Maximum surrender is £20,000.

103   C

Aston Ltd can surrender any amount of trading loss up to £100,000 subject to the available profits of Martin Ltd for the corresponding AP (27,000 – 5,000 = £22,000).

104   A

	£
Schedule D Case I	14,000
Less: Loss b/f	(6,000)
	8,000
Schedule D Case III	3,000
	11,000
Less: Charges	(2,000)
Available profits for group relief	9,000

105   C

The 75% subsidiary test requires a holding of not less than 75% of the ordinary share capital.

106   A

No claim is required for intra-group relief on no gain/no loss transfers.

107   A

Transfer to Seeds – no gain/no loss, same 75% group.

The sale of Seeds to Milton is not within six years of the intra-group transfer, thus no gain arises on the building.

108   D

The gain is computed on a deemed disposal by C Ltd on 15 December 2003 and accrues on the first day of the accounting period in which C Ltd leaves the group (within six years of the transfer), ie on 1 January 2004.

Objective Test Answers (Pilot Paper)

109   C

The supply of services is standard rated unless it is zero rated or exempt or outside the scope of VAT. The payment of wages to employees is outside the scope of VAT but that is not the situation here as the accounting firm is paying J Ltd.

110   B

				£
Allowances	Jaguar	27,000-13,000		14,000
	Pool	$8,300 \times 25\%$ WDA		2,075
	Computer	$5,500 \times 100\%$ FYA*		5,500
				21,575

* This assumes SD Ltd is a 'small' business.

111   A

Entertaining staff is allowable (although it can give rise to a benefit in kind). Gifts costing less than £50 per donee and carrying a conspicuous advert for the donor's business are allowed unless in the form of tobacco, drink or food. Advertising is allowed as wholly and exclusively for the trade.

112   B

P9D –   used for reporting expenses paid to 'lower paid' employees.
P45 -   records PAYE hand over information when employee leaves.
P60 -   summarises PAYE/NIC etc totals for tax year.

113   A

The tax point for a supply of services is the date of completion unless a tax invoice is raised or payment received earlier. The actual tax point is then the earlier of invoice or payment.

114   B

The final quarter payment is due on 14th day of the sixteenth month after the start of the accounting period.

115   D

The CTSA enquiry rules specify quarter dates of 30 April, 31 July, 30 October and 31 January. If a return is submitted late the enquiry time limit becomes 12 months from the following quarter date.

Objective Test Answers (May 2001)

116   D

A completed form P46 enables the employer to apply the correct PAYE treatment to the employee's remuneration until the Revenue issue further instructions.

117   B

The basic tax for goods arises when they are collected or delivered or made available to the customer - ie delivery on 2 October 2003. Payment or invoicing before the basic tax point would supersede the basic tax point. An invoice raised within fourteen days after the basic tax point would similarly displace the basic tax point. Neither of these situations arise so the basic tax point stands.

118 B

If the AP is less than twelve months each instalment is 3/n ^{ths} of the liability due by instalments where n = number of months of AP. If n does not divide exactly by 3 the final instalment will be the balance of the amount due by instalments.

Final instalment: $1 - \frac{3}{8} - \frac{3}{8} = \frac{2}{8}$

$$800,000 \times \tfrac{2}{8} = £200,000$$

119 B

Turnover exceeds £56,000 on 30 November 2003 (6 × £6,500 + 2 × £9,000). Customs must be informed by 30 December 2003 and registration takes effect from 1 January 2004.

120 D

If a CT 600 is submitted late the enquiry period is extended to the first anniversary of the quarter day falling after the submission date - the quarter days being 31 January, 30 April, 31 July and 31 October.

121 D

The PAYE code is constructed as:

PA		4,615
Add:	Professional sub	300
Less:	Benefit of car £10,000 × 23% (15% + (195 – 155) × $\frac{1}{5}$)	(2,300)
	Benefit of asset £3,000 × 20%	(600)
	Tax due for 2002/03: 110 × $^{100}/_{22}$	(500)
		1,515
Results in code		151L

122 A

FY 2002/FY 2003		
	30,000 × 19%	5,700
	Less: $^{19}/_{400}$ (50,000 – 30,000)	(950)
		4,750

Objective Test Answers (November 2001)

123 C

124 D

125 C Disallowed expenses:

	£
Tax appeal	6,500
Breach of Health and Safety Regs	800
Planning permission	1,200
	8,500

126	C	CT liability			£

$$36,000 \times 19\% \qquad 6,840$$

Less $^{19}\!/_{400}$ (50,000 – 36,000) (665)

6,175

127 A Wholly zero rated supplies would attract repayments of input tax which could be recovered earlier if the company remained outside the group registration and had monthly return periods.

128 D Regardless of length of AP the final quarterly instalment is always payable three months and 14 days after the end of the AP.

129	C		Plant Pool £	Expensive Car £	Total CAs £
		Tax wdvs b/f	90,000	18,000	
		Disposal proceeds	(3,000)		
			87,000		
		WDA @ 25%/(max)	(21,750)	(3,000)	24,750
		Purchase qualifying for 100% FYA			25,000
		c/f	65,250	15,000	49,750

Answers

Adjustment of profits

Answer 1

C Ltd

> *Tutorial note:*
>
> This is a question on profit adjustment and follows a style used more than once before under the old syllabus. There seems to be very little variety in the situations shown. It is generally either the application of the loan relationship rules or the distinction between capital and revenue. There are a number of other principles of profit adjustment available to test but the examiner choses to ignore them.
>
> In short, it is not a stimulating question but it does offer a lot of easy marks.

Notes on the deductibility of expenses for Schedule D Case I purposes

(a)   The valuation fees and solicitors' fees were incurred in the prospective purchase of a capital asset and are therefore not allowable for Schedule D Case I purposes. Normally they would form part of the base cost of the asset but as the asset was never acquired there is no relief at all. *Add back £8,000 and £5,000 to profit.*

(b)   The loan is acquired for a trading purpose - to refurbish fixed assets. The incidental costs of acquiring the loan are allowable as a trading expense. The valuation cost would qualify as an incidental cost. Relief would usually be allowed on an accruals basis so strictly the £60,000 cost should be written off evenly over the life of the loan. *As there is insufficient information make no adjustment.*

(c)   Similarly the legal fees of £15,000 and the finder's fee of £5,000 would be allowable as an incidental cost of obtaining a loan for trading purposes. *No adjustment required.*

(d)   The £45,000 cost of a report on a group of companies is disallowed as it is a capital expense. If the purchase goes ahead the cost will be part of the acquisition cost of the shares. *Disallow £45,000.*

(e)   As for (d), the £38,000 legal and accountancy fees are disallowed as a trading expense but are added to the base cost of the shares acquired. *Disallow £38,000.*

(f)   The £5,000 legal costs of selling the restaurant are not allowed as a trading expense but are allowed an incidental cost of disposing of a capital asset.

Similarly, the cost of setting up the lease is disallowed as a capital expense. It will be allowed in calculating any capital gain on the grant of a lease. *Disallow £5,000 and £3,000.*

(g)   The £380,000 fees incurred in making the rights issue are disallowed as a capital cost - the cost of raising share capital. *Disallow £380,000.*

(h)   The insurance proceeds are taxable under Schedule D Case I as they are offset against an allowable trading expense - repair costs. They are taxable in the year of recovery assuming that a debtor for the amount due had not been created in the previous year's accounts. *No adjustment required.*

Examination tip - *You earn the easy marks by stating clearly the adjustment needed (if any) to trading profits. Otherwise marks are earned for a clear explanation of the treatment.*

Answer 2

K Ltd

EXPENDITURE

(1)   The loan interest of £20,000 would be added back to profit as it is not in respect of a loan taken out for a trade purpose. Instead the amount payable (ie accruals basis) for the year to 31 March 2004 would be allowed against Schedule D Case III income.

(2)   The repair costs of £28,000 would be added back to profit under the principle established in the Law Shipping case. If an asset is not in a useable condition when purchased, any costs incurred to make it useable are instead added to its capital cost. If the warehouse qualifies as an industrial building the £28,000 may attract IBAs.

(3)   Assuming the interest has been charged on an accruals basis the £50,000 will be allowed as interest incurred on a loan for a trading purpose. The legal fees of £18,000 are also allowable although strictly they should be written off over the period of the debentures.

(4)   The £60,000 would be added back to profit on the principle established in *Strong v Woodifield*. The expense is too remote from the trade.

(5)   Assuming the amount charged is commercial and is therefore wholly and exclusively for the benefit of K Ltd's trade, it would be allowed in full.

INCOME

(1)   The £40,000 recovery relates to a trading expense and therefore no adjustment would be required. The £5,000 relates to the letting activity and should be excluded from Schedule D Case I profit but included as a Schedule A receipt.

(2)   Interest received on the loan to the supplier should be excluded from Schedule D Case I profits as it is not a loan granted for a purpose of K Ltd's trade. Instead the interest receivable in the period should be included as Schedule D Case III income.

Capital allowances on plant and machinery

Answer 3

Expenditure on a building

> *Tutorial note:*
>
> The original question that this is based on has been modified to replace a 'listing exercise' with an exercise which tests your understanding of the different ways of relieving 'capital' expenditure. This brings it more in line with the likely emphasis of the new syllabus.

(a)   **Tax relief for expenditure on retail buildings**

      (i)   *Repairs*   The cost of repairing or refurbishing existing buildings is generally an allowable trading expense. This also applies to repairs to newly acquired buildings provided they were usable before the repairs were carried out.

      (ii)   *Improvements*   Improvements are treated as part of the capital cost of the building and will be relieved through the capital gains rules when the building is sold provided the improvement expenditure is reflected in the state of the building on sale.

(iii)	*Plant*	Plant installed in a building, thereby becoming part of the fabric of the building, is normally treated as a capital improvement to the building.

Plant which is removable from the building, such as shop counters, qualifies for capital allowances of 25% writing down allowances. For a 'small' or 'medium' sized business a 40% first year allowance would be available.

Plant which is short lived – perhaps with a life expectancy of less than two or three years – could be written off as a trading expense in the year of expenditure. This could apply to special display units which are expected to 'age' quickly.

(iv)	*Buildings*	Building works for the retail trade will not generally attract tax relief until capital gains are computed as disposal.
(v)	*Works not carried out*	There is no relief whatsoever for the costs of unsuccessful applications for planning permission and other capital costs that do not bring a capital asset into existence.

Examination tip - *Where different parts of a question appear to 'overlap' it is good technique to decide how to avoid presenting the same information twice. For example, don't go into detail on 'plant' definition in part (a) if that has to be covered for part (b).*

(b) **Plant and case law**

Where plant is installed or housed in a building, it is important to decide whether it retains its separate identify as plant or is subsumed into the fabric of the building and no longer qualifies for capital allowances as plant.

The Courts have developed a functional test. If the item has some active function in the owner's trade, it is likely to be regarded as plant. On the other hand, if it has become part of the setting in which the trade is conducted, it is no longer plant.

This is a notoriously difficult area and the following tax cases only throw some light on the dividing lines.

Cole Brothers Ltd v Phillips

A building would be considered as incomplete without an electrical wiring system. Thus general wiring is not 'plant'. However, specialist lighting and associated wiring (eg for display units) would count as plant as they played an active part in the trade.

CIR v Scottish and Newcastle Breweries Ltd

Artistic objects used in hotels and restaurants to create atmosphere and thereby attract customers qualify as plant. Even items that are part of the setting can be treated as plant.

Hampton v Fortes Autogrill Ltd

False ceilings used to support and mask-off ventilation pipes and other services were held not to be plant as they did not meet the function test.

Dixon v Fitch's Garage Ltd

A canopy over a garage forecourt did not qualify as plant even though without it customers for petrol might have gone elsewhere in inclement weather. Its setting nature outweighed any supposed function of attracting customers.

Examination tip - *Do not give more cases than asked for. You should choose carefully the cases you are going to describe to start with rather than remembering more appropriate cases when you've already written on the requisite number.*

Revenue practice

The Revenue have a longstanding practice to allow certain items installed in a building to be treated as plant as follows:

♦ Main services into the building - eg cost of wiring up to the main switchboard and bringing in the water main to the stop cock.

♦ Hot water and central heating equipment and pipes (but not cold water pipes).

♦ Ventilation and air conditioning systems.

♦ Bathroom fittings - WCs, wash basins etc.

♦ Fire alarm and sprinkler systems.

Examination tip - You earn marks in part (a) for mentioning and describing the tax relief of the obvious sorts of expenditure envisaged by the company - eg repairs and improvements.

For part (b) you are expected to discuss 'plant' in relation to a retail trade. Certain cases are clearly more relevant than others. For example the 'Dry Dock' case and the 'Grain Silo' case, though both succeeded for the tax payer, are not immediately relevant to a retail trade.

If you cannot remember a case name, describe it instead. You should not be penalised for just forgetting the name if you can present the facts and the outcome correctly.

Answer 4

D Ltd

> ### Tutorial note:
>
> This is based on a capital allowances question set for the November 1998 exam sitting. The original question concerned a sole trader – a topic no longer examinable under the new syllabus. This modified 'corporate' version attempts to show the type of capital allowance question which might appear under the new syllabus. Points of interest are as follows:
>
> ♦ Capital allowances for a 'long period' of account have to be calculated separately for each constituent accounting period.
>
> ♦ Plant bought prior to commencing trade is treated as if purchased when the trade commenced.
>
> ♦ Similarly, plant sold after trade ceases is deemed sold at the date of cessation at the amount subsequently realised.
>
> ♦ If plant is gifted to an employee – thereby resulting in an income tax charge on the employee – the proceeds for capital allowance purposes is taken as nil.
>
> ♦ Computer equipment attracts a 100% rate of FYA for a 'small' business where the cost is incurred between 1 April 2000 and 31 March 2004.

Computation of maximum capital allowances

		Plant pool £	Expensive car £	CA summary £
AP:	**1.10.00 – 30.9.01**			
	Additions not qualifying for FYA		26,000	
	WDA @ 25% (maximum £3,000)		(3,000)	3,000
	Plant attracting 40% FYA	210,000		
	Less: 40% FYA	(84,000)		84,000
				―――――
				87,000
				―――――

AP : **1.10.01 – 31.12.01** (3 months)

Tax wdvs b/f	126,000	23,000	
Additions not qualifying for FYA	11,000		
	137,000		
WDA @ 25%/3,000 × $\frac{3}{12}$	(8,562)	(750)	9,312
Additions qualifying for FYA	20,000		
Less: 40% FYA	(8,000)		8,000
			17,312

AP : **1.1.02 – 31.12.02**

Tax wdvs b/f	140,438	22,250	
Disposals	(16,000)	(21,000)	
Balancing allowance		1,250	1,250
	124,438		
Additions not qualifying for FYA		32,000	
WDA @ 25%/£3,000	(31,109)	(3,000)	34,109
			35,359

AP : **1.1.03 – 31.12.03**

Tax wdvs b/f	93,329	29,000	
WDA @ 25%/£3,000	(23,332)	(3,000)	26,332
Additions attracting 100% FYA	65,000		
Less: 100% FYA	(65,000)		65,000
			91,332

AP : **1.1.04 – 30.4.04**

Tax wdvs b/f	69,997	26,000	
Disposals	(66,000)	(18,000)	
Balancing allowances	3,997	8,000	11,997

Examination tip - *You must use a capital allowance layout for your answer but it is a good idea to 'economise' where possible especially if you otherwise risk having to use more than 4 or 5 columns. For example, recycle the expensive car column if you never finish an AP with more than one expensive car. Also, there is no real need to use an inset column for FYA expenditure provided you take care over which figure qualifies for FYA.*

If you have time, check that the total of CAs agrees to the total of purchases less sales. Remember to restrict the January 2002 disposal to £16,000 and to ignore the gift to the salesman.

There are 5 capital allowance totals for the 5 APs and if each one is correct you will receive full marks. However, the computations are progressive so an earlier error may have a knock-on effect. Part of your mark earning strategy must therefore be to give sufficient explanation of your calculations so you can be awarded marks for correct principles even if you make mistakes.

Industrial buildings allowance

Answer 5

R Ltd

> **Tutorial note:**
>
> This is a relatively straightforward question on 'other' category of capital allowances – IBAs. The only difficulty concerned the factory in the EZ (Enterprise Zone). Usually an initial allowance of 100% is taken in the year of purchase but if a lesser allowance is claimed, the balance is written off as a WDA of 25% of the original cost until it is fully relieved. Thus, if no IA is taken it will be written down to nil for tax purposes over four years. The IA is a matter of choice but the WDA has to be taken.
>
> Part (b) concerns the IBA position on leasing a building. The basic rule on IBAs is that to claim IBA you need to hold the 'relevant' interest.

(a) **Computation of IBAs available to R Ltd for the year to 31 March 2004**

		£
FACTORY A:	No IBAs as its 25 year tax life has expired.	
FACTORY B:	Original qualifying cost (less than second-hand price)	50,000
	Tax life remaining when purchased by R Ltd (25 – 6) years	19 years
	WDA : $\dfrac{50,000}{19}$ =	£2,632 pa

	FACTORY C:	Qualifying cost:	
		Site preparation	10,000
		Factory	100,000
		Office	25,000
			135,000

The office cost is allowed as it is less than 25% of the total.
WDA : 135,000 × 4%   £5,400

It is assumed that the building is in use by 31 March 2004.

FACTORY D:	Qualifying cost (1.4.02)	120,000
	Portion of initial allowance claimed in y/e 31.3.03	(30,000)
	WDA: 120,000 × 25%	(30,000)
		60,000

Year to 31 March 2004
25% WDA : 120,000 × 25%   £30,000

FACTORY E:	Qualifying cost (1.4.93)	70,000
	Initial allowance 20%	14,000
	WDA 4% for y/e 31.3.94 – y/e 31.3.00 (7 years)	19,600
	Allowances actually given	33,600

As the building is sold above cost all the IBAs actually given will be clawed back:

	Balancing charge	£33,600

Summary:	FACTORY	£
	A	-
	B	2,632
	C	5,400
	D	30,000
	E	(33,600)
		4,432

Examination tip - *It is usually better exam technique to make a separate summary than to keep a running total in the far right hand column.*

(b) **MEMORANDUM**

To: The Directors of R Ltd

Re: Availability of IBAs on leased buildings

Date: 10 May 2004

From: Chartered Management Accountant

The company is considering leasing factories rather than buying them and advice is therefore required on the IBA position.

Basically IBAs are available on leased buildings only to the landlord of the building as he has incurred the expense on the 'relevant interest' – ie he still retains the freehold reversionary interest in the building.

This seems unfair as it is the tenant's use which makes the building 'industrial'. In fact there are usually lease terms which require the tenant to make such use of the building that ensures the entitlement to IBAs for the landlord.

If the lease is for a period of over 50 years the landlord and the tenant can elect jointly to treat the consideration paid by the tenant for the grant of the lease as if it were paid to acquire the freehold interest. In other words, entitlement to IBAs passes to the tenant. This will usually be attractive where the landlord has no use for the IBAs but does not wish to make an outright sale of the asset (eg a statutory development corporation).

Whether or not this election is made, the tenant is entitled to IBAs on any capital improvements that he makes to his interest (ie the leasehold interest) in the building.

Please let me know if I can provide further information.

Signed: Chartered Management Accountant

Examination tip - For awarding full marks in part (a) the marker is probably just looking for the correct five figures relevant to the five factories. It would be sensible, however, to include explanations of your treatment where it seems appropriate. For example, just putting nil for Factory A's WDA without saying its tax life is up or not mentioning the 25% de minimis limit for Factory C might lose you marks. As a rule you should show that you understand what you have done or chosen not to do. Otherwise the marker could think you achieved the right answer by default!

In part (b) you should receive most of the marks for being aware of the election for IBA transfer on a long leasehold.

Answer 6

JAY Ltd

> **Tutorial note:**
>
> This is an easy capital allowance computation on plant with a minor part on IBAs. You should recognise that a 15 month period of account requires a 12 month followed by a 3 month capital allowance computation.
>
> The next key to success is the indispensable plant CA layout. How many columns? A careful read of the details shows the need for a short life asset column and perhaps an inset column for FYA additions. You should be able to survive on a single expensive car column keeping to a maximum of four or five columns – the manageable limit.
>
> Finally, fill in the layout in the correct order dealing with the events up to 31 December 2003 in the first computation and those after in the second.
>
> The IBA computation requires you to spot two figures – the allowable cost remaining and the tax life unexpired. As long as the second-hand price exceeds original qualifying cost and there has been no non-industrial use, the second-hand purchaser's allowable cost is the original qualifying cost. You do not have to prove this.

(a)   **Computation of maximum capital allowances**

(i)   **Plant and machinery**

	General pool £	Expensive car £	Short life asset £	CA summary £
Year to 31 December 2003				
Balances b/f general pool	48,000	9,000		
Addition without FYA				
12.9.03 VW Polo	11,600			
Disposals				
30.3.03 Plant	(8,000)			
3.7.03 Car	(6,000)			
	45,600			
WDA @ 25%	(11,400)	(2,250)		13,650

		£			
Additions for 40% FYA					
28.6.03 Meat slicer		2,500			
1.1.03 Plant		24,000			
5.7.03 Vehicles		28,000			
		54,500			
40% FYA		(21,800)	32,700		21,800
10.2.03 Sandwich machine				14,000	
40% FYA				(5,600)	5,600
					41,050
			66,900	6,750	8,400
3 months to 31 March 2004					
Balances b/f			66,900	6,750	8,400
Disposals					
31.1.04 Expensive car				(14,000)	
Feb 04 Sandwich machine					(3,000)
Balancing (charge)/allowance				(7,250)	5,400 (1,850)
Additions without FYA					
1.1.04				24,000	
WDA @ 25% × 3/12			(4,181)	(750)	4,931
Additions for 40% FYA					
15.1.04 Meat slicer	6,000				
2.2.04 Wrapping m/c	12,000				
10.3.04 Vehicle	32,000				
	50,000				
FYA @ 40%	(20,000)		30,000		20,000
					23,081
Balances c/f			92,719	23,250	

Examination tip - Note that to keep the layout to a manageable width, the expensive car column has been 'recycled'.

(ii) **Industrial buildings allowances**

Second-hand factory acquired 1 January 2003 for	£100,000
Original qualifying cost	£80,000
Tax life remaining 25 – (1.1.97 to 1.1.03)	19 years
WDA : $^{80,000}/_{19}$ =	£4,210 pa
AP : 12m to 31.12.03 : WDA	£4,210
AP : 3m to 31.3.04 : WDA $^3/_{12}$ × 4,210	£1,052

(iii) **Summary**

	AP year to 31.12.03 £	AP 3m to 31.3.04 £
Plant CAs	41,050	23,081
IBAs	4,210	1,052
	45,260	24,133

Notes:

(i)   The shop front is part of the cost of the retail unit (ie shop) and will not qualify as plant. There are no capital allowances for shops other than in an Enterprise Zone or as a de minimis part of an industrial building.

(ii)   The full cost of the wayward sandwich plant is relieved over the two periods by claiming short life asset treatment.

Examination tip - *The question only requires the two amounts of maximum capital allowances and this should be sufficient for full marks. However, the examiner indicated in his own published answer that some commentary on the treatment of the shop front and the 'short life asset' was expected. It may be advisable, therefore, to comment on the less obvious parts of your computations where time permits. A better use of your time might be to check that the total of qualifying plant cost less disposals reconciles with the total of capital allowances and unrelieved balances carried forward.*

Answer 7

W Ltd

(a)   **W Ltd – maximum capital allowances for the year to 31 March 2004**

Plant and machinery

	General pool £	Expensive cars 1 £	Expensive cars 2 £	Lathe SLA £	Capital allowance totals £
Tax written down values b/f	64,000	22,000	30,000	18,000	
Additions:					
Car	11,000				
Lorry (part)	10,000				
	85,000				
Disposals	(85,000)	-	(22,000)	(20,000)	
Balancing Allowance/charge	-		8,000	(2,000)	6,000
WDA 25% (maximum 3,000)		(3,000)			3,000
Additions qualifying for FYA					
Computer	20,000				
100% FYA	(20,000)				20,000
Lorry (18,000-10,000)	8,000				
40% FYA	(3,200)				3,200
Tax written down values c/f	4,800	19,000			
Total plant capital allowances					32,200

Old factory

	Original cost £	£	Extension £
Qualifying cost	120,000		40,000
4% WDA (y/e 31.3.93 – y/e 31.3.03) × 11	(52,800)		
4% WDA (y/e 31.3.95 – y/e 31.3.03) × 9			(14,400)
Tax wdvs	67,200		25,600
		92,800	
Less proceeds		100,000	
Balancing charge		7,200	(7,200)
			25,000

New factory (purchased second hand)

		£	
Original qualifying cost (less than purchase price)		180,000	
Life remaining on purchase 25-10	=	15 years	
WDA = 180,000/15			12,000
Total maximum allowances			37,000

(b)   **Treatment of lorry**

£10,000 of the £18,000 cost has been treated as an addition not qualifying for FYA so that it can cover £1 for £1 the potential balancing charge on the plant disposals. The balance of £8,000 is included as an addition qualifying for FYA at 40%.

Computer system

As the company is a 'small enterprise' it attracts 100% FYA on certain information technology equipment such as computers. There is no point in electing for short life asset treatment as no balance remains after 100% FYA. Any subsequent sale proceeds would result in a balancing charge if it was kept in a separate column. By keeping it in the general pool the proceeds could be covered by the balance in the pool or by pool additions.

Answer 8

P Ltd

(a)   **Maximum capital allowances - year to 31 December 2003**

(i)   *Plant and machinery*

	General Pool	Computer (SLA)	Mercedes /Lexus	Capital allowances total
	£	£	£	£
Tax written down values b/f	70,000	2,362	13,000	
Disposals (other than pool)				
20.4.03 Mercedes			(9,000)	
20.4.03 Computer		(2,000)		
Balancing allowances		362	4,000	4,362
Additions without FYA				
30.1.03 3 Ford cars	27,000			
31.10.03 Lexus car			28,000	
Disposals from pool				
20.4.03 4 machines	(5,000)			
31.12.03 Cars	(35,000)			
	57,000			
WDA @ 25%	(14,250)		(3,000) max	17,250

	£			
Additions with FYA				
1.1.03 Installed machines	30,000			
3.3.03 Vans	42,000			
20.5.03 Machines	30,000			
31.10.03 Machines	9,000	111,000		
FYA @ 40%		(44,400)		44,400
20.5.03 Computer		12,000		
FYA @ 100%		(12,000)		12,000
Tax written down values c/f		109,350	25,000	
Total of capital allowances on plant and machinery				78,012

(ii)   *Industrial buildings*

Balance of expenditure taken over : 180,000 - 30,000	£150,000
(Less than original qualifying cost of £220,000)	
Life remaining 25 - 10 = 15 years	
WDA : 150,000/15	£10,000
Total allowances for the year : 78,012 + 10,000	£88,012

Note

1   The expensive column is recycled to save space in the layout.

2   A short life asset election should not be made for the computer acquired during the year as it qualifies for 100% FYA. If the election was made it would attract a balancing charge if sold before transfer to the general pool.

(b) **Situations where a de-pooling election is not tax efficient**

(i) The advantage of a SLA election is being able to crystallise a balancing allowance where the asset is sold within four years of the end of the AP of purchase. If, therefore, the asset is likely to be sold above tax written down value and would crystallise a balancing charge the election should not be made.

(ii) Currently computer equipment attracts a 100% FYA so if it is likely to be sold before it has to be transferred to the general pool a balancing charge would result. It would therefore not be advisable to make the election.

(iii) If there is likely to be a disposal of plant from the general pool using proceeds in excess of the tax written down value of the pool a balancing charge may arise. Pooling new expenditure on plant - instead of de-pooling - enables such a balancing charge to be covered £1 for £1. In this way, new expenditure would be effectively relieved at 100%.

Introduction to corporation tax – the computation of the CT liability

Answer 9

PGD Ltd

> *Tutorial note:*
>
> This style of corporation tax computational question was commonly met under the old syllabus and is likely in the future. The requirements of the question lead you through the necessary stages rather than just asking for the MCT figure so you are not left worrying about which workings to produce on your way to the final answer.

(a) **Capital allowance computation for the year to 30 September 2003**

	General pool £	Expensive car £	Short life asset £	CA summary £
Tax wdv b/f	67,500	11,200	12,000	
Additions not qualifying for FYA				
Motor car	10,500			
Disposals (excl VAT)	(8,000)		(4,000)	
Balancing allowance			8,000	8,000
	70,000	11,200		
Less: WDA @ 25%	(17,500)	(2,800)		20,300
Additions qualifying for FYA				
Machinery	16,000			
FYA @ 40%	(6,400)			6,400
Tax wdvs c/f	62,100	8,400		
Total capital allowances				34,700

Examination tip - It would be difficult to produce the capital allowance figure without using a columnar layout. It is important to minimise the number of columns, however. An inset column for FYA additions can be avoided as shown above. As long as figures to deduct are shown in brackets there is also no need to sub-total after every step. The emphasis is on speed without sacrificing clarity.

(b)   **Schedule D Case I adjusted profit for the year to 30 September 2003**

		£	£
Profit per the accounts			226,300
Add back:	Loan interest		8,000
	Depreciation		11,000
			245,300
Deduct:	Capital allowances	34,700	
	Loan interest receivable	6,000	
	Rents receivable	7,000	
	Patent royalties received	30,000	
	FII	8,000	85,700
			159,600

Interest paid

The interest paid on the debentures issued to build a factory extension is allowable as it is paid on a loan taken out for a trading purpose. It is charged through the accounts on an accruals basis so no adjustment is required.

The interest paid on the 10 year loan is an expense under Schedule D Case III as the loan was taken out for a non-trading purpose.

Patent royalties paid

Patent royalties paid for the purpose of the trade on or after 1 April 2002 are allowed as a trading expense on an accruals basis, therefore no adjustment is necessary.

Interest received

Unless the company lends money as a trading activity - which is clearly not the case - interest receivable is assessable under Schedule D Case III and not Schedule D Case I.

(c)   **Computation of mainstream corporation tax for the year to 30 September 2003**

	£
Schedule D Case I	159,600
Schedule A	7,000
Schedule D VI	30,000
	196,600
Less: Schedule D Case III deficit (8,000 - 6,000)	(2,000)
PCTCT	194,600
Add FII	8,000
Profits	202,600

Gross corporation tax (small company limits £150,000 and £750,000 for two associated companies).

	£
194,600 × 30%	58,380
Less: $\frac{11}{400}$ (750,000 – 202,600) × $\frac{194,600}{202,600}$	(14,459)
	43,921
Less: ACT b/f (Working 1)	(5,720)
	38,201
Less: Income tax suffered still recoverable (Working 2)	(3,040)
Mainstream corporation tax payable 1 July 2004	35,161

Examination tip - *As with all computational questions, it is fairly obvious at which point your answer is complete. In part (b) the treatment of interest etc has to be explained and it is important not to waste the easy marks given for so doing. Mark earning in part (c) is enhanced if the ACT and IT workings are shown separate from the main answer. If time is short you could dispense with commenting on the non-effect of straddling between FY 2002 and FY 2003 - as done in the answer.*

Workings

1 **Treatment of surplus ACT**

		£	£
Maximum set-off (ignoring shadow ACT)			
PCTCT× 20% 194,600×20%			38,920
Less: Shadow ACT			
Dividend paid		140,000	
Less: Dividend received: 8,000×90%		(7,200)	
		132,800	
Shadow ACT @ $\frac{20}{80}$			(33,200)
ACT set-off limited to			5,720
Surplus ACT b/f			14,700
Less: Set-off			(5,720)
Surplus ACT carried forward at 1 October 2003			8,980

2 **Income tax suffered**

		£	£
Income tax deducted on patent royalties received:			
30,000×22%			6,600
Income tax withheld on payments:			
Debenture interest	9,000×20%	1,800	
Patent royalties	8,000×22%	1,760	
			3,560
Income tax recoverable			3,040

Answer 10

K Ltd

Tutorial note:

This question tests basic knowledge of the loan relationship rules including relief for a deficit on Schedule D Case III. Part (a) needs merely a 'description' but part (b) clearly requires a more formal presentation – as a 'memo' or a report properly addressed to the directors. You have to be careful to spot which figures have to be adjusted for – the £50,000 loan write-off has been excluded from the Schedule D Case I expenses but the £2,000 interest does require adjustment.

As most of the marks are given in part (a), this is where you are expected to detail the loan relationship treatment. Part (b) has to be answered in the light of any point arising from part (a) – ie what to do with the deficit.

(a) **Taxation treatment under the loan relationship rules**

Under the loan relationship rules interest receivable is assessable under Schedule D Case III on an accruals basis. Therefore the interest of £2,000 received on the loan to the supplier and included in the £80,000 trading profits figure must be deducted in arriving at the Schedule D Case I figure.

Interest receivable of, say, £2,000 is assessable under Schedule D Case III. There is clearly no closing accrual as the payer is in liquidation with no funds to meet any of its liabilities. However, if there was an opening accrual, that part of the interest is strictly assessable in the previous period.

The write-off of the £50,000 loan to a supplier is an allowable expense against Schedule D Case III income. It is assumed that no part of the £50,000 had accrued before the current period. The loss has already been added back so no adjustment is needed to the Schedule D Case I figure. The write-off would have been a Schedule D Case I expense had the loan been made for a trading purpose but this seems unlikely.

There is therefore a net Schedule D Case III deficit of £48,000 (£50,000 - £2,000) which may be relieved by:

(i) Set-off against total profits after charges of the current period.

(ii) Carry back against Schedule D Case III profits of the previous 12 months.

(iii) Carry forward against non-trading profits of future periods.

(iv) Set-off against profits of L Ltd for the year to 31 March 2004 under a group relief claim.

(b) **MEMORANDUM**

To:	The directors of K Ltd
Re:	Relief for the loss on the loan to a supplier
Date:	10 May 2004
From:	Chartered Management Accountant

There is a £48,000 deficit on Schedule D Case III income for the year to 31 March 2004 attributable to the write-off of a loan to a supplier.

The loss could be set against other profits of K Ltd for the current period or surrendered as group relief against the profits of L Ltd for the same accounting period - ie year to 31 March 2004.

The relief should be used by the company with the higher marginal tax rate. As there are two group companies, the upper limit for the starting rate marginal band is £25,000 (£50,000 × ½) and the lower limit for the small company rate marginal band is £150,000. In other words, profits between £25,000 and £150,000 attract a marginal rate of 19% and those above £150,000 are taxed marginally at 32.75%.

As K Ltd's profits and L Ltd's profits for the period are £78,000 (£80,000 - £2,000 loan interest) and £220,000 respectively, the relief will be maximised by surrendering the £48,000 deficit as group relief to L Ltd. This saves tax of £15,720 (£48,000 × 32.75%) compared to £9,120 (48,000 × 19%).

Signed: Chartered Management Accountant

Examination tip - *As you should have concluded in part (a) that a Schedule D Case III deficit arises, part of your answer must cover the various reliefs available for the deficit including, as there is a subsidiary, group relief.*

You could have omitted a detailed discussion of whether the £50,000 and £2,000 were the correct 'accrued' figures without sacrificing any marks.

Further aspects of corporation tax

Answer 11

WJ Ltd

Tutorial note:

This is a conventional question on a long period (ie over 12 months) of account. There are therefore two accounting periods (chargeable periods) – one for the first 12 months and one for the balance of 4 months. The rules for allocating profits should be well understood. The original question has been developed to avoid uncertainty over the Schedule D Case III and Case VI items. The object is to apply the accruals basis separately to each period but the examiner may not always provide enough information. If you are only given the amount accrued for the entire period you would have to time apportion it to the separate accounting periods.

The examiner has tended to expect the MCT pay days to be shown even when not specifically asked for – as evidenced by his own suggested answers. It is worth supplying the dates therefore as it takes no time to do so.

If quarterly instalments were needed for the MCT payment, it should be specifically required as it is more complicated to produce. Note that here, even though the company pays the full CT rate in the second accounting period, the instalment payments are not required as the company was not 'large' in the previous accounting period.

(a) **Computation of capital allowances for the periods ending 29 February 2004**

	General pool £	Expensive car £	Short life asset £	CA summary £
Year to 31 October 2003				
Tax wdvs b/f	168,000	20,000	8,000	
Disposals	(6,000)	(12,000)		
		———		
Balancing allowance		8,000		8,000
		———		
Additions without FYA		14,000		
	———			
	162,000			
Less: WDA @ 25%	(40,500)	(3,000)	(2,000)	45,500
Additions qualifying for FYA				
(10,000 + 24,000)	34,000			
FYA @ 40%	(13,600)			13,600
				———
				67,100
				———

4 months to 29 February 2004

Tax wdvs b/f	141,900	11,000	6,000	
Disposals			(2,000)	
Balancing allowance			4,000	4,000
Less: WDA @ 25% × $\frac{4}{12}$	(11,825)	(917)		12,742
				16,742
Tax wdvs c/f	130,075	10,083		

Examination tip - *Although a columnar layout for plant capital allowances is essential, there is usually some scope to reduce the number of columns. For example:*

♦ *Recycle the expensive car column if an expensive car is sold and another purchased in the same year.*
♦ *Try to avoid using an inset column for FYA additions - see above approach.*

(b) **Computation of mainstream corporation tax for the periods ending 29 February 2004**

	Year to 31 October 2003 £	*4 months to 29 February 2004* £
Trading profits (before CAs) 12 : 4	451,500	150,500
Less: Capital allowances	(67,100)	(16,742)
Schedule D Case I	384,400	133,758
Capital gains (Working 1)	10,000	360,000
Schedule A (Working 2)	17,000	7,000
Schedule D Case VI (Working 3)	15,250	5,000
	426,650	505,758
Less: Charge paid (Gift Aid)	(8,000)	-
	418,650	505,758
Less: Schedule D Case III deficit (Working 4)	(5,000)	(1,667)
PCTCT	413,650	504,091
FII	20,000	-
Profits for small company purposes	433,650	504,091
Corporation tax thereon (Working 5) 413,650/504,091 × 30%	124,095	151,227
Less: Marginal relief $\frac{11}{400}$ (1,500,000 – 433,650) × $\frac{413,650}{433,650}$	(27,972)	
	96,123	151,227
Less: ACT b/f (Working 6)	(47,230)	(13,318)
	48,893	137,909
Less: Income tax recoverable (Working 7)	(5,280)	-
Mainstream corporation tax	43,613	137,909
Due date	1.8.04	1.12.04

Examination tip - *Both parts of the question are fully computational so full marks are given by simply generating the required figures. A certain amount of annotation - particularly for the ACT and income tax workings - would make your answer more presentable and easier for marks to be allocated.*

Workings

1   **Capital gains**

	£
Year to 31 October 2003	
Capital gains	40,000
Less: Capital loss b/f	(30,000)
	10,000

2   **Schedule A**

Rents receivable (12 months paid in advance)	
Year to 31 October 2003	17,000
4 months to 29 February 2004 - 21,000 × $\frac{4}{12}$	7,000

3   **Schedule D Case VI**

	Year to 31 October 2003 £	4 months to 29 February 2004 £
Patent income (accruals basis)	24,000	10,000
Less: Written off @ $\frac{180,000}{12}$ = £15,000 pa ($\frac{7}{12}$; $\frac{4}{12}$)	(8,750)	(5,000)
	15,250	5,000

4   **Schedule D Case III deficit**

As the rate of both the loan interest paid and debenture interest received is unchanged over the periods concerned, the annual rate of deficit is £5,000 (£15,000 - £10,000).

The deficit for the 4 months to 29 February 2004 is therefore:

$$\frac{4}{12} \times £5,000 = £1,667$$

5   **Small company limits**

	Lower £	Upper £
Year to 31 October 2003	300,000	1,500,000
4 months to 29 February 2004 (× $\frac{4}{12}$)	100,000	500,000

Although the year to 31 October 2003 straddles FY 2002 and FY 2003 the marginal relief calculation does not need to be done in two parts as the marginal relief fraction has not changed.

6   **ACT set-off**

	Year to 31.10.03 £	4m to 29.2.04 £
Maximum set-off (ignoring shadow ACT) PCTCT @ 20%		
413,650/504,091 × 20%	82,730	100,818
Shadow ACT		
Dividend paid	160,000	350,000
Less: Dividend received 20,000 × 90%	18,000	-
	142,000	350,000
Shadow ACT @ $^{20}/_{80}$	35,500	87,500
Reduced available set-off	47,230	13,318
Surplus ACT b/f	(63,000)	(15,770)
Surplus ACT c/f	15,770	2,452

7   **Income tax recoverable**

Income tax suffered on income:	
Patent royalties - 24,000 × 22%	5,280

Answer 12

EIS Funding

> *Tutorial note:*
>
> When this question was set under the old syllabus, candidates also had to comment on the capital gains implications of EIS share investment for individual investors. Under the new syllabus the capital gains taxation of individuals is not examinable so the updated version of this question excludes those aspects.

REPORT

To:	The Board of Directors
Re:	Raising finance under the Enterprise Investment Scheme (EIS)
Date:	10 May 2004
From:	Chartered Management Accountant

Issuing shares

The purpose of this report is to review the tax implications of raising finance through the issue of shares and in particular to consider the specific rules for issuing shares that qualify under the Enterprise Investment Scheme.

The costs of issuing shares are disallowed for corporation tax purposes. Similarly, any VAT incurred on such costs is irrecoverable.

Dividends paid on shares are also not allowable for corporation tax and are instead an appropriation of post-tax profits.

The issue of shares contrasts with the raising of finance through the issue of debenture stock. The issue costs and the interest payable on debentures are allowable expenses. However, dividends are only paid when the directors choose to do so whereas debenture interest generally has to be paid.

Advantages for investors under the EIS

♦ Amounts invested under the EIS can give rise to an income tax credit equal to 20% of the amount invested.

♦ The investment must be in new ordinary shares of an unquoted trading company.

♦ The maximum qualifying for relief in one tax year is £150,000. However, up to £25,000 (or half the amount invested if less) subscribed to EIS shares before 6 October in a tax year can be carried back for relief in the previous tax year.

♦ The shares must be held for a minimum of three years or the tax credit will be clawed back.

EIS conditions for the company

♦ The EIS shares issued by the company must be new ordinary fully paid shares carrying no preferential rights to dividends or assets.

♦ The company must be unquoted and must exist mainly to carry on a qualifying trade. All trades qualify if they are conducted commercially unless they fall on a 'black list'. These are mainly trades which are less risky because they are backed by property (eg farming and property development) or which need little encouragement such as banking or legal or financial services.

♦ The qualifying trade which will use the funds raised by the EIS shares issue must be carried on mainly in the UK.

These conditions must apply for the relevant period of three years after the EIS share issue. There is an exception for unquoted status. It is sufficient that when the EIS shares are issued there are no arrangements in existence for the company to become quoted other than becoming listed on the Alternative Investment Market. EIS relief is not clawed back if the company subsequently becomes quoted in the following three years.

In addition, at the date of issue the gross assets of the company must not exceed £15 million directly before the issue nor £16 million directly after the issue.

EIS conditions for the investor

♦ The investor must not be connected with the company in the period of two years before the issue and three years after the issue.

♦ An investor is connected if he or she controls more than 30% of the company's share capital or voting rights or entitlement to assets in a winding up.

♦ An investor is also connected if he is an employee or director of the company although a director does not count as 'connected' if he was not 'connected' before the EIS share issue and only receives reasonable remuneration for his services as a director.

This report only gives an outline of the EIS rules. They are very complicated and in practice they are difficult to satisfy. Please let me know if you require further information.

Signed: Chartered Management Accountant

Examination tip - *Marks are earned most efficiently by producing the report in the format suggested in the question. Although the question concentrates on raising finance through a share issue, it is fair to comment on the main alternative of issuing a debenture. The marks are given for answering each of the four 'questions'.*

Corporation tax losses

Answer 13

STD Ltd ceasing

Tutorial note:

Because of subsequent changes in the legislation concerning ACT, this question is somewhat easier than when originally set. Where information is provided in a tabular form the best layout of your answer is also likely to be a tabular form.

Relief for trading losses is far less complicated than most candidates seem to think. Losses are first set against profits of the same year (here there are none) and then they are carried back against profits but not to displace trade charges. The loss of the 12 months to the date of cessation is carried back for three years (later years first) instead of just one year.

Loss carry back can have a knock-on effect for ACT set-off. However, dividends paid after 5 April 1999 do not require an ACT payment so the problem does not arise in this question.

(a)   **Computation of MCT (before loss relief) for the three years to 31 March 2003**

	Y/e 31.3.01 £	Y/e 31.3.02 £	Y/e 31.3.03 £
Schedule D Case I	140,000	180,000	45,000
Schedule A	20,000	11,000	5,000
Capital gains (net) (Working 1)	10,000	-	-
	170,000	191,000	50,000
Less: Charges paid:			
Patent royalties	(15,000)	(15,000)	-
Gift Aid	(11,000)		(8,000)
PCTCT	144,000	176,000	42,000
CT thereon at small company rate (20%/19%)	28,800	35,200	7,980
Less: Marginal relief (Working 2)	-	-	(380)
MCT payable	28,800	35,200	7,600
Due	1.1.02	1.1.03	1.1.04

Examination tip - A common mistake is to treat the tax deducted and paid over on charges as somehow recoverable. The company is only acting as a collecting agent. It would be like trying to claim back PAYE deductions!

(b)   **Corporation tax repayable following loss claims**

	Y/e 31.3.01 £	Y/e 31.3.02 £	Y/e 31.3.03 £
Profit before charges	170,000	191,000	50,000
Less: Trade charges	(15,000)	(15,000)	-
	155,000	176,000	50,000
Less: S393A(1)(b) relief	(94,000)	(176,000)	(50,000)
	61,000	-	-
Less: Non-trade charge	(11,000)		(8,000) wasted
PCTCT	50,000	-	-
GCT @ 20%	10,000	-	-
Previously paid	28,800	35,200	7,600
Repayment due (total £61,600)	18,800	35,200	7,600

Loss memorandum:

Loss of the year to 31 March 2004	320,000

Less: Relief under S393A(1)(b) (carry back)

y/e 31.3.03	(50,000)
y/e 31.3.02	(176,000)
y/e 31.3.01	(94,000)
	-

Unrelieved amounts remaining:

Non-trade charges (y/e 31.3.03)	£8,000
Capital losses (Working 1) 15,000 + 50,000	£65,000

Examination tip - *Full marks are given if you correctly calculate all the figures required - ie MCT for each of the three years before loss relief, the amount repayable following loss relief and any amounts remaining unrelieved. It is, however, advisable to make your workings sufficiently clear that you can be awarded marks for correct principles even if you've made arithmetical errors along the way.*

Workings

1   **Capital gains and losses**

	£
Gains of y/e 31.3.03	15,000
Less: Losses of y/e 31.3.02 b/fwd	(30,000)
Losses to carry forward	(15,000)

2   **Starting rate marginal relief**

y/e 31.3.03

	£
$\frac{19}{400}$ (50,000 - 42,000)	380

Answer 14

L Ltd (losses)

> *Tutorial note:*
>
> This is a straightforward corporation tax loss computation. The only slight complication is the 12 month carry back period which encompasses part of a period. You are expected to use a columnar layout and to modify the standard PCTCT layout to fit in the loss. The loss must be used against profits of the same period first and profits for this purpose are taken before deducting charges. Any excess trade charges resulting can only be carried forward. Next the trade charges for earlier periods are deducted as these cannot be displaced by a loss carry back claim. The remaining profits can then be reduced by the carried back loss.
>
> Remember, patent royalties paid on or after 1 April 2002 are no longer relieved as charges on income but as a trading expense so excess trading charges are rapidly becoming extinct. Unless told otherwise, you should assume patent royalties paid have been incurred for a trading purpose.
>
> Royalties received before 1 April 2002 are included as 'taxed income' on a paid basis (not accruals basis).
>
> This question has been updated to avoid the transitional problems of switching from a 'paid' to an 'accruals' basis for patents (income or expenditure) with effect from 1 April 2002. However, the transitional rules are quite simple. The accruals basis is not allowed to include amounts already brought into PCTCT on a paid basis nor is any amount allowed to 'escape' on the changeover. Any adjustments to satisfy these two simple rules are made to the accruals basis figure(s).

(a) **Mainstream corporation tax computations for the first two APs**

	Year to 31.1.02 £	8 months to 30.9.02 £
Schedule D Case I	17,000	21,000
Schedule A	3,000	2,000
Patent royalties	6,000	4,000
Chargeable gains	7,000	-
	33,000	27,000
Less: Charges on income		
Patent royalties	(4,000)	-
Gift Aid	-	(2,000)
PCTCT	29,000	25,000

*(24,000 – 3,000 patent royalties)

Gross corporation tax	£	£
FY00/FY01 $29,000 \times 20\%$	5,800	
FY00/FY01 starting rate marginal relief		
Less: $\frac{1}{40} \times (50,000 - 29,000)$	(525)	
FY01 $25,000 \times 20\% \times \frac{2}{8}$		1,250
FY02 $25,000 \times 19\% \times \frac{6}{8}$		3,562
Less:		
FY01 $\frac{1}{40} \times (50,000 \times \frac{8}{12} - 25,000) \times \frac{2}{8}$		(52)
FY02 $\frac{19}{400} \times (50,000 \times \frac{8}{12} - 25,000) \times \frac{6}{8}$		(297)
	5,275	4,463

Less: Income tax recoverable
        Patent royalties (received less paid)
                6,000 - 4,000 = 2,000 × 22%   (440)
                4,000 - 3,000 = 1,000 × 22%   (220)

MCT   4,835   4,243

Pay day   1.11.02   1.7.03

(b)   **Revised computations after claiming loss relief**

	Year to 31.1.02 £	8 months to 30.9.02 £	Year to 30.9.03 £
Schedule D Case I	17,000	21,000	-
Schedule A	3,000	2,000	4,000
Patent royalties	6,000	4,000	2,000
Chargeable gains	7,000	-	-
	33,000	27,000	6,000
Less: S393A(1)(a) relief			(6,000)
Less: Trade charges	(4,000)	-	
	29,000	27,000	-
Less: S393A(1)(b) relief	(9,667)	(27,000)	
PCTCT	19,333	-	-
Non-trade charge wasted	-	2,000	-
Gross corporation tax			
19,333 × 20%	3,867	-	
Less: $\frac{1}{40}$ × (50,000 – 19,333)	(767)		
	3,100		
Less: Income tax recoverable (as before)	(440)	(220)	
MCT after loss relief	2,660	(220)	
MCT originally payable	4,835	4,243	
MCT refundable	2,175	4,463	

(c)   **Loss memorandum**

	£
Loss of year to 30 September 2003 (62,000 + 5,000)	67,000
Used against total profits of same year (S393A(1)(a))	(6,000)
	61,000
Used by carry back under S393A(1)(b)	
8 months to 30.9.02	(27,000)
4 months of profits of year to 31.1.02 - $\frac{4}{12}$ × £29,000	(9,667)
Loss remaining carried forward under S393(1)(a) ICTA 1988	24,333
Capital loss to carry forward:	
Allowable loss of the 8 months to 30.9.02	8,000
Less: Used in the year to 30.9.03	(4,000)
Unrelieved capital loss to carry forward	4,000

Examination tip - *The loss can only be carried back 12 months in total so only four months of carry back period applies for the year to 31.1.02. The examiner would accept the total profits available calculated as $^{4}/_{12} \times £33,000 = £11,000$ although the above answer apportioning profits net of trade charges is usually accepted as the correct approach.*

Usually a loss memorandum would be prepared as part of the loss application exercise but it will be required anyway for the answer to part (c) so it is more mark efficient to exclude it in part (b). Similarly, there is no need to explain the treatment of the capital loss other than as part of your answer to part (c). You could explain how 'total profits' for loss relief purposes differs between current year relief and carry back relief but your understanding of this should be clear from the way the computation is performed.

Employee's taxation - benefits

Answer 15

Mr K

> **Tutorial note:**
>
> This is an easy question if you understand the employment benefit rules and the scope of NIC for employed earnings and benefits.
>
> In part (b) Class 1 applies on benefits paid in cash – eg settling Mr K's legal costs. This would result in a primary NIC Class 1 contribution if Mr K's income was below the upper earnings limit. Benefits received in kind attract a Class 1A charge almost without exception. Even where benefits are small or irregular and have been charged to income tax under a PAYE Settlement Agreement (PSA) there is a place for them in the NIC net under Class 1B. The employer pays 12.8% under Class 1, Class 1A or Class 1B. The employee can only be liable to NIC under Class 1.

(a) **Computation of assessable benefits for 2003/04**

			£	£
(i)	*Mercedes motor car*			
	$24,000 \times 31\% \times ^{4}/_{12}$			2,480
	Mr K had the car for 4 months (6.4.03 – 5.8.03) and the percentage is found by: $15\% + (235 – 155) \times ^{1}/_{5} = 31\%$			
	Fuel benefit : $14,400 \times 31\% \times ^{4}/_{12}$			1,488
	Lexus motor car			
	$36,000 \times 35\% \times ^{6}/_{12}$			6,300
	Mr K had the car for 6 months. Percentage is found by: $15\% + (265 – 155) \times ^{1}/_{5} = 37\%$ but restricted to a maximum of 35%			
	Fuel benefit: $14,400 \times 35\% \times ^{6}/_{12}$			2,520
	Net costs of fine and legal expenses: 1,200 – 300			900
(ii)	*Suits*			
	$800 \times 20\% \times 2$			320
(iii)	*Housing*			
	Annual value		8,000	
	Less: Rent paid by Mr K		(5,000)	3,000
	Expensive property charge: $(125,000 – 75,000) = 50,000 \times 5\%$			2,500
	Total value of benefits assessable on Mr K			19,508

(b) **Additional costs for the company**

	£
Net cost of fines etc attracts an NIC liability under Class 1 - 900 × 12.8%	115
The rest of the benefits fall under Class 1A - (19,508 - 900) = 18,608 × 12.8%	2,382
Class 1B applies to the benefits agreed under a PSA - 9,600 × 12.8%	1,229
	3,726

Examination tip - As a computational question with clear requirements, the marks are earned by generating the assessable benefits (part (a)) and the NIC payable by the company (part (b)).

Employees' taxation – remuneration and compliance

Answer 16

Reporting benefits

> *Tutorial note:*
>
> This is a difficult question to answer satisfactorily. There are a few pointers on what to emphasise. For example, the 'requirements' mentions 'forms', 'broad content' and 'time limits'. The question also refers to salary ranges of £7,000 to £20,000 so the 'lower' paid and 'higher' paid treatment must be covered.
>
> Before launching into your answer, jot down the main topic headings you think are needed and arrange them in a logical order. Review your list and decide if it is complete or, for that matter, covering unnecessary items. If you haven't got 'dispensations' add it in. If you plan to explain exactly how car benefits are calculated – cross it off! This report is mainly about reporting requirements and clearly not concerned with the actual calculating of benefits.

REPORT

To: The Directors of Jay and Co

Re: Reporting requirements for employment benefits

Date: 10 May 2004

From: Chartered Management Accountant

The purpose of this report is to outline the legal duties of employers to report benefits supplied to their employees.

In the past you have run your business as a partnership with minimal help from part-time employees who, presumably, did not receive benefits. Now that the business has been transferred to a company and is set to expand, it will be necessary to address the reporting requirements in detail.

Categories of employees

For the purpose of benefits-in-kind the tax rules distinguish between 'lower paid' and 'higher paid' employees.

♦ Higher paid : These are employees remunerated at the rate of £8,500 pa or more.

♦ Lower paid : These are employees remunerated at less than £8,500 pa.

Note that directors are generally 'higher paid' regardless of their level of earnings. Also, the test of remuneration level applies to the total emoluments including benefits and before any deduction for expenses. Benefits are calculated on the basis that the employee is 'higher paid' to see whether the £8,500 limit is breached. If it is not breached, the benefits are recalculated on the 'lower paid' basis.

The term 'lower paid' is used in the legislation. Although the term 'higher paid' is not found in the legislation (it would be rather a misnomer), it is commonly used as an easy label to remember.

There are special benefit rules that apply to both higher paid and lower paid employees. This arises where a benefit is supplied via a cash voucher, a non-cash voucher or a credit card and where an employee is allowed to occupy accommodation or granted share options.

For higher paid employees

♦ There are further special rules for calculating the chargeable value of certain benefits such as low interest loans, company cars, private use fuel and the use of assets such as suits.

♦ If special rules do not apply, the benefit is valued at the cost of the employer to provide the benefit – eg the cost of a holiday or private health insurance.

♦ After each year a form, P11D, has to be completed for each 'higher paid' employee to record the taxable value of every benefit supplied.

For lower paid employees

♦ Apart from the special rules on accommodation and vouchers, a lower paid employee is taxed on the amount of a benefit which could be obtained if sold for cash – ie the second-hand value. In many instances, eg the loan of a suit, this amounts to nil especially where the employee is formally prohibited from 'trading' it in anyway.

♦ After each tax year the employer has to complete a form P9D for each lower paid employee who has received taxable benefits.

Dispensations and PAYE Settlement Agreements (PSAs)

For many years the Revenue have been prepared to grant dispensations from reporting benefits on P11Ds and P9Ds where the benefits concerned are cancelled by an equal employment expenses claim. Typically, if the employee is only reimbursed for actual expenses incurred for his employment duties, the reimbursement which should be shown on the P11D will be cancelled by an equal expense claim against taxable income. It may be advisable to apply for a dispensation to cover certain categories of reimbursements.

The Revenue also operate a statutory system of PAYE Settlement Agreements (PSAs). Basically the company can agree with the Revenue to pay the employee's tax on small or irregularly occurring benefits as a global sum. The tax is found by grossing up the benefit values at the average marginal income tax rate of the employees in question. The advantage of a PSA is the avoidance of having to report the benefits covered in the individual employee's P11Ds/P9Ds.

Exemptions from the benefit rules

Certain benefits are exempt from income taxation and present a useful opportunity for employers to remunerate staff tax efficiently as the costs of providing exempt benefits remain allowable against corporation tax. Examples include:

♦ Free or subsidised canteen facilities.

♦ Up to £5,000 interest free loans.

♦ Employer contributions to approved pension schemes.

♦ The first £8,000 of relocation expenses paid by an employer.

♦ Shares acquired under 'approved' schemes (although a CGT charge may arise in some circumstances).

♦ The provision of workplace nurseries.

♦ The private use of a mobile phone (but not if it involves using vouchers to pay for call time).

♦ Staff Christmas parties (or similar) up to £150 per head pa.

The further advantage of exempt benefits is not having to show them on a P11D/P9D.

Year end reporting requirements

The employer has to complete a form P11D (or P9D as appropriate) for each employee in receipt of taxable benefits in the tax year and send a copy to the Revenue by 6 July following the year end. By the same date a copy has to be given to the employee concerned to assist them in completing his own self-assessment tax return. The P11D reporting duty can be onerous as there are special calculation rules for many categories of benefit and the employer has a duty to calculate the correct taxable amount. There are supplementary sheets available to help with these calculations.

The employer must also complete a form P11D(b), which is used to calculate the Class 1A NICs due on employee benefits. This form must also be filed by 6 July; there are automatic penalties for late filing.

This report raises a number of matters which you will no doubt wish to discuss further.

Signed: Chartered Management Accountant

Examination tip - *The above answer is probably more detailed than would be required for full marks. The important point is not to ramble from one topic to another. The answer is broken down into labelled sections to help with the mark earning and force a structure on the report. There are more marks to earn by mentioning most relevant topics, albeit briefly, rather than going into depth on just one or two.*

Answer 17

F Ltd

> **Tutorial note:**
>
> This is quite a demanding question although the tax and NIC concepts are fairly straightforward. It is good practice to prepare the computations in separate Appendices. The report should outline the choices, explain the tax effects of each choice with reference to the relevant Appendix and show the conclusion.
>
> Where the question is posed: bonus or dividends?, you have to concentrate on the relative tax costs. As the directors are also the shareholders, the key issue is how to extract profits at the least tax cost. The question, however, confuses the issue, perhaps deliberately. With a dividend the recipient has a higher after tax receipt but this overlooks the lack of tax relief in the company. £1 for £1 it is less expensive for a 32.75% corporation tax rate company to pay a bonus. It is usually more revealing to decide on the required net receipt for the shareholder/employee and see the tax cost of the alternative ways of achieving it.

REPORT

To: Mr and Mrs F, the directors of F Ltd

Re: The tax implications of paying a bonus v paying a dividend

Date: 23 February 2004

From: Chartered Management Accountant

The purpose of this report is to show the tax effects of:

(i)   paying a bonus of £20,000 to each director, and

(ii)   paying a dividend of £20,000 to each director/shareholder.

The intention is for these alternative disbursements to be paid out of the profits for the year to 31 March 2004. From the company's viewpoint there is no need for either the bonus or the dividend to be paid or even decided by 31 March 2004 although, in the case of the bonus, payment must not be made later than 9 months after the year end.

Bonus payments

A bonus payment has to be made under PAYE. Any PAYE and NIC due on the payment has to be paid to the Revenue Accounts office within 14 days of the end of the tax month of payment.

In view of each director's annual earnings of £45,000 the payments will require PAYE deducted at 40%, employee's Class 1 NIC payment of 1% and an employer's Class 1 NIC payment of 12.8%. NIC is not due on the employee at the full 11% rate as the upper earnings limit is already exceeded.

Normally a salary amount enters the PAYE system when it is actually paid or, if earlier, when it is made available. However, for directors an earlier date could apply:

♦ if the payment is determined before the year end and it is treated as paid at the year end (unless paid earlier).

♦ if the payment is determined after the year end and it is 'paid' when it is determined.

For cash flow reasons, a bonus should not be determined significantly in advance of the date it is intended to be paid.

Appendix 1 shows the tax effects of paying a bonus. Although employer's NIC is payable, the bonus and the NIC are allowable against corporation tax at 32.75% - the marginal tax rate applying for profits above £150,000. The existence of the associated company N Ltd halves the lower limit of £300,000.

Dividend payments

A dividend is payable out of after tax profits and is not an allowable business expense. On the other hand it does not attract NIC liability.

The shareholder receives the dividend with a 10% imputed tax credit. The dividend therefore has to be grossed up at $^{100}/_{90}$. For a higher rate taxpayer, there is an income tax charge of 32½% but with a 10% tax credit reducing it to a rate of 22½%. This extra tax is payable on 31 January following the tax year of receipt. It would delay the tax payment by 12 months if the dividend was paid after 5 April 2004.

The tax effects are quantified in Appendix 2 below.

Conclusion

The payment of a bonus of £20,000 results in £11,800 after tax for the director but at a tax and NIC cost of £3,371 (Appendix 1). The payment of a dividend of £20,000 results in £15,000 after tax for the shareholder director but at a tax cost of £5,000 (Appendix 2).

For each £1 of net receipt there is a higher cost if it is paid as a dividend (Appendix 2).

As the directors own the company they should be concerned with minimising the total tax and NIC charge for extracting profits regardless of whether the tax charge falls on the director or the company.

In the longer term the directors should also be interested in profit extraction which reduces retained profits as there may be a future tax cost of removing those profits from the company.

However, as the company has a marginal tax rate of 32.75% it is currently more tax efficient to take out profits as extra salary rather than as dividends.

Please let me know if I can provide further explanations.

Signed: Chartered Management Accountant

Examination tip - *Marks depend significantly on concluding that a bonus is preferable.*

Appendix 1 – Taking extra salary

(i)   *Effect on the company*

		£
Profit before tax		280,000
Less:	Bonus 2 × 20,000	(40,000)
	Employer's NIC 40,000 × 12.8%	(5,120)
		234,880
Corporation tax:		
	234,880 × 30%	70,464
	Less: $\frac{11}{400}$ (750,000 – 234,880)	(14,166)
		56,298
Net profits retained in the company		178,582

(ii)   *Effect on the shareholders*

	£
Each director retains income of 20,000 × 59%	11,800

(They are clearly higher paid individuals and earnings are well in excess of the UEL for NIC so an IT rate of 40% plus a NIC charge of 1% applies.)

(iii)   *Overview*

	£
Income tax/NIC paid by directors 40,000 × 41%	16,400
NIC paid by company	5,120
CT saving 45,120 × 32.75%	(14,777)
	6,743
Per director ½	£3,371

It costs £3,371 of tax/NIC to provide a director with £11,800 net.

Appendix 2 – Paying profits out as dividends

(i)   *Effect on the company*

		£	£
Profit before tax			280,000
Less:	CT: 280,000 × 30%	84,000	
Less:	$\frac{11}{400}$ (750,000 – 280,000)	(12,925)	(71,075)
Profit after tax			208,925
Less:	Dividends (2 × 20,000)		40,000
Profits retained in the company			168,925

(ii)   *Effect on the directors*

		£
For each director :	Net dividend received	20,000
	Gross up $\frac{100}{90}$	22,222
	IT due at 32½%	7,222
	Less: 10% tax credit	(2,222)
	Extra tax to pay	5,000
	Net dividend retained	15,000

(iii)   *Overview*

Income tax paid per director   £5,000

It costs £5,000 of tax to provide a director with £15,000 net.

To make a comparison with the bonus payment in Appendix 1, it costs £3,933 (5,000 × $^{11,800}\!/_{15,000}$) to provide a director with £11,800 net.

Answer 18

Advertising Company

(a)   **Report to the Head of Payroll**

        Subject: Employment benefits

        Date: 10 April 2004

        From: Debbie Mills – Chief Accountant

        Report's focus

        The company has recently taken on a number of employees who had previously acted for the company on a freelance basis. Certain benefits are being provided to these employees and this report will explain how the taxable amounts are calculated and the associated compliance requirements.

        1   **Company cars**

        This form of benefit is already being provided to the directors. A brief reminder of the rules is as follows:

        ♦   The benefit is calculated as a percentage of the car's list price.

        ♦   The percentage is based on the car's carbon dioxide emission rate as recorded in the car's registration document. An emission rate of 155 gms/km or less gives a 15% charge. An extra 1% applies for every additional 5 gms/km (eg 163 gms/km = 16% charge). There is a 3% supplement if the car uses diesel fuel but there is an overall maximum of 35%.

        ♦   List price is the manufacturer's published price inclusive of VAT applying when the car was first registered (even if acquired second hand).

        ♦   List price includes the price of any accessories fitted after purchase unless costing under £100.

        ♦   A reduction is allowed for any capital contribution the employee makes up to a maximum of £5,000.

        ♦   If the list price exceeds £80,000 it is capped at that amount.

        ♦   If the car is only available for part of the tax year – ie, use commences after 6 April or ends before 5 April – the charge is reduced on a time basis.

        ♦   If, during the period of use, the car is unavailable for more than 30 consecutive days the charge is reduced on a time basis. No reduction is made for lesser periods.

        ♦   The charge covers all associated costs such as insurance, road fund tax and servicing.

        ♦   Contributions by the employee towards the running costs are deductible from the amount of the charge.

2   **Fuel provided for private motoring**

If fuel is provided for private use in a company car there is a fuel benefit charge dependant on the car benefit percentage.

- For 2003/04 the benefit is £14,400 multiplied by the car benefit percentage.

- Employee contributions have no effect unless they fully repay the actual cost of the private mileage – in which case the charge is extinguished.

- Mileage undertaken between home and the normal place of work is private mileage, not business mileage.

- The fuel benefit charge is reduced on a time basis if the availability of the fuel is permanently discontinued during the tax year.

3   **Help with relocation costs**

Contribution by the company of up to £8,000 to an employee in respect of most relocation costs are an exempt benefit. However the exemption only applies if the employee has to move house in order to be within a reasonable daily travelling distance of work.

4   **Interest-free loans**

If the total of loans to an employee does not exceed £5,000 at any time in the tax year no chargeable benefit arises. Otherwise the benefit is valued at the amount of interest at the 'official rate' (currently 5%) which the employer has foregone.

If the loan is written off the employee is taxed on the amount of the write-off in the tax year of write-off.

5   **Class 1A NIC**

Where a director or an employee earning over £8,500 pa receives one or more of the above chargeable benefits the employer has to pay Class 1A NIC calculated at 12.8% on the taxable value of the benefit. This is due for payment on 19 July following the tax year.

6   **Year end returns of benefits**

For every director and 'higher paid' employee in receipt of benefits the company has to complete a form P11D and send it to the Revenue by 6 July following the tax year. Failure to meet that deadline can result in penalties.

A form P11D consists of 2 main pages on which to record the taxable value of the benefits. The employee is entitled to receive a copy of the form – also by 6 July – and uses the detail to complete his own tax return. The employer has available a selection of working sheets to help calculate the figures to put on the P11D. Where a Class 1A liability arises the box on the P11D has a 1A 'marker'.

Please let me know if you need further clarification.

Signed: Debbie Mills – Chief Accountant

(b)   **Staff memorandum**

Subject: Tax on employment benefits

Date: 10 April 2004

From: Debbie Mills – Chief Accountant

Where you receive a benefit such as a company car the taxable value will be shown on your form P11D which should be available to you from the Payroll department shortly after the end of the tax year.

The figures on the forms have to be transferred onto the employment pages issued with your Tax Return.

Usually you would not need to check the calculation of your benefit amounts but if you want an explanation you should ask the Payroll Department.

The tax on your benefits is normally collected by restricting your PAYE code number. If the restriction exceeds the amount of your allowances a 'K code' results – this is just a negative PAYE code and means that an amount is added to your gross pay each month for the tax calculation.

If benefits have not already been factored into your tax code – eg, as for new employees – your self assessment return will show an amount of tax to pay by the following 31 January. If instead you prefer the tax to be collected through PAYE the Revenue require you to submit your tax return by 30 September following the tax year.

Answer 19

Mr K

(a) *Benefits assessable for 2003/2004*

				£	£
(i)	Cars:	Jaguar used for 5 months Emission rate > 255 gms/km so percentage of 35% applies $£32,000 \times 35\% \times \frac{5}{12}$			4,667
		Mercedes used for 5 months Percentage: $15\% + (225 - 155) \times \frac{1}{5} = 29\%$ $£40,000 \times 29\% \times \frac{5}{12}$			4,833
(ii)	Suits:	Two suits for 5 months $£600 \times 2 \times 20\% \times \frac{5}{12}$			100
(iii)	House:	Annual value	12,000		
		Less: Contribution	(5,000)		
			7,000		
		Add: Expensive accommodation charge $240,000 - 75,000 = 165,000 \times 5\%$	8,250		
		Running costs (2,800 + 1,500)	4,300	19,550	
(iv)	Gift:	MV of TV/audio system when new	4,000		
		Less: Assessed 2001/02 and 2002/03 $2 \times 20\% \times 4,000$	(1,600)		
			2,400		
		Less: Paid by Mr K	(1,200)	1,200	
		(Higher than 1,500 - 1,200 = 300)		30,350	

(b) *Additional cost for the company*

Class 1A NIC $£30,350 \times 12.8\% = £3,885$ (due 19 July 2004)

(c)   *Estimate of Mr K's PAYE code number for 2004/2005*

	£
Car benefit 40,000 × 29%	11,600
Suits £600 × 2 × 20%	240
Accommodation	19,550
	31,390
Less PA	(4,615)
	26,775
This results in a K code	K2,676

Capital gains – principles and computation

Answer 20

L Ltd (rents)

> *Tutorial note:*
>
> When this question was originally set there were differences in tax treatment between tenant repairing and landlord repairing leases. Such leases are still a commercial feature of property letting but the tax rules now make no distinction. All letting by a company is treated for tax as a single business with income and expenses dealt with as if the business was a trade – ie accruals basis. It is not actually a trade so, for example, there are separate rules for relieving Schedule A losses.

(a)   **Schedule A income for the year to 31 October 2003**

Property		Expenditure £	Rent £
A		3,000	5,000
B	$\frac{7}{12} \times 12,000$	3,100	7,000
C	$\frac{4}{12} \times 6,000$	7,400	2,000
D		2,800	7,200
E		4,800	16,000
F	$\frac{1}{12} \times 20,000$	9,000	1,667
		30,100	38,867
		-	(30,100)
Amount to be included in PCTCT			8,767

Examination tip - *Note that using a columnar layout is a neat and efficient way of presenting your answer.*

(b)   **MEMORANDUM**

To: The Directors of L Ltd

Re: Tax treatment of premiums received for granting short leases

Date: 10 May 2004

From: Chartered Management Accountant

If the company receives a premium for granting a lease on freehold property for a period of less than 50 years (a 'short' lease) it will be assessable partly as an income profit and partly as a capital gain.

Rationale

A lease premium is regarded for tax purposes as a forward payment of rent. Without a premium the annual rents would be higher in a given situation. However, the longer the period of a lease the more the premium becomes akin to a capital payment.

Capital/income split

The capital element is equal to 2% of the premium for every complete year for which the lease can last disregarding the first year. So a 21 year lease has a capital element of 40% ((21 – 1) × 2%). The income element is the balance – here, 60%. The Revenue will examine the lease if necessary to decide on the likely minimum term of the lease. For example, a 21 year lease determinable by either party every five years is obviously just a five year lease.

Income

Although rental income is assessable on an accruals basis without regard to when it is actually received, the income element of a premium is assessable under Schedule A in full in the accounting period in which it is granted. There is no question of spreading the assessment over the period of the lease.

Capital

The capital element of the premium is taxed as a capital gain. In effect it is a part disposal of the freehold so the calculation uses the following fraction of the original cost or March 1982 value:

$$\frac{\text{Capital element of premium}}{\text{Full premium} + \text{freehold reversionary value}}$$

The freehold reversionary value is the market value of the freehold when the lease has been granted taking account of the terms of the lease.

Please let me know if I can provide further details.

Signed: Chartered Management Accountant

Examination tip - *It is relatively easy to earn the marks in part (a) and it should be possible to earn full marks without providing lengthy explanations. For part (b) there are eight marks so it will be necessary to bring out a number of facts. For example, it is not enough to say what proportion is treated as capital. You have to go on to outline how a part disposal gain is calculated. Mark earning is more assured if you use paragraph headings to organise your answer.*

Capital gains – shares and securities

Answer 21

B Ltd and Z Ltd

Tutorial note:

This question sub-divides into several quite separate capital gains calculations. You should label each calculation clearly so the marker can see which disposal is being dealt with. If you know the rules for short leasehold disposals and for the sale of nil paid rights shares there are some easy marks on offer.

(i) *Leasehold*

The cost depreciates on a 'curved line' using the lease table percentages provided in the question.

(ii) *Rights issues*

If rights issues are taken up they are added to the pool. An indexed rise is added just before pooling the rights shares and cost.

However, if the shareholder chooses he can instead sell the right to take up the rights shares at the (usually) preferential rights price – known as selling the rights 'nil paid'. In effect, the shareholder is making a part disposal of the pool shares (the value but not the number) and the normal $^A\!/_{A+B}$ calculation technique applies. However, if the rights sale proceeds are less than 5% of the current value of the holding (including the rights proceeds), no gain is computed. Instead the proceeds are deducted from the pool cost. It is Revenue practice to apply this treatment even if the proceeds exceed 5% provided less than £3,000 is received.

(a) **B Ltd – Computation of gains for the year to 31 March 2004**

(i) *Disposal of painting – 30 September 2003*

	£
Proceeds (deemed)	6,000
Less: Cost	(7,100)
Allowable loss	(1,100)

Examination tip - *The question requires gains and losses to be summarised. This can either be done by using a column running down the right hand side of the answer or by having a separate summary at the end. The latter approach is easier to produce in the exam.*

(ii) *Disposal of lease – 31 October 2003*

	£
Proceeds	100,000
Less: Cost × $\dfrac{\%\text{ at disposal (31 years)}}{\%\text{ at acquisition (35 years)}}$	
$45,000 \times \dfrac{88.371}{91.981}$	(43,234)
	56,766
Less: Indexation allowance: $43,234 \times 0.091$	(3,934)
Chargeable gain	52,832

(iii)   *Destruction of warehouse – December 2003*

	£
Proceeds	5,000
Less: March 1982 value	(7,000)
Allowable loss	(2,000)

Examination tip - *It seems unfair but the examiner expects you to know that a S.35 TCGA 1992 election is made to rebase all assets held at March 1982 ignoring their original cost. You should be able to guess this from the context. As a general exam technique, if a similar problem arises you have to make a sensible guess – usually a little thought will reveal the examiner's meaning.*

Summary of gains and losses

		£
(i)	Painting	(1,100)
(ii)	Lease	52,832
(iii)	Warehouse	(2,000)
Net chargeable gains		49,732

(b)   **Z Ltd – Sale of rights nil paid**

(i)   *Sale of rights for £9,800*

	£
Proceeds	9,800
Less: Cost	
$110,000 \times \dfrac{9,800}{9,800 + 10,000 \times 16}$	(6,349)
	3,451
Less: Indexation allowance - $6,349 \times 0.300$	(1,905)
Chargeable gain	1,546

Examination tip - *Strictly an FA 1985 pool should be shown but this is an acceptable short cut.*

(ii)   *Sale of rights for £8,000*

As £8,000 is less than 5% of (£8,000 + 10,000 × £16) – ie 4.76% < 5% - the proceeds are simply deducted from the cost of the shares:

1985 Pool:

		No	Cost £	Indexed cost £
June 1992 :	Purchase	10,000	110,000	110,000
January 2004 :	Indexed rise - $110,000 \times 0.300$			33,000
				143,000
	Sale nil paid	-	(8,000)	(8,000)
	c/f	10,000	102,000	135,000

Examination tip - *In computations marks are given primarily for correct answers – obviously. Any labels or explanations can be kept to a minimum provided you make it clear what you are trying to do. You could mention, where appropriate, that indexation allowance cannot increase or create a loss but if you have acted on that principle it is hard to see why it should be worth a mark. In fact the examiner did not supply the indexation factor for the warehouse disposal thereby pre-empting the point anyway. The advice must be to provide annotation and explanation but only in reasonable measures and only if you have the time. They are no substitute for the correct numerical results.*

Answer 22

BD Ltd

> *Tutorial note:*
>
> This is a relatively straightforward question on capital gains. In the granting of a sub-lease out of a short lease, the cost to apply is the part of the head lease cost expiring during the period of the sub-lease using the 'curved line' depreciation percentages. Part of the sub-lease premium is assessable under Schedule A as an income element and this has to be excluded from the gain.
>
> In the share disposal calculation it was necessary to apportion the original cost between the replacement assets produced by the reorganisation. This is normally done on the basis of the relative market values immediately after the reorganisation.

(a)   **Chargeable gains and allowable losses for the year to 31 March 2004**

(i)   *Grant of a sub-lease*

		£
Proceeds		12,000
Less:	Cost expiring during the sub-lease period	
	$48,000 \times \dfrac{\text{\% at start of sub-lease } - \text{ \% at end}}{\text{\% at acquisition of head lease}}$	
	$48,000 \times \dfrac{83.816 \ (27 \text{ years}) - 74.635 \ (21 \text{ years})}{91.981 \ (35 \text{ years})}$	(4,791)
		7,209
Less:	Indexation allowance - $4,791 \times 0.213$	(1,020)
		6,189
	Relief for income element in the sub-lease premium	
	$12,000 \times (100\% - 2\% \ (6 - 1))$	(10,800)
Chargeable gain		Nil

(ii)   *Sale of office block*

		£
Proceeds		42,000
Less:	Part disposal cost	
	$100,000 \times \dfrac{42,000}{42,000 + 190,000}$	(18,103)
		23,897
Less:	Indexation allowance – $18,103 \times 0.540$	(9,776)
Chargeable gain		14,121

(iii)   *Sale of 20,000 ordinary shares in X Ltd*

		£	£
Proceeds		75,000	75,000
Less:	Cost/31.3.82 MV (see below)	(10,385)	(13,846)
		64,615	61,154
Less:	Indexation allowance - $13,846 \times 1.277$	(17,681)	(17,681)
		46,934	43,473
Lower gain applies			43,473

Split of cost on reorganisation:

	MV July 1992 £	Cost £	31.3.82 MV £
20,000 ordinary shares @ £1.80	36,000	10,385 $(^{36}\!/_{52})$	13,846 $(^{36}\!/_{52})$
20,000 preference shares @ £0.80	16,000	4,615 $(^{16}\!/_{52})$	6,154 $(^{16}\!/_{52})$
	52,000	15,000	20,000

(b)   **Amount of corporation tax payable on the gains**

			£
Gains:	(i)	Sub-lease premium	-
	(ii)	Office block	14,121
	(iii)	Shares in X Ltd	43,473
			57,594
CT @ 32.75%			£18,862

As BD Ltd has one associated company, Mince SA, the small company bands are divided by 2 – ie £150,000 and £750,000.

As BD Ltd' s profits for the period already exceed £150,000 and there is no FII, the gains attract the marginal rate of 32.75%.

Examination tip - *As long as the figures are correctly applied to produce the required computational results, there is no need to supply detailed annotations. For example, it should be sufficient in the first computation to just calculate the expiring cost without trying to explain the rationale of the approach. The rule is to leave enough of a trail for the marker to follow your reasoning just in case you trip up on the arithmetic.*

Capital gains – rollover and holdover reliefs

Answer 23

P Ltd, G Ltd and R Ltd

Tutorial note:

Part (a) involves reconstructing an FA 1985 pool and a 'frozen' (FA 1982) pool. The complications of bonus or rights issues did not arise. Nevertheless, care is needed especially to slot in indexed rises where appropriate. The techniques were frequently tested under the old syllabus. Constructing an FA 1985 pool should be an easy way of earning marks even if somewhat tedious!

Part (b) looks at first glance to be a 'groups' capital gains problem but it is not. It is just a disposal of an asset which had been used to rollover a gain. Note that whenever 'cost' is adjusted for whatever reason – eg rollover relief as here or lease cost depreciation – the resulting figure is also used in calculating indexation allowance. It is often overlooked that rollover using a non-depreciating asset reduces the potential indexation allowance when the replacement asset is sold. For this reason a company may decide not to claim rollover relief in some circumstances.

Part (c) requires advice (based on your computations) on whether to make a 'global' election – sometimes described as a S.35 TCGA 1992 election or just a 'Section 35' election. The examiner's own published answer did not bother with the 'report' headings although on past papers this would have been expected.

(a)   **P Ltd – Chargeable gain on disposal of T Ltd shares**

The 25,000 shares sold are matched first with the 20,000 shares in the FA 1985 pool (see Working 1) and then with 5,000 of the 7,000 shares in the FA 1982 pool (see Working 2).

	£
FA 1985 pool:	
Proceeds $^{20,000}/_{25,000} \times 150,000$	120,000
Less: Cost (Working 1)	(80,000)
	40,000
Less: Indexation allowance: 118,995 – 80,000 (Working 1)	(38,995)
Chargeable gain	1,005

***Examination tip** - Although it is clear that a loss does not arise, it is still good exam practice to show the 'cost' and the 'indexation allowance' deducted separately instead of just deducting the indexed cost.*

FA 1982 pool:	£
Proceeds: $^{5,000}/_{25,000} \times 150,000$	30,000
Less: 31.3.82 MV (Working 2)	(6,000)
	24,000
Less: Indexation allowance: $6,000 \times 1.277$	(7,662)
Chargeable gain	16,338
Total chargeable gain (£1,005 + £16,338)	£17,343

(b)   **G Ltd – Computation of net funds generated in H Ltd**

	£	£
Sale of surplus premises:		
Proceeds		150,000
Less: Cost	40,000	
Reduced by gain rolled over	(10,000)	(30,000)
		120,000
Less: Indexation allowance: $30,000 \times 0.299$		(8,970)
Chargeable gain		111,030
Corporation tax at 32.75%		36,362

	£
Proceeds	150,000
Less: Corporation tax	(36,362)
Net funds remaining	£113,638

Note: The CT rate for additional profits is 32.75% as profits already fall into the marginal relief band of £150,000 to £750,000. The £300,000/£1,500,000 limits are halved as G Ltd and H Ltd are associated for the year to 31.3.2004.

(c)   **R Ltd – Chargeable gains on the disposal of two factories**

Factory A:

	Cost £	31.3.82 MV £
Proceeds	70,000	70,000
Less: Cost/31.3.82 MV	(80,000)	(100,000)
	(10,000)	(30,000)

Indexation allowance cannot increase a loss so is ignored.

Factory B:

	Cost £	31.3.82 MV £
Proceeds	125,000	125,000
Less: Cost/31.3.82 MV	(27,000)	(40,000)
	98,000	85,000
Less: Indexation allowance: 40,000 × 1.277	(51,080)	(51,080)
	46,920	33,920

Advice:

As this is the first disposal of assets held at 31 March 1982 the company can still make a global election to use the 31 March 1982 market value ignoring original pre-March 1982 cost.

Without an election:

			£
Factory A	:	smaller loss	(10,000)
Factory B	:	lower gain	33,920
Net chargeable gains			23,920

With an election:

			£
Factory A	:	loss based on 31.3.82 MV	(30,000)
Factory B	:	gain based on 31.3.82 MV	33,920
Net chargeable gains			3,920

If these are the only two assets held by R Ltd which are affected by a global election, the election should be made as it reduces net chargeable gains by £20,000.

If there are other assets which would be affected, the likely impact of a global election on any future disposals should be reviewed. Any probable disadvantage would have to be balanced against the current saving on £20,000 of extra loss relief.

An election has to be made within two years of the end of the AP in which the first relevant disposal occurs (ie the AP containing July 2003).

Examination tip - In parts (a) and (b), as for computational questions in general, full marks are given for a completely correct final answer but it is advisable to leave a clear trail through your workings.

In part (c), full marks were probably given for advising the Board to make the election with figures to show the advantage. The suggested answer goes further. It explains why an election is still possible (in practice now uncommon), the potential problems if other assets are affected and the time limit for the election.

Workings

1   **T Ltd FA 1985 pool**

		No	Cost £	Indexed cost £
April 1985 :	Bring in acquisitions since April 1982			
	Jan 1984	5,000	10,000	10,000
	Indexed rise: 0.091 × 10,000			910
				10,910
March 1990 :	Indexed rise: 10,910 × 0.281			3,066
				13,976
	Purchase	10,000	50,000	50,000
		15,000	60,000	63,976
April 1996 :	Indexed rise: 63,976 × 0.257			16,442
	Purchase	5,000	20,000	20,000
		20,000	80,000	100,418
July 2003 :	Indexed rise: 100,418 × 0.185			18,577
				118,995
	Sale	(20,000)	(80,000)	(118,995)
		-	-	-

2   **T Ltd FA 1982 pool**

		No	31.3.82 MV £
Acquisition/disposal date:			
January 1980		3,000	3,600
February 1982		4,000	4,800
		7,000	8,400
July 2003:	Sale (25,000 – 20,000)	(5,000)	(6,000)
		2,000	2,400

Answer 24

V Ltd

> *Tutorial note:*
>
> This question tests a number of standard capital gains topics and touches on the income tax treatment of gifts to employees.
>
> Note that if a global rebasing election has been made, the original cost is completely ignored. The election has clearly produced a higher gain on the painting as its value had dropped by 31 March 1982. However, the company must have decided on making the election following an earlier disposal that it was generally beneficial even if there would be some 'losers'.
>
> The two sculptures were bought together and are being disposed to two related ('connected') individuals. The gains rules apply by treating the pair as a single asset. In fact, even if the two sculptures had been acquired separately, they might still be deemed to be a single asset or set. In this way the Revenue can prevent the £6,000 chattel exemption from applying. The problem can arise where any assets could be realistically seen as forming a set – for example, similar paintings or antique chairs or silverware.
>
> The report has to consider the income tax treatment of gifts to employees. Whether a 'higher paid' employee is taxed on the market value of the asset or a 'lower paid' employee is taxed on the second-hand value probably makes no practical difference. The 'market value' should be the net sale proceeds that a seller would expect to receive – ie the second-hand value.

(a)   **Computation of chargeable gains and allowable losses**

A   *Gain on March 1995 disposal crystallising*

	£
Proceeds (March 1995)	250,000
Less: Cost (May 1986)	(120,000)
	130,000
Less: Indexation allowance: 0.507 × 120,000	(60,840)
Chargeable gain	69,160
Less: Proceeds not reinvested (250,000 – 210,000)	(40,000)
Gain held over	29,160

When the plant which is used for the hold over relief is destroyed, the held over gain becomes chargeable.

The plant was presumably 'sold' for less than original cost so no chargeable gain results. Any loss is relieved through the capital allowance computation.

B

(i)   *Disposal of a painting*

	£
Proceeds	8,000
Less: Selling costs	(200)
	7,800
Less: 31 March 1982 MV	(1,000)
	6,800
Less: Indexation allowance: 1.277 × 1,000	(1,277)
	5,523
Gain cannot exceed $\frac{5}{3}$ (8,000 – 6,000) =	£3,333
The actual chargeable gain is therefore	£3,333

(ii)   *Disposal of sculptures*

	£
Proceeds	10,000
Less: Cost	(4,000)
	6,000
Less: Indexation allowance: 4,000 × 0.282	(1,128)
Chargeable gain	4,872

The two sculptures are treated as a single asset, not two assets sold for £5,000 each.

The marginal relief calculation is not beneficial.

$\frac{5}{3}$ (10,000 – 6,000) =	£6,667

(iii)   *Disposal of three tables*

Each asset costs less than £6,000 and is sold for less than £6,000 so there is no capital gains or allowable loss.

C   **Sale of 10,000 ordinary shares in X Ltd**

	MV after reorganisation £		Cost apportioned £
15,000 ordinary shares @ 1.40	21,000	$^{21}/_{36}$	17,500
8,000 preference shares @ 1.25	10,000	$^{10}/_{36}$	8,333
£5,000 debentures @ par	5,000	$^{5}/_{36}$	4,167
	36,000		30,000

Proceeds	60,000
Less: Cost $^{10}/_{15}$ × 17,500	(11,667)
	48,333
Less: Indexation allowance: 11,667 × 0.611	(7,129)
Chargeable gain	41,204

(b)   **REPORT**

To:	The Board of V Ltd
Re:	Tax implications of disposals to employees
Date:	10 May 2004
From:	Chartered Management Accountant

Gifts or sales at an undervalue of company assets to an employee can give rise to a benefit taxable on the employee.

If the employee is a director or an employee earning more than £8,500 pa, the gift of an asset is valued at the asset's market value at the date of the gift. Similarly, if the asset is sold to the employee at below market value, the discount is the taxable value of the benefit.

If the employee is 'lower paid' – ie paid less than £8,500 pa – the value of a gifted asset is its second-hand value. This is taken as the amount which the employee would receive if he tried to sell the asset immediately after receiving it.

The gift of the sculptures to the manager and his wife should be reported as a taxable benefit of £10,000. Even if the wife is 'lower paid' a value of, say, £5,000 would be taxable on her. If the gift was only made to her by virtue of her husband's employment, the gift of both sculptures should be taxable on him.

If the three tables sold to the employees only have a market value of £1,000 each, there would be no benefit taxable on them.

Please let me know if I can provide further information.

Signed: Chartered Management Accountant

Examination tip - *The computations in part (a) should be accompanied by some explanation. You have to judge how much to give. For example, you could explain that the held over gain (A) will become chargeable by the end of 10 years of ownership of the plant at the latest. This is not particularly relevant as the gain has already become chargeable.*

There are only four marks in part (b) so the examiner is only looking for the main points. Perhaps the employees had had private use of the tables and this would influence the benefit calculation. It is, however, an insignificant factor and is unlikely to earn any marks.

Answer 25

S Ltd

(a) **Computation of chargeable gains**

(i) April 2003 - Sale of warehouse

		£
Proceeds		120,000
Less:	Cost	(80,000)
		40,000
Less:	Indexation allowance: $80,000 \times 0.245$	(19,600)
		20,400

(ii) May 2003 - Sale of two offices out of six

Proceeds		40,000
Less:	Cost $50,000 \times \dfrac{40,000}{40,000 + 60,000}$	(20,000)
		20,000
Less:	Indexation allowance: $20,000 \times 0.425$	(8,500)
		11,500

(iii) June 2003 - Sale of 10,000 out of 14,000 shares in T Ltd

From FA 1985 Pool	Proceeds $8,000 \times £10$	80,000
	Less: Cost	(23,500)
		56,500
	Less: IA (35,710 - 23,500)	(12,210)
		44,290
From 1982 Pool	Proceeds $2,000 \times £10$	20,000
	Less 31.3.82 MV	(3,200)
		16,800
	Less: IA $3,200 \times 1.272$	(4,070)
		12,730

Total gains: (20,400 + 11,500 + 44,290 + 12,730)	88,920

Working

1   FA 1985 Pool of T Ltd shares

		No	*Cost* £	*Indexed cost* £
April 1985	Shares acquired May 1983	5,000	9,500	9,500
	Indexation to date			
	9,500 × 0.120			1,140
				10,640
June 1985	1 for 5 bonus	1,000	-	-
August 1998	Indexed rise			
	10,640 × 0.727			7,735
	Purchase	2,000	14,000	14,000
		8,000	23,500	32,375
June 2003	Indexed rise			
	32,375 × 0.103			3,335
				35,710
	Disposal	(8,000)	(23,500)	(35,710)
		-	-	-

2   1982 Pool of T Ltd shares

		No	*Cost* £	*31.3.82 MV* £
May 1979	Purchase	5,000	10,000	
June 1985	1 for 5 bonus	1,000	-	-
		6,000	10,000	9,600 @ 1.60
June 2002	Disposal	(2,000)	(3,333)	(3,200)
	c/f	4,000	6,667	6,400

(b)   **Report to the Directors of S Ltd**

Re: Deferring corporation tax on capital gains

This report sets out the opportunities for deferring corporation tax payable on the gains arising in the accounting period to 31 March 2004.

The relief for deferring gains is called rollover relief. It is only available on certain categories of assets and it can only be claimed if the asset on which the gain arises has been used in the company's own trade.

The qualifying categories of asset include land and buildings and fixed plant and machinery but does not include shares.

Therefore the only assets on which a gain can be rolled over are the two offices as they fall into a qualifying category (land and buildings) and have been used in the company's own trade.

Relief is not available for the gain on the warehouse as it was never used in the company's trade and neither do the T Ltd shares qualify as they are shares (not a qualifying asset).

For the entire gain of £11,500 on the offices to be rolled over, a qualifying asset or assets costing at least £40,000 - the proceeds of the offices - must be acquired by S Ltd in the period commencing in May 2002 (12 months prior to the disposal) and ending in May 2006 (three years after the disposal).

The replacement asset does not have to be of the same type (ie land and buildings). It would be possible to acquire instead fixed plant. The new asset does not even have to be used in the same trade as the offices but it must be used in a trade carried on by S Ltd - even a trade which did not commence until after the offices were sold.

If less than £40,000 is reinvested, the gain equal to the surplus proceeds remains chargeable. For example, if only £35,000 was reinvested, £5,000 would remain chargeable and only the balance of £6,500 (£11,500 - £5,000) would be rolled over.

Where the gain is rolled over it is deducted from the base cost of the replacement asset. In the above example the base cost of £35,000 would be reduced to £28,500 (£35,000 - £6,500), thereby ensuring that the gain becomes chargeable when the replacement asset is sold. Note, however, that any indexation allowance is calculated on the reduced base cost and this could make a rollover claim unattractive.

The gain on the replacement asset could itself be rolled over again so, for an expanding company, rollover relief could defer gains indefinitely.

If the replacement asset is a depreciating asset, ie one with an expected life at purchase of less than 60 years, the gain is not 'rolled over' but is merely put into suspense or 'held over'.

Typical depreciating assets are leasehold interests of less than 60 years and fixed plant and machinery.

The holdover gain becomes chargeable ('crystallises') on the earliest of the following three events:

♦ When the replacement assets ceases to be used in the company's trade.
♦ When the replacement asset is sold.
♦ When ten years have elapsed from the acquisition of the replacement asset.

It is possible to achieve a 'permanent' roll over where the gain has been 'held over' if a non-depreciating replacement asset is acquired before the gain crystallises.

To summarise, only the gain on the offices can be deferred and for full deferral at least £40,000 must be reinvested in a qualifying assets or assets.

Please let me know if I can be of further assistance.

Value added tax

Answer 26

Partial exemption

Tutorial note:

This is a standard question on partial exemption from VAT. The general principle is that only input tax on supplies used to make taxable supplies is recoverable. Where it is not possible to allocate input tax to either taxable or exempt supplies (eg in the case of general overhead expenses) there has to be a mechanism for apportioning. As VAT is very much a practical tax needing to be sorted out as it happens the solution is understandably pragmatic and not necessarily precise. Furthermore, there is a de minimis limit and an annual adjustment to review the approach taken quarter by quarter.

Whether partial exemption is tested by applying it to figures or, as here, by explaining it in a report, it is an easy topic to gain marks on.

REPORT

To:	The Board
Re:	Extending turnover to exempt supplies
Date:	10 May 2004
From:	Chartered Management Accountant

At present the company has only supplied goods which are standard-rated for VAT purposes and has therefore been able to recover any input tax that it has suffered. There have been minor exceptions to this rule such as input tax on buying cars and on most forms of entertainment but these disallowances are general and not related to the type of supplies made.

When part of the supplies made by the company are exempt from VAT, input tax recovery will be allowed as follows.

(i)   Input tax will be fully recoverable if it is incurred wholly for making taxable supplies.

(ii)   Input tax will not be recoverable (subject to the de minimis limits mentioned below) if it is incurred wholly for making exempt supplies.

(iii)   Where input tax is incurred on purchases which cannot be wholly attributable to either type of supply, it is apportioned usually on the basis of the ratio of taxable turnover to exempt turnover. Using the 'standard' method about 25% of non-attributable input tax would be disallowed.

Note that Customs may be prepared to agree a more appropriate means of apportioning 'mixed' input tax. It is up to the company to devise a suitable alternative method. It could be based, for example, on the proportion of employees involved or factory space allocated if appropriate.

The disallowance is ignored if the total of exempt-related input tax is less than £625 per month on average and does not exceed 50% of total input tax – the de minimis limits.

The recovery portion is calculated independently for each VAT quarter but with an annual adjustment following every fourth quarter.

Please let me know if I can provide further information.

Signed: Chartered Management Accountant

Examination tip *- It is possible to obtain full marks without mentioning 'fringe' items such as the annual adjustment and the possibility of non-standard apportioning of non-attributable input tax. As usual you should decide the key issues and ensure that these are given prominence in your answer. Here the question is clearly saying 'What is the impact on VAT recovery if we make some exempt supplies?'. If you answer that coherently and in the required 'report' format, you will probably earn most of the available marks.*

Answer 27

Export sales

> **Tutorial note:**
>
> VAT is not a popular topic and the treatment of exports even less so. Nevertheless, the rules are straightforward and allow zero rating for exports of goods other than to non-registered EU customers. The EU is supposed to be a 'Single Market'. However, until VAT rates and rules are harmonised across all the member states, sales between EU states have to be covered by special rules. Otherwise there would be a distortion of trade with customers in one state shopping around the Community to buy where the VAT rates were lowest for the goods in question.

REPORT

To: The Board

Re: The VAT treatment of export sales

Date: 10 May 2004

From: Chartered Management Accountant

I understand that the company intends to make export sales partly to customers in other EU member states and partly to customers in North America. The purpose of this report is to set out briefly the VAT implications of making export sales distinguishing between those made to the EU and those made to non-EU countries such as North America.

(i)   *Exports to EU member states*

Two alternative situations can apply depending on whether or not the customer in the other EU member state is VAT registered in that state.

Export sales to EU VAT registered customers are zero-rated and the customer will account for the appropriate rate of home country VAT as if he had sold the goods to himself. A similar treatment applies when we acquire goods ('make acquisitions') from other EU member states. In order to zero rate such outputs we must show the customer's EU VAT number on our invoice to him and retain evidence that the goods have actually left the UK.

If the customer is not VAT registered we must treat it as though the sale had been made to a UK customer. However, if the sales that are made in this way to an individual EU state exceed a certain threshold, we would be required to register for VAT in that state and account for VAT under the rules applying in that state. We could avoid the need to register if we appointed an agent in that state to account for VAT on our behalf.

Where sales levels to EU customers exceed certain thresholds, we become liable to submit regular statements to Customs showing the amounts of sales.

(ii)   *Exports to North America*

If we hold evidence that the goods in question have been exported from the UK, the sales must be zero-rated.

If I can provide further information please let me know.

Signed: Chartered Management Accountant

Examination tip -*There are basically three situations to cover – sales to non EU countries, sales to EU VAT registered customers and sales to EU non-registered customers – and this should give most of the marks.*

Answer 28

Tax points and entertainment

Tutorial note:

This is a fairly straightforward question on two of the main VAT topics – tax points and irrecoverable input tax. The question does not indicate any particular types of supply or invoicing practices so you have to explain tax points to cover most possible situations. There has been a long running debate on the recovery of VAT on staff entertaining. It is safest to explain Customs' position even though this is not universally accepted.

INSTRUCTION SHEET FOR STAFF INVOLVED WITH VAT RECORDS

Re:	(1)	Identifying tax points
	(2)	Recovering VAT on entertaining

Following a recent VAT control visit by Customs Officers, penalties have been imposed on the company for errors made in recording VAT and in completing VAT returns. In particular, staff now need to be aware of the correct recognition of tax points and the allowed recovery of input tax on entertaining expenditure.

(1)   **Tax points**

The tax point of a supply is important because it fixes the date on which the event enters the VAT system. Its main significance is in determining which VAT return quarter the supply falls into. The legislation defines a 'basic tax point' but this may be modified to an 'actual tax point' in certain circumstances.

The basic tax point

For a supply of goods the basic tax point is the date the goods are removed for delivery to a customer or made available to the customer.

For a supply of services the basic tax point is the date the services are performed. If they are performed over a period it is the date the service is completed. Where services are continually supplied without ever being completed, the tax point is the invoice date or, if earlier, the date of payment.

The actual tax point

If payment is made before the basic tax point or if a VAT invoice is made before the basic tax point, the earlier of payment date or invoice date becomes the actual tax point.

Note that a refundable deposit does not constitute payment and cannot therefore trigger a tax point. Also a proforma invoice which purports not to be a tax invoice does not create a tax point.

In the absence of an earlier payment, an invoice issued within 14 days following the basic tax point creates an actual tax point in place of the basic tax point. Customs could agree a later date if appropriate. This could apply if invoicing was only done monthly in arrears. An invoice is only 'issued' when it is delivered to the customer.

If goods are supplied on a sale or return basis the tax point is the earlier of the date the customer accepts the sale and 12 months after they are despatched.

(2)   **Entertaining**

At present for corporation tax purposes we disallow all entertaining other than staff entertaining. Any input VAT charged on such entertaining is similarly disallowed for VAT purposes and must not be posted to the recoverable input VAT account.

The VAT rules on staff entertaining are more stringent than the corporation tax rules. Basically the input tax is only allowable for the costs incurred on the staff. Where spouses or partners are also entertained – eg the staff Christmas dance – Customs expect input tax to be apportioned. The non-staff portion is disallowed for VAT recovery. Customs may accept that if a payment is made for spouse tickets all the input VAT is recoverable. The VAT element in the ticket price ($^{40}/_{47}$ ths) has to be accounted for as output tax. The ticket price need not reflect the full cost of the entertainment.

Examination tip - *Most of the marks are earned by explaining the main rules for 'tax point' and for recovering VAT on staff entertaining. You are probably not expected to know the device of charging non-staff for entertainment. Despite the circumstances leading to the information sheet issue, there is no requirement to explain the penalties being imposed and there would be no marks for covering them.*

Answer 29

TC Ltd and D Ltd

(a)   **Brief notes on three specific means of remunerating staff**

(i)   *Cars and fuel for private use*

Employee: Assessable benefit on percentage of list price.

Carbon dioxide emission rating 155 gms/km or less	15%
For every extra 5 gms/km	+ 1%
For diesel fuel	+ 3%
Overall maximum	35%

Benefit time apportioned if only available for part of year or if off the road for over 30 consecutive days.

Additional charge for private use fuel calculated as £14,400 multiplied by the percentage calculated for the car benefit.

No NIC charge on employee.

Employer: Capital allowances on car – 25% WDA maximum £3,000.

Full expense relief for all running costs.

Class IA NIC charge at 12.8% on the value of the assessable benefit – allowed as a trading expense.

VAT not recoverable on car cost – claim capital allowances on VAT inclusive cost.

VAT recoverable on fuel but a scale VAT output charge arises to cover private element.

(ii)   *Loans at low interest rate or interest free*

Employee: Benefit charge on difference between interest that would have been charged at official rate (currently 5%) and interest actually paid.

For fluctuating loans, average loan between start and end of year is used but inspector or employee could insist on basing calculation on day to day balance. If loan balance never exceeds £5,000 there is no benefit charge.

No NIC charge on employee.

Employer: No expense relief for nominal interest foregone.

Class 1A NIC charge at 12.8% on income tax value of benefit.

(iii)   Private use of assets

Employee: Assessable annual benefit of 20% of asset's value when first used to provide benefit.

Deduction for any business use portion and employee's contribution to employee.

Exemption for first £500 of benefit of computer equipment, provided available not just to directors.

No NIC charge on employee.

Employer: Capital allowances normally allowed on asset.

Class 1A NIC charge at 12.8% on income tax value of benefit.

Private use portion of asset requires a VAT output tax charge. If asset is originally wholly for private use, input VAT should not be reclaimed.

Tutorial note:

There are other forms of benefit some of which you could write a lot on (eg use of accommodation) and others which could be covered adequately in a couple of lines (eg medical insurance). It is best in this situation to choose mainstream popular items such as cars which give scope for sufficient detail rather than slightly fringe benefits on which you can say very little, such as late night taxis home.

(b)   **MEMORANDUM**

To: The Managing Director

Re: VAT implications of making exempt supplies

Date: 21 November 2004

From: Chief Accountant

This memorandum outlines the VAT implications of making VAT exempt supplies.

In order to recover input VAT on purchases and expenses it must be incurred in making taxable supplies – either at the zero rate or standard rate.

If the company makes exempt supplies it can recover the input tax incurred wholly in making taxable supplies.

Input tax incurred wholly in making the exempt supplies is irrecoverable.

Input tax that cannot be allocated wholly to either category of supply – for example, most types of general overhead – has to be prorated. This is normally done in proportion to the value of turnover – ie allow the portion equal to taxable supplies over total turnover.

If the total of disallowed input tax as calculated above is both less than £625 a month on average and 50% of total input tax, it is allowed on a de minimis basis.

The position is calculated at the end of each quarter with an annual adjustment at the end of each year.

Chief Accountant

Groups of companies

Answer 30

A Ltd and B Ltd

> **Tutorial note:**
>
> Parts (a) and (b) are quite separate from each other. In part (a) the key working is group relief. Only overlapping period profits and losses can be matched and the lower amount determines the maximum loss that can be surrendered. It is a straightforward concept but important to get it right.
>
> Part (a) could have been more complicated if the question had not required a maximum group relief claim. For example, reducing the group relief claim results in more PCTCT taxed at the small company rate but there is a corresponding increase in the amount of surplus ACT that becomes usable. If B Ltd was likely to have significant profits in the following AP it might have been preferable to reduce a group relief surrender and carry the bulk of the loss forward. There are tactical reasons for relieving surplus ACT in priority to group losses.
>
> Part (b) involved a straightforward group gains tax planning exercise recognising that 'pre-entry' losses were the problem.

(a) **Corporation tax payable by A Ltd after group relief**

Nine months accounting period to 30 September 2003.

	£
Schedule D Case I (36,000 + 18,000 – 8,000)	46,000
Schedule A	20,000
Schedule D Case III (8,000 + 15,000)	23,000
	89,000
Less: Charges on income Gift Aid	(5,000)
	84,000
Less: Group relief (Working 1)	(56,000)
PCTCT	28,000
Add FII	8,000
'Profits' for small company/starting rate purposes	36,000
GCT @ 19% (Working 2)	5,320
Less: ACT b/f (Working 3)	(4,400)
	920
Less: Income tax recoverable (Working 4)	(1,320)
Tax repayable to A Ltd	£(400)

Examination tip - It is good exam technique to relegate any detailed workings to a working note cross-referenced to the appropriate point in the main answer.

(b) **MEMORANDUM**

To:	The directors of A Ltd
Re:	Tax advice on proposed asset disposals
Date:	10 May 2004
From:	Chartered Management Accountant

It is currently intended for A Ltd to dispose of a capital asset at a gain and for B Ltd to dispose of an asset at a loss – both disposals to occur in the next accounting period.

It is possible for A Ltd and B Ltd to elect that the disposal of an asset by one of them is deemed made by the other. The election is to be made within two years of the end of the accounting period in which the disposal was made. For example, the loss of B Ltd could, by election, be deemed made by A Ltd. The loss would then be available to offset against A Ltd's gains.

However, the following matters should be considered.

(i)   If the asset giving rise to B Ltd's loss was owned by B Ltd before it joined the group (ie before 1 April 2003) only part of the loss can be used. The 'pre-entry' part of the loss is not available to relief gains on assets held, or originally held, by other group companies. The pre-entry portion is usually computed by time apportioning the loss although it is possible to elect for the pre-entry loss to be calculated using the market value of the asset as at 1 April 2003.

(ii)   A Ltd and B Ltd do not have the same year ends so it is important that the loss is not realised after the end of the AP in which A Ltd makes the gain. Losses can be carried forward but not back.

(iii)   If the post entry loss does not exceed the gain resulting in unrelieved gain, it would be preferable to match the disposals in the company with the lower marginal tax rate.

Signed: Chartered Management Accountant

Examination tip - For part (a) there is little scope for non-mark earning effort. Marks are given for satisfactorily completing the main computation and producing workings to support figures where necessary. Workings in note form (see 1 and 2) are sufficient if the marker can see your conclusion and how you arrive there.

For part (b) there are only six marks available so you have to decide if there is a topic uppermost in the examiner's mind. The main point is 'pre-entry' losses. You might still earn full marks even without working in the year end differences between A Ltd and B Ltd or mentioning where net gains should be allowed to fall.

Workings

1   **Group relief**

		£
A Ltd Profits	1.1.2003 – 30.9.2003	84,000
B Ltd Losses	1.4.2003 – 31.3.2004	(130,000)
Overlapping AP (since acquisition 1.4.2003):		
A Ltd Profits	1.4.2003 – 30.9.2003 : $^6/_9$	56,000
B Ltd Losses	1.4.2003 – 30.9.2003 : $^6/_{12}$	(65,000)

Group relief limited to £56,000 of loss.

2   **CT rates**

One associated company (counted even though owned for just part of AP)

Starting rate upper limit	$^{50,000}/_2 \times {}^9/_{12}$:	18,750
Small company rate lower threshold	$^{300,000}/_2 \times {}^9/_{12}$:	112,500
Therefore all of A Ltd's PCTCT are taxable at the small company rate:		19%

3   **ACT set-off**

	£	£
Maximum set-off (ignoring shadow ACT)		
PCTCT @ 20% 28,000 × 20%		5,600
Dividend paid	12,000	
Dividend received 8,000 × 90%	(7,200)	
	4,800	
Shadow ACT @ 20%	1,200	(1,200)
Set-off limited to		4,400
Surplus ACT b/f		22,000
Set-off in period to 30.9.2003		(4,400)
Surplus ACT c/f		17,600

4   **Income tax recoverable**

		£
Income tax suffered on:		
Patent royalties	$12,000 \times 22\%$	2,640
Income tax deducted on:		
Patent royalties	$6,000 \times 22\%$	(1,320)
Income tax still recoverable		1,320

Answer 31

S Ltd and T Ltd

Tutorial note:

The basic concept of taxing capital gains is straightforward even with indexation allowance to cater for. However, there are a number of special situations where the simple idea of 'proceeds – cost – IA' is not enough.

In this question you have to deal with:

♦   *Sale of rights nil paid* – think of it as a part disposal of value. No shares are sold but the value of the shares in issue will be diluted by issuing new rights shares at below current market value. Selling the right to buy shares at a reduced cost is compensation to this loss of value. It requires an $^A/_{A+B}$ part disposal approach.

♦   *Held over gain crystallising.* A reinvestment in 'depreciating' assets allows gains on business assets to be deferred or held over (not rolled over in the sense of setting off against the new base cost) for up to 10 years.

♦   *Gains crystallising on leaving a group.* Whenever a company leaves a capital gains group, the gains on intra-group transfers acquired in the previous six years will crystallise in the company leaving.

(a)   **Chargeable gains and allowable losses of S Ltd for the year to 31 March 2004**

(i)   *Sale of rights nil paid – November 2003*

	£
Proceeds	18,000
Less: Cost $120,000 \times \dfrac{18,000}{18,000 + (20,000 \times £9)}$	(10,909)
	7,091
Less: Indexation allowance $10,909 \times 0.371$	(4,047)
Chargeable gain	3,044

Note: This cannot be treated as a 'small' disposal as the proceeds of £18,000 exceed both £3,000 and 5% of the value of the holding, ie

$5\% (18,000 + (20,000 \times £9)) = £9,900$

(ii)   *Crystallising of held over gain – 1 March 2004*

			Cost £	31.3.82 MV £
Disposal in March 1994:				
	Proceeds		175,000	175,000
	Less:	Cost/31.3.82 MV	(80,000)	(90,000)
			95,000	85,000
	Less:	Indexation allowance		
		90,000 × 0.794	(71,460)	(71,460)
			23,540	13,540
	Lower gain was chargeable			13,540

As the reinvestment in plant took place on 1 March 1994, the held over gain will crystallise 10 years later on 1 March 2004.

(iii)   *Gain on intra company disposal crystallising – 31 October 2003*

S Ltd is leaving the capital gains group (T Ltd's holding reduced below 75%) within six years of receiving an asset from another group company on a no gain/no loss basis. This triggers the gain which would otherwise have been chargeable on the transfer of the factory from T Ltd to S Ltd. The gain is chargeable on S Ltd in the accounting period in which it leaves the group – ie year to 31 March 2004.

Disposal in May 1999:

		£
'Proceeds'		105,000
Less:	Cost	(80,000)
		25,000
Less:	Indexation allowance 80,000 × 0.174	(13,920)
Gain now becoming chargeable		11,080

(iv)   *Summary*

		£
(i)	Sale of rights nil paid	3,044
(ii)	Held over gain crystallising	13,540
(iii)	Gain crystallising on leaving group	11,080
		27,664

Examination tip - *It is good exam technique to summarise gains and losses even where the question does not specifically mention this as a requirement.*

(b)   **Corporation tax due on S Ltd's gains**

S Ltd has one associated company for the year to 31 March 2003 so the lower limit of the small company marginal relief band is £150,000 (£300,000 ÷ 2).

Using marginal rates, the gains of £27,664 will attract tax as follows:

	£		£
150,000 – 140,000	10,000 × 19%	=	1,900
	17,664 × 32.75%	=	5,785
	27,664		
Corporation tax due to gains			7,685

Examination tip - *It is likely that if the marker can spot '£27,664' and £7,685' he will award full marks. However, most candidates under exam conditions may make arithmetical errors so the computations should be laid out to show you understand the principles. The brief commentary accompanying the above computations would help the marker to allocate marks for understanding principles. You should not be too brief where 20 marks are on offer.*

Answer 32

M Ltd and B Ltd

Tutorial note:

The following suggested answers to parts (a) and (b) cover the required details. Part (a) starts by explaining the following computational steps. In the exam you should similarly jot down your analysis of the group relationships etc as part of your answer. This helps you to focus on how the computations of MCT have to be tackled.

(a) **B Ltd and M Ltd – Computation of mainstream corporation tax payable**

M Ltd is a consortium owned company because at least 75% of its share capital is owned by companies which hold at least 5% but no more than 75% each.

A Ltd, B Ltd and C Ltd are the consortium members each owning at least 5% of the share capital. D Ltd is not a consortium member – at least for tax purposes – as it owns less than 5% of the share capital.

Loss making consortium members can surrender their loss to the consortium company up to the portion of the consortium company's profits corresponding to the consortium members' percentage ownership.

B Ltd and M Ltd are associated companies so the lower and upper small company marginal relief limits become £150,000 and £750,000.

				B Ltd £	M Ltd £
PCTCT before consortium relief				160,000	220,000
Less: Consortium relief					
A Ltd to M Ltd					
Lower of	(1)		60,000		
	(2)	15% × 220,000	33,000		(33,000)
C Ltd to M Ltd					
Lower of	(1)		20,000		
	(2)	5% × 220,000	11,000		(11,000)
				160,000	176,000
Corporation tax thereon:					
PCTCT @ 30%				48,000	52,800
Less: $^{11}/_{400}$ (750,000 – 160,000)				(16,225)	
$^{11}/_{400}$ (750,000 – 176,000)					(15,785)
MCT payable 1.1.05				31,775	37,015

(b)   **REPORT**

To: The Directors of K Ltd

Re: Responsibilities under self assessment

Date: 10 May 2004

From: Chartered Management Accountant

The company has recently changed its accounting reference date from 30 September to 31 December and has prepared one set of accounts covering the period of 1 October 2002 to 31 December 2003.

The period of account is split for tax purposes into the 12 month period to 30 September 2003 and the three month period to 31 December 2003.

Corporation tax is payable for each period nine months after the period end – ie 1 July 2004 and 1 October 2004 respectively – whether or not the company receives any notice to submit a tax return.

The effect on the filing requirements of changing the accounting date is slightly more complicated. Shortly after 30 September 2003, the Revenue, not being aware of the change, will issue a notice to the company to submit a tax return for the year just ended. Normally the company then has 12 months (ie by 30 September 2004) in which to file its return. However, by extending the period of account to 31 December 2003, the submission date for the period to 30 September 2003 is put back to 31 December 2004.

The filing date for the three months to 31 December 2003 depends on what the Revenue does:

(i)   If the Revenue issues the next tax return notice in October 2004 – ie without realising the accounting date has been changed – it will specify the period of 12 months to 30 September 2004. This is deemed to be addressed to the three months to 31 December 2003 as it falls wholly within the specified period. The return must be filed by the later of three months from the issue date and the normal filing date (ie 31 December 2004 being 12 months after the period end). Therefore if the return is issued on, say, 15 October 2004 the return filing date becomes 15 January 2005.

(ii)   If the Revenue gets wind of the changed date – perhaps from the company or from information passed to them by the Registrar of Companies – and issues the return before 30 September 2004, the normal filing date of 31 December 2004 will apply. This is because it falls after the date three months after the issue of the return.

Please let me know if I can provide further information.

Signed: Chartered Management Accountant

Examination tip *- Part (a) is primarily a computational question but you should provide some explanation of the computational steps to earn full marks. The report needed in part (b) has to explain the principles for recognising the filing dates. You may have earned full marks without covering the position of the return being issued after 30 September 2004 provided you put up a convincing reason for the Revenue issuing a tax return before 30 September 2004.*

Answer 33

Group disposals

Tutorial note:

This is a difficult question to answer satisfactorily because it is fairly open ended. The best approach is to note down the various topics which you think are relevant. This is bound to include the 'group gains' topics such as relief for intra-company transfers and the charge on subsidiaries leaving a group within six years of such a transfer.

You then have to organise all the points you intend to make under a set of section headings. It seems sensible to start by explaining how gains and losses are calculated. However, there is no single satisfactory way of choosing section headings.

REPORT

To: The Board

Re: The capital gains implications of disposing of assets and subsidiaries

Date: 10 May 2004

From: Chartered Management Accountant

The group is about to undergo a reorganisation of its business activities and intends to dispose of certain assets held by different group companies and some of the subsidiary companies themselves. This gives rise to potential exposure to tax on capital gains and other tax implications.

The purpose of this report is therefore to outline the likely tax effects of the reorganisation.

General impact of asset disposals

The disposal of a chargeable asset such as freehold premises to a purchaser outside the group could result in a chargeable gain or allowable loss.

The result is calculated by deducting the cost of the asset from the sale proceeds and reducing the gain by an allowance for inflation. This allowance is found by multiplying the cost of the asset by the increase in the retail prices index.

If the asset had been acquired before 1 April 1982 the calculation is repeated using the value of the asset on 31 March 1982 in place of cost. For both the 'cost' and the '1982 value' calculation the indexation allowance is based on the higher of cost and the 1982 value.

If the asset had been acquired from another company in the group, it would have been automatically transferred at such a price that gave rise to neither a gain nor a loss – ie cost plus indexation allowance to date. In this case, when the asset is sold outside the group the gain is calculated as if the original group cost and acquisition dated applied. The vendor company effectively 'stands in the shoes' of the original purchasing company.

An indexation allowance cannot turn a gain into a loss nor increase a loss.

Corporation tax on gains

The gains on disposals made during an accounting period are included as part of the chargeable profits of that accounting period.

The rate of tax depends on the total of profits and is generally either 19% or 30% or an intermediate rate. Although the average rate of CT will not exceed 30%, the marginal rate could be 32.75% if the gains fall in the small company marginal relief band.

Relief for allowable losses

If the disposal of an asset results in an allowable loss this will be set-off automatically against any gains realised by the same company in the same accounting period.

Where losses exceed gains the excess loss is carried forward to relieve future gains of the same company as soon as they arise.

Where the asset giving rise to the loss was already owned by the subsidiary when it joined the group, the 'pre-entry' part of the loss cannot be used except against gains on assets which the subsidiary already owned when it joined. It is not possible to relieve pre-entry losses against gains on assets acquired intra-group.

The pre-entry loss is normally found by time apportioning it over the period of ownership but it is possible to elect to calculate it using the asset's market value when the subsidiary joined the group.

There are also restrictions to prevent relief of a subsidiary's gains arising before it joined the group by routing loss making disposals through it.

Minimising group gains

It used to be normal practice to arrange for gains and losses (non pre-entry) to be realised in the same company so that they can be matched. For example, assets would be transferred intra-group on a no loss – no gain basis before sale to a third party.

Actual transfers are not, in fact, necessary. An election can be made within two years of the end of the accounting period of a disposal to deem that the disposal (or part of it) was made by another group company. In this way the group can decide retrospectively where losses and gains are best matched to relieve losses to the maximum extent and to ensure any gains remaining attract the lowest marginal rate in the group. This election is more versatile than would be the case if it were simply possible to 'group relieve' capital losses.

Gains on business assets (not shares) can be rolled over against replacement business assets on a group wide basis. In other words the gains of one company can be rolled over against reinvestment by another group company.

Disposals of subsidiaries

When a subsidiary is sold the normal capital gains share rules apply. A disposal is being made of the shares held in an FA 1985 share pool. If the holding was acquired by a single acquisition, the gain or loss calculation follows the rules described above. Provided the subsidiary is a trading company any gain (or loss) is exempt. This applies to the disposal out of a 'substantial' holding ie where 10% or more of the shares are held. It is also necessary for the disposing company to be a trading company or a member of a trading group.

The sale of a subsidiary normally has no capital gains effect on the assets held by the subsidiary. However, if an asset had been acquired intra-group within the previous six years, the gain that would otherwise have arisen on the intra-group transfer crystallises. It becomes chargeable on the subsidiary company as at the start of the accounting period in which it leaves the group.

The crystallised gain could, by election, be transferred to another 'old' group company and/or rolled over by a company in the old group (including the subsidiary leaving) acquiring a replacement asset.

Although the subsidiary is liable for any tax that remains chargeable on the crystallising gain – after all it holds the asset – if it remains unpaid six months after it was payable, the Revenue can collect the tax from the company which originally transferred the asset.

Other tax implications

The transfer of an asset could be a taxable supply for VAT purposes. If the transfer is made as part of the transfer of a business as a going concern the supply is outside the scope of VAT. It is important to charge

VAT if it is a taxable supply or Customs would assess output VAT of $\frac{7}{47}$ of the sale price.

If a trade ceases any trading losses can be carried back for up to three years. Redundancy payments can be made to employees in excess of the statutory amount but, as the trade does not continue, there is strictly no trading purpose for the excess. The tax rules, however, allow relief for up to three times the statutory amount in addition to the statutory redundancy amount.

Stamp duty land tax of up to 4% of market value can be payable on a transaction which results in the disposal of land. It is an expensive tax to overlook.

Please let me know if I can provide further details on any of the above points.

Signed: Chartered Management Accountant

Examination tip - *It is important to make a reasonable number of points without necessarily going into every detail. Marks are easy to earn if you use a number of headed sections. The marker can then find his way around your answer and you can allocate your time productively over the different parts of your answer.*

Answer 34

Acquiring shares or assets

> *Tutorial note:*
>
> With this type of question it is important to identify a suitable framework for your answer. It splits clearly into four parts – the tax implications for the purchaser and the target company for each of the two situations. Before answering each part it is advisable to jot down notes of the points to make. You are unlikely to cover all the possible topics in such an open ended question but you will easily achieve a pass mark if you cover the most important areas and mention other relevant points.
>
> The tax implications of acquiring a business either by acquiring the company or by acquiring the assets of the company are discussed below.

1   **Acquiring a majority holding of voting shares in the target company**

Effect on purchaser

There is no immediate tax relief for the purchase of shares. Stamp Duty of 0.5% is payable on the market value of the shares and forms part of the base cost for a subsequent disposal.

The acquiring company increases the number of its associates by one and thereby potentially increases the corporation tax payable on its own profits as the band limits are further reduced.

The acquiring company will take on the target company not just its assets. The value acquired may be reduced by liabilities unforeseen at the date of acquisition. Warranties and indemnities should therefore be obtained from the vendors so that legal redress is available where unexpected problems arise after the purchase.

The vendor may be prepared to accept a discounted price if any gain made by the vendor on the disposal is exempt under the rules for substantial shareholdings.

Effect on target company

The change of ownership of the company does not generally impact on the company. For example, the company continues to own its own assets and will continue to claim capital allowances. However, the change of ownership can have the following results.

♦   Gains will crystallise on assets acquired intra-group in the past six years.

♦   Relief for trading losses being carried forward is denied if there is also a major change in the nature or conduct of the trade within a three year period including the date ownership changed.

♦   There are similar restrictions for the carry forward of surplus ACT.

♦   Both losses and ACT are similarly cancelled if the target company's trade becomes negligible and there is a change of ownership before the trade revives.

For the accounting period of sale, the target company is associated with both the old group and the new group for the purpose of reducing the lower and upper small company band limits.

2   **Purchasing the assets and trade of the target company**

Effect for the purchaser

The purchaser acquires assets which may attract relief as capital allowances. It is also possible to use the chargeable assets acquired, such as freehold property, to roll over other gains made by the purchaser.

Stamp Duty land tax is payable at up to 4% on the value of any land transferred.

The purchaser acquires assets 'clean', ie without necessarily taking over the liabilities of the target company. The trade cannot be taken over without assuming the statutory employment responsibilities to the workforce but such problems as a potential PAYE audit remain with the target company for the period prior to the transfer.

The purchaser cannot take over unrelieved tax amounts such as capital losses, trading losses, Schedule D Case III deficits and Schedule A losses.

However, the purchaser does not increase the number of its associate companies as it is not acquiring a further subsidiary.

Effect on the target company

The target company is disposing of its assets and ceasing to trade. The effect will be:

♦   Any trading losses of the final 12 months can be carried back up to three years.

♦   The disposal of plant and industrial buildings will result in balancing allowances/ charges.

♦   The disposal of chargeable assets will result in capital gains/ allowable losses.

♦   There may be scope for tax saving if the global price agreed for the assets and trade can be reallocated.

Examination tip - *It is likely that the marks are allocated evenly between the two parts of the question and there are separate marks for discussing the vendor's and the purchaser's position. As the question asks for the taxation implications, it is advisable to cover as many relevant areas as possible rather than going into depth on just a few topics.*

Answer 35

H Ltd Group

> *Tutorial note:*
>
> The first two stages of the question lay the ground work for the final stage and are just an exercise in analysing group relationships for their tax implications.
>
> Part (c) requires some thought and a lot of number crunching. Essentially there are three companies with losses, J Ltd, M Ltd and X Ltd. Deal first with those losses that are most heavily restricted. For example, M Ltd's loss can only go to L Ltd and X Ltd's loss is only usable by G Ltd. Note that G Ltd is not part of H Ltd's 75% group so it stands alone. Finally deal with the loss which is the least restricted remembering that group relief claims can be made for specific amounts of loss but a S393A claim is not capable of being limited to a specific amount. The trick is to make the S393A claim last when the loss has been whittled down by group relief to the required amount. The loss claims for J Ltd's loss are made to relieve the highest marginal rates in priority. If you reach a level where two potential claimants have the same marginal tax rate, and there is no special instruction in the question, you are generally free to choose – but say what you have done.

(a) **Diagram of group structure**

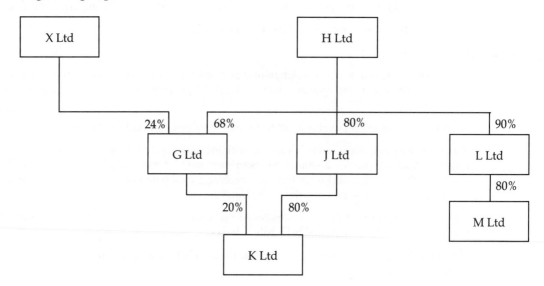

(b) **Group/consortium relationships**

(i) All of the companies except X Ltd are associated for the purposes of small company rate and small company marginal relief.

G, H, J, K, L, M = 6 associates

	Small company rate		*Starting rate*	
Lower limit	$300{,}000 \times \frac{1}{6}$ =	£50,000	$10{,}000 \times \frac{1}{6}$ =	£1,667
Upper limit	$1{,}500{,}000 \times \frac{1}{6}$ =	£250,000	$50{,}000 \times \frac{1}{6}$ =	£8,333

(ii) *Consortia*

G Ltd is a consortium company as over 75% of its share capital is held by companies each holding at least 5% but less than 75%. The consortium members are X Ltd and H Ltd.

(iii) *Groups*

A 75% group for group relief purposes exists between:

♦ L Ltd and M Ltd

♦ H Ltd, L Ltd, J Ltd and K Ltd

K Ltd is included because at least 75% is held indirectly by H Ltd:

via J Ltd	:	80% × 80%	=	64.0%
via G Ltd	:	68% × 20%	=	13.6%
				77.6%

A 75% capital gains group exists between:

♦ H Ltd, J Ltd, L Ltd, K Ltd and M Ltd

(c) **Mainstream corporation tax payable assuming reliefs taken tax efficiently**

	H £	G £	J £	L £	K £	M £
Schedule D Case I	48,000	60,000	-	30,000	90,000	-
Schedule D Case III	4,000	5,000	6,000	-	10,000	1,000
	52,000	65,000	6,000	30,000	100,000	1,000
Less: S393A(1)(a) relief			(1,333)			
	52,000	65,000	4,667	30,000	100,000	1,000
Less: Gift Aid	(2,000)	(4,000)	(3,000)			(1,000)
	50,000	61,000	1,667	30,000	100,000	-
Group relief M Ltd to L Ltd				(30,000)		
Consortium relief X Ltd to G Ltd		(14,640)				
Group relief J Ltd to K Ltd					(62,667)	
PCTCT	50,000	46,360	1,667	-	37,333	-
Corporation tax at 19%/Nil%	9,500	8,808	-		7,093	

Loss memorandum

	J £	M £	X £
Loss of the year to 31 March 2004	64,000	42,000	24,000
Group relief M Ltd to L Ltd		(30,000)	
Consortium relief X Ltd to G Ltd limited to 24% of 61,000			(14,640)
Group relief J Ltd to K Ltd	(62,667)		
S393A(1)(a) relief in J Ltd	(1,333)		
Losses remaining	-	14,000	9,360

The losses of M Ltd can only be group relieved to L Ltd. This is limited by the available profits in L Ltd.

The loss of X Ltd can only be consortium relieved to G Ltd and is limited by the profits of G Ltd proportionate to X Ltd's holding.

However, the loss of J Ltd is not sufficient for all the possible reliefs so it is rationed by the marginal rate of tax savings. First it should reduce K Ltd's profits to £50,000 saving tax at 32.75%. Next it saves tax at 23.75% in J Ltd by reducing its profits to £1,667. This requires a S393A(1)(a) claim which cannot be restricted. Therefore the group relief claims must be made first to leave the £1,333 necessary in J Ltd. This extra loss can either be group relieved to H Ltd at 19% or further relieved in K Ltd at 19%. It is simpler to continue the group relief claim in K Ltd.

In all cases of group relief and consortium relief it is assumed that a claimant company pays for the relief in fairness to minority interests in the surrendering company.

Examination tip - Most of the content needed for earning marks is self-explanatory. The diagram in part (a) could include the shareholdings of individuals but they are not relevant to the tax breaks available. In part (b) there is a mark for mentioning the capital gains group although this point does not reappear in part (c), unlike group relief and consortium relief. In part (c) you are expected to show a 'loss memorandum' working. The explanation at the foot of the loss memorandum is more detailed than necessary for the marks although it is a useful reminder of the approach for maximising tax relief.

Answer 36

D Ltd

(a)   **D Ltd – Computation of chargeable gains and allowable losses**

1   Disposal of building in May 1994:

	£
Sale proceeds	280,000
Less: 31 March 1982 value *	(130,000)
	150,000
Less indexation allowance 130,000 × 0.822	(106,860)
	43,140
Unreinvested proceeds: 280,000 – 270,000	10,000
Balance of gain rolled over	33,140
	43,140

* Cost is irrelevant as a global rebasing election has been made.

Scrapping of plant in May 2003:

Original gain deferred becomes chargeable	£33,140

Loss relief is not available on the plant itself as the loss is relieved through the capital allowance rules.

2   Transfer of factory to D Ltd in June 1998

As the transfer is within a capital gains group it would originally be treated on a no gain/no loss basis. However the gain that would have otherwise arisen is taxable on D Ltd as the company leaves the group within 6 years of the transfer.

Market value (June 1998)	260,000
Less: Cost (June 1989)	(180,000)
	80,000
Less: indexation allowance: 180,000 × 0.416	74,880
	5,120

This gain crystallises in the accounting period in which D Ltd leaves the group – the year to 31 December 2003.

3   Sale of office block in June 2003

Disposal proceeds	300,000
Less: 31 March 1982 value	(150,000)
	150,000
Less: indexation allowance 150,000 × 1.272	(150,000) max
	-

4   Part disposal of land in September 2003

Disposal proceeds	180,000
Less: $500,000 \times \dfrac{180,000}{180,000 + 1,200,000}$	(65,217)
	114,783
Less: indexation allowance 65,217 × 0.302	(19,696)
	95,087

(b)   **Potential deferral of gains**

1   The gain that crystallised when the plant was scrapped could have been rolled over if a suitable business asset (ie, non-depreciating) had been acquired before the gain crystallised.

3   There is no scope for deferring the gain on the investment property (had there been a gain) as it was not used in D's trade.

2 and 4 Provided the factory and the plots of land had been used for the purposes of D Ltd's trade the gains can be rolled over against the base cost of suitable business assets acquired within the period from 12 months before to three years after the disposal. The 'disposal' of the factory for this purpose is treated as occurring when the gain accrued, ie 1 January 2003, the start of the accounting period in which D Ltd left the T Ltd group.

Answer 37

Reliefs for groups and consortia

(a)   **The role of non-UK companies in groups and consortia**

The UK tax rules recognise that large groups of companies operate both in the UK and abroad, and may include non-resident companies. Whilst generally not extending UK tax reliefs to these non-resident companies, the rules are cast so as not to disadvantage the UK members of the group. The rules are:

♦   A company can be a member of a group or a consortium without regard to its residence status.

♦   *Illustrations of effect on a group*

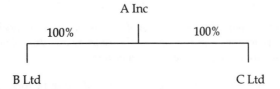

A Inc is non-UK resident but B Ltd and C Ltd are both UK resident.

A Inc, B Ltd and C Ltd form a group.

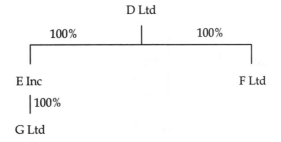

E Inc is non-UK resident but D Ltd, F Ltd and G Ltd are UK resident. E Inc, D Ltd, F Ltd and G Ltd form a group.

Illustration of effect on a consortium

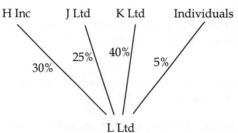

H Inc is non-resident, whilst J Ltd, K Ltd and L Ltd are all UK resident. L Ltd is a consortium owned company and H Inc, J Ltd and K Ltd are consortium members.

♦   Although a non-UK resident company can be a group or a consortium member only the profits or losses of a UK trading branch can participate in a group relief or consortium relief claim.

♦   Similarly a non-UK resident company can now be part of a capital gains group but only in respect of its assets which are within the charge to UK corporation tax on gains. In effect only assets used by a non-UK company for a UK trading branch would be covered.

(b)   **Strategy to maximise loss claims in a group**

There are three main factors to take into account when considering the loss relief claims to make within a group.

(i)   *The rate at which relief is given.* If companies in a group are subject to different marginal tax rates it is advantageous to relieve profits at the highest rate first. Note that companies can suffer marginal tax rates of Nil%, 19%, 23.75%, 30% and 32.75% depending on their level of profits (ie PCTCT + FII).

(ii)   *The timing of the cashflow generated.* A relief which generates cashflow earlier should be preferred over one where there is a delay. For example, group relief for the current year would be preferable to s393(1) relief against future trading profits.

(iii)   *The wastage of other reliefs.* Loss relief claims can have a knock-on effect for non-trading charges, relief for ACT and set off of foreign tax credits. Claims should be chosen that minimise any wastage or delay of other reliefs.

Any consideration of loss relief claims may have to weigh conflicting factors. For example a group relief claim might give immediate relief at 19% but a s393(1) claim might give relief at 30% albeit in twelve months' or perhaps twenty four months' time.

(c)   **Relief for a consortium of E Ltd and F Ltd owning G Ltd**

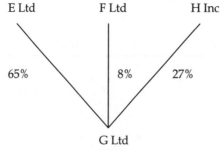

G Ltd is a consortium owned company as at least 75% of its shares are owned by companies holding at least 5% with no one company owning 75% or more.

E Ltd to G Ltd

E Ltd   loss   £54,000
G Ltd   profit   £30,000

E Ltd can surrender its loss to G Ltd under consortium relief but only up to £19,500 (65% of £30,000).

F Ltd to G Ltd

F Ltd   loss   £60,000
G Ltd   profit   £30,000

F Ltd can surrender up to £2,400 (8% of £30,000) of its loss to G Ltd.

H Inc to G Ltd

As H Inc's loss does not arise in respect of any UK trading activity, consortium relief is not available.

Answer 38

S Ltd

(a)   **Chargeable gains for S Ltd for the year to 31 March 2004**

(i)   *30 September 2003 : S Ltd leaves the H Ltd capital gains group*

This crystallises the chargeable gain which had been exempted in June 1998 on the no gain/no loss group transfer as it is within six years of leaving the group.

	£	£
Proceeds (ie MV in June 1998)		220,000
Less: Cost (Aug 1985)	90,000	
Improvement (June 1991)	30,000	(120,000)
Unindexed gain		100,000
Less: Indexation allowance		
90,000 × 0.711	63,990	
30,000 × 0.218	6,540	(70,530)
Gain crystallising in AP of leaving group		29,470

(ii)   *June 2003 : Sale of rights nil paid*

The £15,000 proceeds exceeds 5% of the total value of the holding (£15,000 + £270,000 = £285,000 × 5% = £14,250) and exceeds the de minimis limit of £3,000 so it cannot be treated as a small part disposal.

	£
Proceeds	15,000
Less: Cost × $^A/_{A+B}$	
$160,000 \times {}^{15,000}/_{15,000+270,000}$	(8,421)
	6,579
Unindexed gain	
Less: Indexation allowance 8,421 × 0.336	(2,829)
Chargeable gain	3,750

(iii)   *September 2003 : sale of an office building*

			£	£
Proceeds			230,000	230,000
Less:	Cost/31 March 1982 MV		(50,000)	(70,000)
	Improvements:	Dec 1981	(10,000)	n/a
		Oct 1991	(20,000)	(20,000)
		June 2003	(30,000)	(30,000)
Unindexed gains			120,000	110,000
Less:	Indexation allowance			
	70,000 × 1.283		(89,810)	(89,810)
	20,000 × 0.343		(6,860)	(6,860)
	30,000 × 0.005		(150)	(150)
Indexed gains			23,180	13,180
Lower gain applies				13,180

Summary:	
(i)	29,470
(ii)	3,750
(iii)	13,180
	46,400

(b)   **S Ltd: CT computation for year to 31 March 2004**

	£
Chargeable gains	46,400
Other income	13,500
PCTCT	59,900

As S Ltd had one associate (H Ltd) at some time during the AP the lower small company limit becomes £150,000 and the upper starting rate limit becomes £25,000 ∴ 19% rate applies.

CT payable : 59,900 × 19% = £11,381 due 1.1.05.

International aspects

Answer 39

Z Ltd

> **Tutorial note:**
>
> This is a straightforward question on double tax relief and its knock-on effect of limiting ACT set-off. It is conventional to use a columnar layout to analyse between UK and foreign income although the figures are sufficiently simple in this question to cope without.

Mainstream corporation tax payable by Z Ltd for the year to 31 March 2004

	Total	*Schedule DI*	*Schedule DV*
	£	*£*	*£*
Schedule D Case I	500,000	500,000	
Schedule D Case V	90,000		90,000
Less: Charges paid	(10,000)	(10,000)	
PCTCT	580,000	490,000	90,000
GCT @ 30% (Working 1)	174,000	147,000	27,000
Less: DTR	(17,000)		(17,000)
	157,000	147,000	10,000
Less: ACT b/f (Working 2)	(6,000)	(6,000)	-
MCT	151,000	141,000	10,000

Examination tip - Although the suggested answer seems fairly brief, it shows all the computational results required and should be sufficient for full marks.

Workings

1   **Gross corporation tax**

There are two wholly owned subsidiaries so the upper limit becomes £500,000 (£1,500,000 × $\frac{1}{3}$) and therefore the full rate applies.

2   **ACT set-off**

Maximum set-off (ignoring shadow ACT):

			£	£
UK:	490,000 × 20%			98,000
DV:	Lower of 90,000 × 20% and 10,000 (UK CT net of DTR)			10,000
				108,000
	Less: Shadow ACT			
	Dividends paid		408,000	
	Shadow ACT @ $\frac{20}{80}$			102,000
	ACT set-off limit			6,000
	Surplus ACT b/f		56,000	
	ACT set-off in the year to 31 March 2004		(6,000)	
	Surplus ACT c/f		50,000	

Answer 40

X Ltd

Tutorial note:

This is a good example of a lengthy but fairly straightforward corporation tax computational question favoured under the old syllabus. Similar questions are likely under the new syllabus and it is essential to practice the technique of constructing such answers.

Part (a) is an easy 'warm-up' to calculate the capital allowances – you need the result anyway later. Part (b) is less helpful and leaves you to organise your answer yourself although there is a clue to the difficult bits – eg ACT. Any MCT question requires:

♦   a PCTCT/profits layout

♦   a GCT to MCT layout

♦   working notes for items in these layouts where comments or computational steps are best kept on the side.

You have to fill in the layouts by taking figures direct from the question or via working notes. Some candidates find it difficult to spot what to do next but there are obvious signposts. For example, you cannot do 'GCT' until you've completed PCTCT/Profits and DTR (if any) takes precedence over ACT.

For part (c) you have to describe the operation of the shadow ACT rules. This is still a practical problem for a lot of companies and is likely to remain so for some time.

(a)   **Capital allowances claimable for the year to 31 March 2004**

	£	General pool £	Expensive car £	CA summary £
Tax wdvs b/f		108,000	18,000	
Less: Disposals		(6,000)		
		102,000		
WDA @ 25%		(25,500)	(3,000)	28,500
		76,500	15,000	
Additions qualifying for FYA:				
30.5.03 Plant	12,000			
FYA @ 40%	(4,800)	7,200		4,800
31.7.03 Computer system	23,750			
FYA @ 100%	(23,750)		-	23,750
Total capital allowances				57,050
Total wdvs c/f		83,700	15,000	

(b)   **Computation of mainstream corporation tax for the year to 31 March 2004**

		£
Adjusted trading profit before CAs (226,000 + 12,000 – 6,000)		232,000
Less: Capital allowances		(57,050)
Schedule D Case I		174,950
Chargeable gains		28,000
Schedule DV		4,000
		206,950
Less: Charges paid		
Gift Aid		(2,000)
		204,950
Less: Schedule A loss		(22,000)
		182,950
Less: Schedule D Case III deficit (Working 1)		(1,000)
PCTCT		181,950
Add: FII		15,000
Profits for small company rate purposes		196,950

Gross corporation tax: (Working 2)

		£
$181,950 \times 30\%$		54,585
Less: $^{11}/_{400} \times (500,000 - 196,950) \times {}^{181,950}/_{196,950}$		(7,699)
		46,886
Less: DTR (Working 3)		(1,031)
		45,855
Less: ACT (Working 4)		(8,965)
		36,890
Less: Income tax recoverable (Working 5)		(120)
Mainstream corporation tax payable 1.1.05		£36,770

Examination tip - *Note that the layout of an exam answer is greatly improved where the face of the answer is not cluttered-up with detailed workings. Even if you are not asked for the MCT payday, it is good practice to include it.*

(c)   **Relief for the remaining surplus ACT**

The surplus ACT remaining at 31 March 2004 will be carried forward to set against gross corporation tax of future APs. The set-off limit is 20% of PCTCT as reduced first by any 'shadow ACT'. This is the notional ACT taking $^{20}/_{80}$ of the net of UK dividends paid less UK dividends received.

If a surplus of shadow ACT (ie in excess of 20% of PCTCT) arises in an AP it will be carried back to the previous AP to displace any set-off of actual ACT. Any remaining surplus shadow ACT is carried forward to use as shadow ACT – ie restricting ACT set-off – in a future AP.

Examination tip - *Parts (a) and (b) require computational answers. Even where you are required to show how certain items have been treated, this is done primarily by computations. In theory, full marks are given for the correct computational results but as insurance against inevitable arithmetical slips you should leave a clear trail through your workings to show your understanding of principles. This adds to your burden but there are 23 marks to earn so you should take time to produce explanations where necessary. For example, explain why there are three associated companies (Working 2).*

For part (c) you are explaining the technique you have already applied in part (b) albeit for a future set-off. There are five marks so, as in the suggested answer above, try to show a good understanding.

Workings

1   **Schedule D Case III**

	£	£
Loan Stock interest receivable		14,000
Loan interest on loan to customer		1,000
		15,000
Loss on loan to customer	10,000	
Loan interest paid on a non-trade loan	6,000	(16,000)
Schedule D Case III deficit		(1,000)

2   **CT rate**

Even though at any time X Ltd only has one subsidiary and for one month it had no subsidiaries, it has a total of two associates counting other companies which were in the group for at least part of the year to 31 March 2004.

Lower limit	:	$£300,000 \times \frac{1}{3}$	£100,000
Upper limit	:	$£1,500,000 \times \frac{1}{3}$	£500,000

X Ltd is therefore a 'marginal relief' company.

3   **Double tax relief**

Average CT rate : $\frac{46,886}{181,950} \times 100\%$ 25.769%

The Schedule D Case V income remaining chargeable is £4,000 assuming any set-offs are made against UK source income/gains.

DTR is the lower of:

(i)   UK CT on foreign income £4,000 × 25.769%   £1,031

(ii)   Foreign tax credit: £4,000 × 35%   £1,400

Excess foreign tax credit to carry forward   £369

Examination tip - *It is good exam practice to identify the amount of any foreign tax credit that cannot be set off in the current period.*

4   **ACT set-off**

	£	£
Maximum set-off (ignoring shadow ACT)		
UK PCTCT @ 20%		
181,950 – 4,000 = 177,950 × 20%		35,590
(As UK CT – DTR on DV income is nil, this part of PCTCT does not contribute to the ACT set-off limit.)		
Less: Shadow ACT		
Dividend paid	120,000	
Less: Net dividend received 15,000 × 90%	(13,500)	
	106,500	
Shadow ACT @ $\frac{20}{80}$	26,625	(26,625)
Maximum set-off		8,965
Surplus ACT b/f		24,000
Less: ACT set-off for the year to 31.3.04		(8,965)
Surplus ACT c/f at 31 March 2004		15,035

5   **Income tax recoverable (per CT61)**

		£	£
IT suffered on income:			
Patent royalties received	12,000 × 22%		2,640
Less: IT deducted on payments			
Patent royalties paid	6,000 × 22%	1,320	
Debenture interest paid	6,000 × 20%	1,200	(2,520)
Income tax remaining recoverable against MCT			120

Answer 41

A Ltd

> **Tutorial note:**
>
> The question is conveniently divided into four parts. For the first three parts you are being guided to the computation of the MCT figure. It should be clear from the question that certain standard layouts are needed – a simplified plant CA layout and a PCTCT/Profits layout. Most of the information supplied will end up in these layouts or in an IBA working.
>
> The only non-standard problem for part (b) is fitting the CFC details into a standard CT layout. Parts (c) and (d) are not too difficult if you can remember the basic principles of the shadow ACT rules.

(a)   **A Ltd – Maximum capital allowances for the nine months to 31 December 2003**

	General pool £	Capital allowances £
Capital allowances on plant:		
Tax WDV b/f	84,000	
WDA @ 25% × $^9/_{12}$	(15,750)	15,750
	68,250	
Additions qualifying for FYA	40,000	
FYA @ 40%	(16,000)	16,000
Tax wdv c/f	92,250	
		31,750
Industrial buildings allowance (Working 1)		4,500
Total capital allowances		£36,250

Examination tip - It is easy to overlook the time restriction on the WDA. On the other hand don't fall into the trap of time restricting the FYA.

(b)   **A Ltd – Corporation tax computation for the nine months to 31 December 2003**

	£	£
Adjusted profit (before CAs)		475,250
Less: CAs (see (a) above)		(36,250)
Schedule D Case I		439,000
Schedule D Case VI (Working 2)		14,000
Capital gains		122,000
		575,000
Less: Charge on income		
Gift Aid payment to charity		(8,000)
		567,000
Less: Schedule A loss set-off	24,000	
Less: Schedule D Case III deficit set-off (Working 3)	3,000	(27,000)
PCTCT		540,000
Add: FII $9,000 \times {}^{100}\!/_{90}$		10,000
'Profits'		550,000

Examination tip - This is recognisable as the standard PCTCT/Profits layout you have learnt with modifications for the Schedule A loss (which must be set-off) and the Schedule D Case III deficit for which relief can be claimed against total profits.

Gross corporation tax: $540,000 \times 30\%$	162,000
Less: Marginal relief (Working 4)	
$\qquad {}^{11}\!/_{400} \times (562,500 - 550,000) \times \dfrac{540,000}{550,000}$	(337)
	161,663
Add: CT on CFC income (Working 5)	12,000
Less: Income tax suffered on income to recover (Working 6)	(520)
Mainstream corporation tax (before ACT set-off)	173,143

Examination tip - Be careful to tax PCTCT and not 'Profits' – a common mistake.

(c)   **A Ltd – Amount of ACT which may be relieved**

	£	£
PCTCT $540,000 \times 20\%$		108,000
Restricted by Shadow ACT		
Dividend paid	360,000	
Less: Dividend received	9,000	
	351,000	
Shadow ACT @ ${}^{20}\!/_{80}$		(87,750)
		20,250
Surplus ACT b/f	40,000	
Less: Maximum set-off	(20,250)	(20,250)
		-
Surplus ACT c/f	19,750	

Examination tip - ACT can also be set against the UK CT on the apportioned CFC profits as follows:

	£
Apportioned profits (Working 4) 48,000 × 20%	*9,600*
Less: DTR	*(2,400)*
Additional ACT set-off	*7,200*

The examiner overlooked this point in the original answer and we have therefore excluded consideration of the point in our updated version of the question.

(d) **Advice to the directors of A Ltd on future dividend policy**

REPORT

To: The Directors of A Ltd

Subject: Future dividend policy

Date: 10 May 2004

From: Management Accountant

Following the year to 31 December 2003 there is a surplus of ACT of £19,750 to carry forward.

Under the shadow ACT rules any dividends paid net of UK dividends received in a period attract a notional amount of 'shadow' ACT calculated at $\frac{20}{80}$ ths of the net amount paid.

The normal maximum set-off of ACT for a period is calculated at 20% of the profits chargeable to corporation tax (PCTCT). Before actual surplus ACT can be set-off, the shadow ACT is set against the maximum ACT set-off limit.

In order to set-off the whole of the £19,750 surplus ACT brought forward, it may be necessary to restrict the amount of net dividends paid so that the shadow ACT generated does not reduce the maximum ACT set-off below £19,750.

If the shadow ACT of a period exceeds the maximum ACT set-off, the surplus shadow ACT resulting is carried back to the previous accounting period and displaces actual ACT already set-off in that period. It is important therefore that if dividends are restricted in a period to obtain full ACT set-off, the dividends paid in the following period should not exceed the point where surplus shadow ACT is generated.

There are commercial reasons why the dividends declared should not be restricted. These might outweigh the recovery (or early recovery) of the surplus ACT brought forward.

Signed: Management Accountant

Examination tip - The first five marks are easily earned by producing the three key figures of plant WDA, FYA and IBA.

For part (b) the easy tasks of just transferring figures from the question to your layout (eg capital gains) will only earn a small part of the 14 marks available. Marks are more abundant where you have to work on the figures supplied especially for non-standard topics like CFC apportionment.

The seven marks in part (c) are earned by producing the straightforward steps showing the shadow ACT effect.

In part (d) the advice to directors has to take the form of a report. This makes it hard to earn the four marks on offer in the time available. You just have to make the relevant points as succinctly as possible.

Note you were not asked to suggest that L Inc should pay 90% of its distributable profits thereby avoiding a CFC apportionment.

It is invariably good exam technique to attempt all parts of a question. However, the four marks in part (d) could be sacrificed if you needed the time to spend on other questions where the marks were easier to earn.

Workings

1 Industrial buildings allowance

Residue of expenditure on building purchased from B Ltd (lower of original cost and second-hand cost)	£96,000
Part of 25 year tax life remaining 25 – 9 (1.4.94 – 1.4.03)	16 years
WDA : $96,000 \times \frac{1}{16} \times \frac{9}{12}$	£4,500

2 Schedule D Case VI

Patent royalties on accruals basis	20,000
Less: 9 months depreciation – $80,000 \times \frac{1}{10} \times \frac{9}{12}$	(6,000)
	14,000

3 Schedule D Case III deficit

	£
Non-trade loan interest payable (accruals basis)	15,000
Non-trade interest receivable	(12,000)
Schedule D Case III deficit	3,000

4 Small company rate thresholds

There are two associated companies, A Ltd and L Inc, and the AP is only for nine months – all falling in FY 2003.

Lower limit of	£300,000 becomes	$300,000 \times \frac{1}{2} \times \frac{9}{12}$	£112,500
Upper limit of	£1,500,000 becomes	$1,500,000 \times \frac{1}{2} \times \frac{9}{12}$	£562,500

∴ A Ltd's profits are 'marginal'.

5 Effect of CFC apportionment

L Inc appears to be a controlled foreign company (CFC) as its tax rate (5%) is less than 75% of the UK rate of CT and the company is controlled by a UK resident company.

	£
Apportioned profits: $60,000 \times 80\%$	48,000
UK tax at 30% (always the full rate)	14,400
Less: DTR for apportioned tax $48,000 \times 5\%$	(2,400)
UK additional tax	12,000

6 Income tax recoverable

		£
Income tax suffered on income:		
Patent royalties	$16,000 \times 22\%$	3,520
Income tax withheld on payments:		
Loan interest	$15,000 \times 20\%$	(3,000)
Income tax remaining to recover		520

Answer 42

M Ltd

(a)   **M Ltd – computation of MCT payable for the year to 31 March 2004**

	Total £	UK income £	A Inc £	Overseas Income B PG £	C SA £
Schedule D Case I	20,000	20,000			
Schedule D Case V (note 1)	587,500		200,000	200,000	187,500
Less S393A loss	(75,000)	(20,000)	(55,000)	-	-
PCTCT	532,500	-	145,000	200,000	187,500
GCT @ 30%	159,750	-	43,500	60,000	56,250
Less DTR (note 1)	(136,250)		(30,000)	(50,000)	(56,250)
MCT	23,500		13,500	10,000	-

By setting off the S393A loss against first UK income, then against the foreign dividend suffering the lowest foreign tax rate, the utilisation of foreign tax credit has been maximised. The £55,000 of loss could be set instead against the B PG dividend with equal effect as its foreign tax rate is also below the UK CT rate.

Notes:

1   Schedule D V

	A Inc £	B PG £	C SA £
Net dividends	170,000	150,000	120,000
WHT $^{15}/_{85}$; $^{25}/_{75}$; $^{20}/_{80}$	30,000	50,000	30,000
	200,000	200,000	150,000
ULT $^{150}/_{800}$ × £200,000	-	-	37,500
	200,000	200,000	187,500
Foreign tax credit available	30,000	50,000	67,500
Foreign tax rate:	15%	25%	36%

Tutorial note:

There is excess foreign tax on the C SA dividend (36%) of £187,500 (= £67,500) – £56,250 = £11,250. This could be relieved under the 'on-shore' pooling rules but this is specifically excluded by the question as it is outside the syllabus.

(b)   **If C SA was a controlled foreign company (CFC)**

If C SA was a controlled foreign company, 30% of its profits would have to be apportioned to M Ltd and taxed at the full rate of CT. An appropriate portion of C SA's foreign tax would also be apportioned to M Ltd to relieve UK tax on the apportioned profits.

Dividends paid to M Ltd by C SA would still be included in M Ltd's taxable profits. Relief is given by treating the appropriate proportion of tax paid on the apportioned profits as tax eligible for double tax relief.

If C SA distributed at least 90% of its profits the apportionment would not be required.

M Ltd has to decide, under the CTSA rules, whether an apportionment is required. Apportioned profits are entered on the supplementary pages of self-assessment return and the tax due thereon is added into the figure of tax payable.

Answer 43

BG Ltd

(a)   **Computation of CT payable by BG Ltd for the year to 31 March 2004**

	Total £	Schedule D I £	P Inc £	Q SA £
Schedule D I	30,000	30,000		
Schedule D V	430,000		160,000	270,000
Less: Charge on income	(50,000)	(30,000)	(20,000)	
PCTCT	410,000	-	140,000	270,000

As BG Ltd is one of at least four associated companies it will pay tax at 30% - PCTCT of £410,000 exceeds £1.5K ÷ 4.

CT liability @ 30%	123,000
Less: DTR – (WN2) 42,000 + 81,000	(123,000)
CT payable	-

Note that if 'on-shore' pooling is ignored, only £97,000 (£16,000 + £81,000) of foreign tax credits are used leaving a CT liability of £26,000 (£123,000 - £97,000).

WORKINGS

1   *Schedule D Case V*

	P Inc £	Q SA £
Net dividend received	144,000	160,000
Add withholding tax $\frac{1}{9}$; $\frac{2}{8}$	16,000	40,000
	160,000	200,000
Add: underlying tax	n/a	
350,000 × $\frac{200}{1,000}$		70,000
Schedule D V	160,000	270,000
Charge set off	20,000	-
	140,000	270,000

2   *Relief for foreign tax*

UK CT @ 30%	42,000	81,000
Less: ULT		(70,000)
		11,000
Less: WHT	(16,000)	(40,000)
Excess WHT		29,000
Scope to relieve WHT	26,000	
Elect for £26,000 of excess WHT to enter the usable WHT pool	(26,000)	(26,000)
Excess WHT to carry forward	-	3,000
DTR used	42,000	81,000

Tutorial note:

Strictly the P Inc dividend constitutes the 'unrelated pool' ie all dividends on which no ULT was available but for which no DTR restriction arises.

The Q SA dividend is one on which Eligible Unrelieved Foreign Tax (EUFT) arises. As the excess tax is wholly WHT it can be fully offset using the spare capacity in the 'unrelated pool'. The WHT that cannot be offset will be carried forward.

The examiner has since decided that for exams in 2003 onwards, 'onshore pooling' will not be examined. Note, however, that in most exam situations involving past CIMA double tax relief questions, treating all the foreign dividends and foreign tax credit as if arising on a single source usually results in the right answer for MCT and excess DTR.

(b)   **MEMORANDUM**

To: The Chairman

Re: Further acquisition in Q SA

Date: 21 November 2004

From: Chief Accountant

Currently BG Ltd holds 15% of Q SA so acquiring a further 10% would bring the holding up to 25%. At this level Q SA potentially becomes a controlled foreign company (CFC) from BG Ltd's viewpoint. If Q SA is a CFC, 25% of its profits would be taxable on BG Ltd even though they had not been received.

The CFC rules only apply if the tax rates borne by the foreign company are less than 75% of the UK rate which would apply if Q SA was UK resident. At present it pays £350K of tax on pre-tax profits of £1,350K (£1,000 + £350) – ie 25.9%. As this exceeds 75% of the UK rate of 30% the CFC rules do not apply.

This appears to be the area of concern which your business colleague has mentioned to you.

Chief Accountant

Scenario answers

Answer 44

X Ltd

(a)   **Report prepared for the Directors of X Ltd**

      Subject: Corporation tax payments due over the next 21 months

      Date: 10 April 2004

      From: Brian Phelps (Chief Accountant)

      Report's focus

      At a meeting last week we discussed the timetable for paying corporation tax (CT) under the quarterly instalment regulations and the pressing need to prepare figures for the company's cash flow forecasts.

      As the company pays tax at the full corporation tax rate (currently 30%) it is required to pay by quarterly instalments starting in the seventh month of the year – ie, in October 2004 for the year to 31 March 2005.

      For this reason we have to prepare accurate estimates of tax liability and update those estimates as further information comes available.

      Overpayments of tax attract interest payments from the Revenue but underpayments bear interest. The Revenue charges a higher rate of interest than it pays so it is generally advisable to pay the correct amount.

      There are also penalties which can be imposed if the Revenue consider that estimates have been made negligently. It is advisable to keep evidence to show that estimates were considered carefully.

      1   **Estimated CT liability for the year to 31 March 2005**

            The estimated liability for the current year is £238,500 (see Appendix 1).

            X Ltd has one associated company, Z Ltd, so the marginal relief band limit of £1,500,000 is halved to £750,000. As X Ltd's profits exceed £750,000 based on current estimates the full 30% rate of CT will apply.

            There are two reductions to the tax so calculated.

            Firstly credit is allowed for some of the surplus ACT brought forward. Normally the set-off would be limited to 20% of chargeable profits – well in excess of the £30,000 surplus ACT available. However, there is a restriction because the company will pay a dividend in the period. The ACT that would have been payable ('shadow ACT') reduces the set-off limit.

            Secondly a credit is given for the income tax suffered on income received net to the extent that it has not already been recovered through the quarterly accounting system.

      2   **Pay days for CT**

            A schedule of dates and amounts is shown in Appendix 2. There is also an explanation of the rules for determining pay days.

            It will be necessary to revise estimates of CT liability as the profit forecast is amended.

3   **The effect of paying the dividend in May 2004**

Prior to 6 April 1999 the payment of a dividend triggered a liability to pay advance corporation tax (ACT) equal to 20/80 of the net dividend.

Although the payment of ACT is no longer required, X Ltd has surplus ACT being carried forward and a nominal amount of ACT ('shadow ACT') on dividends paid reduces the company's maximum ACT set off.

As shown in Appendix 1, the proposed dividend payable in May 2004 generates sufficient shadow ACT to leave £19,200 of ACT still surplus. To relieve all the surplus ACT, therefore, the dividend must be reduced by £76,800 (19,200 × 80/20)

Note that if the company pays a dividend in the following accounting period any surplus shadow ACT generated is carried back automatically to restrict the actual ACT set off.

4   **The need for reliable estimates of chargeable income**

Under the quarterly instalment regulations, most if not all of the company's CT liability is due before it can be known with certainty. Even the final instalment is due only just over three months after the year end, usually before the accounts are even ready for auditing.

The quarterly payments must therefore be based on estimates of profit. Inevitably these will lead to either over-payments or under-payments of tax. The Revenue will pay interest on amounts that prove to be overpaid but charge interest on underpayments. Interest receivable is taxed under Schedule D Case III and interest payable is a Schedule D Case III expense. There is however a difference in the interest rates in the Revenue's favour. The rate of interest receivable is too low to make overpaying attractive and the rate payable to the Revenue on underpaid tax makes it a costly form of borrowing. It is important therefore to have an accurate estimate of the CT liability.

If quarterly payments are significantly underestimated, the Revenue may impose penalties for negligence. The company should document the steps taken to estimate CT liability and show how it revised those estimates as more accurate information came available.

5   **Statutory obligations under Corporation Tax Self Assessment (CTSA)**

Under CTSA the company must submit a completed form CT600 (corporation tax return) within 12 months of the end of its accounting period along with a copy of its accounts.

Please let me know if I can provide further clarification of the above information.

Signed: Brian Phelps (Chief Accountant)

Appendix 1 – X Ltd's CT liability for the year to 31 March 2004

	£	£
Trading profit	820,000	
Add: Patent royalties receivable	15,000	
Less: Interest payable	(12,000)	
Schedule D Case I		823,000
Schedule A		10,000
Schedule D Case III		5,000
Less: Gift Aid		(4,000)
Profits chargeable to corporation tax		834,000

The full rate of CT applies as the upper limit of £750,000 is exceeded. The £1,500,000 upper limit is halved because X Ltd has an associate, Z Ltd.

Gross CT liability: 834,000 × 30%		250,200
Less: ACT set off (Note 1 below)		(10,800)
Less: Income tax recoverable (Note 2 below)		(900)
Mainstream corporation tax payable		238,500

Note 1   ACT set-off

ACT brought forward		30,000
Maximum set-off: 834,000 × 20%	166,800	
Restricted by Shadow ACT - 624,000 × 20/80	156,000	
Set-off limit	10,800	(10,800)
Surplus ACT remaining to carry forward		19,200

Note 2   Income tax recoverable

Income tax withheld on income:	
Patent royalties: 15,000 × 22%	3,300
Income tax retained on payments:	
Interest: 12,000 × 20%	(2,400)
Income tax still to recover	900

Appendix 2 – Schedule of CT payments for the 21 months to January 2006

As X Ltd pays CT at the full rate it has to account for the tax by quarterly instalments.

(i)   *Year to 31 March 2004*

As there was a surplus of ACT remaining to carry forward at 31 March 2004, and no shadow ACT generated in that year, full ACT set off of £180,000 (£900,000 PCTCT × 20%) must have been applied. Mainstream tax payable would be £90,000 (270,000-180,000).

Pay days		£
14 October 2003	90,000 × ¼	22,500
14 January 2004	90,000 × ¼	22,500
14 April 2004	90,000 × ¼	22,500
14 July 2004	90,000 × ¼	22,500
		90,000

(ii)   *Year to 31 March 2005*

Pay days		£
14 October 2004	238,500 × ¼	59,625
14 January 2005	238,500 × ¼	59,625
14 April 2005	238,500 × ¼	59,625
14 July 2005	238,500 × ¼	59,625
		238,500

(iii)   *Summary of payments up to January 2006*

Pay days	£
14 April 2004	22,500
14 July 2004	22,500
14 October 2004	59,625
14 January 2005	59,625
14 April 2005	59,625
14 July 2005	59,625
14 October 2005	? *
14 January 2006	? *

* The payments due on 14 October 2005 and 14 January 2006 are the first and second quarterly instalments for the year to 31 March 2006. An estimate of, say, £60,000 each may be preferable to leaving them blank as there is otherwise a risk of overlooking the liabilities due at those points.

(b)   **Report prepared for the Directors of B Ltd**

Subject: X Ltd's current corporation tax (CT) position

Date: 5 May 2005

From: Brian Phelps - Chief Accountant of X Ltd

Report's focus

In April 2004 I prepared a report for the directors of X Ltd setting out the estimated CT liability for the year to 31 March 2005 and a schedule of CT paydays and amounts covering the period up to January 2006.

A copy of this report was made available to you at the time of purchase.

The purpose of the following report is to update the estimates in the original report in the light of further information.

1   Revision of CT liability for the year to 31 March 2005

The revised CT liability for the year to 31 March 2005 is shown in Appendix 1. This shows a small reduction of just of over £5,000 resulting from a number of factors. While each factor is significant the net effect is relatively small. These are summarised as follows:

(a)   Trading profits were originally estimated at £820,000 but this was revised down to £810,000.

(b)   A loan of £50,000 to a supplier has been written off as irrecoverable. This is allowable for tax.

(c)   A payment of £24,000 was made to remove Mr Smith as general manager and this has been allowed as a trading expense. However, the Revenue may contend that the payment was part of the arrangements to purchase Mr Smith's 20% shareholding and disallow the payment as a trading expense. This is less likely to apply if it can be shown that the dismissal and the subsequent purchase were quite separate transactions.

(d)   X Ltd acquired an asset from Z Ltd in August 2000 on a no loss/no gain basis since both companies were in the same capital gains group. The gain that would otherwise have arisen – ie, £30,000 – now crystallises as X Ltd leaves the group within six years of the transfer. The gain is treated as arising in the period in which X Ltd leaves the group.

(e)   As the chargeable profits have been reduced the maximum set-off limit for the surplus ACT is restricted. After the shadow ACT restriction the set-off limit is now nil so there is no relief in the current year for the ACT.

2   Revision to the schedule of CT payments

The cash flow effect of the revision of the CT liability for the year to 31 March 2004 is shown in Appendix 2.

The first three instalments have been overpaid by a total of £4,050. This can be recovered by reducing the corrected value of the 4th instalment due on 14 July 2004 to £54,225.

Please let me know if I can provide further clarification of the above information.

Signed: Brian Phelps (Chief Accountant of X Ltd)

Appendix 1 – X Ltd's revised CT liability for the year to 31 March 2005

	£	£
Trading profit (revised)	810,000	
Add: Patent royalties	15,000	
Less: Payment to Mr Smith	(24,000)	
Interest payable	(12,000)	
Schedule D Case I		789,000
Schedule A		10,000
Gain crystallising on earlier transfer intra-group		30,000
Less: Gift Aid		(4,000)
		825,000
Schedule D Case III		
Interest receivable	5,000	
Irrecoverable non-trading loan	(50,000)	
Deficit relieved against other profits	45,000	(45,000)
Profits chargeable to corporation tax		780,000

Full rate of CT (30%) still applies owing to the number of associated companies.

Gross: CT liability: £780,000 × 30%		234,000
Less: ACT (see Note)		-
Less: Income tax recoverable (as before)		(900)
Mainstream corporation tax payable		233,100
Note Maximum ACT set-off 780,000 × 20%		156,000
Shadow ACT (as before)		(156,000)
Set-off permitted		-
Surplus ACT b/f and c/f		30,000

Appendix 2 – Revised schedule of CT payments

(i)   As at May 2005 the first three instalments for the year to 31 March 2005 have been paid based on the original estimated profit:

		£
Paid to date	3 × £59,625	178,875
Due to date	¾ × 233,100	(174,825)
Overpaid		4,050

(ii)   Payable on 4th instalment:

	£
Revised quarterly amount ¼ × 233,100	58,275
Less overpayment to date	(4,050)
	54,225

Answer 45

W Ltd

(a)   **Report to the Directors of W Ltd**

Re: The Corporation Tax matters for the year to 31 December 2003

Date: 5 June 2003

This report considers the tax implications related to the purchase of B Ltd and L Ltd intended to take place on 1 July 2003.

(i)   *Funds generated by the sale of two assets*

The company proposes to sell two assets, the truck parking lot and a building bought in May 1987. The funds net of corporation tax will be approximately £185,000 leaving a shortfall of about £65,000 to borrow to meet acquisition costs of £250,000 (see Appendix A).

(ii)   *Corporation tax liabilities of W Ltd and L Ltd for the year to 31 December 2003*

As shown in Appendix B the corporation tax (CT) liabilities for W Ltd and L Ltd for the current year are expected to be about £280,000 and £6,000 respectively.

This assumes that B Ltd will surrender the maximum group relief for its trading loss anticipated in the current year. As B Ltd only joins the group half way through the year only the time apportioned part of its loss arising after acquisition can be group relieved. W Ltd should be the target of any available group relief as it has the highest marginal tax rate.

W Ltd's CT liability will be reduced by the £30,000 of surplus ACT brought forward. As you may be aware, the payment of a dividend can restrict a company's ability to offset surplus ACT.

This point is considered in Appendix C and concludes that whether a dividend of £20,000 or £100,000 is paid there is no restriction on the ability to offset W Ltd's surplus ACT.

As W Ltd pays the full rate of CT it is required to account for its CT liability (net of ACT) by quarterly instalments. The schedule of pay days for W Ltd is shown in Appendix D.

Note that the first instalment is due on the fourteenth day of the seventh month of the period with the subsequent three instalments due at three monthly intervals thereafter.

The instalments are each a quarter of the CT liability for the current year. As most of the tax is due before the CT liability is finalised the company has to make best estimates and revise the estimates as the year progresses. Instalments may therefore differ as earlier under or over payments are adjusted for. Interest is charged or received where under or over payments have occurred.

As L Ltd does not pay CT at the full rate the quarterly instalment requirement does not apply and the full liability of £5,700 will be payable on 1 October 2003.

(iii)   *Organising VAT arrangements for the group*

As W Ltd will control B Ltd and L Ltd it would be possible for all three companies to be covered by a group registration. This would have the advantage of requiring only one VAT return to be submitted per quarter and for intra-company sales to be ignored for VAT purposes.

It is not necessary to include all the potential companies in a group registration. If L Ltd was in an ongoing input tax repayment situation the group's cashflow would be enhanced by keeping L Ltd out of the registration and being registered separately with monthly return periods. This would have to be weighed against the extra administration of twelve extra VAT returns a year for the group.

L Ltd could be in a repayment situation because it makes exports which are zero rated. This applies to exports outside the EU and to supplies made to VAT registered traders in other EU countries. It does not apply to 'exports' to non-registered persons in other EU countries which remain standard rated. The actual VAT position of L Ltd would have to be reviewed.

Please let me know if there are any further matters arising.

APPENDIX A - Net funds arising from the proposed disposals

(a)   The company intends to dispose of two assets in June 2003:

1   Plot of land used as parking lot for trucks

	£
Sales proceeds anticipated	60,000
Less: Cost (March 1989)	(35,000)
Unindexed gain	25,000
Less: Indexation allowance: $35,000 \times 0.607$	(21,245)
Indexed gain	3,755

2   Building purchased in May 1987 as a replacement

The gain on the original disposal in May 1987 was rolled over and has reduced the base cost of the current building.

	£
Original sale proceeds in May 1987	70,000
Less: Cost	(30,000)
Unindexed gain	40,000
Less: Indexation allowance: $30,000 \times 0.283$	(8,490)
Indexed gain to rollover	31,510

Only half of this rolled over gain reduces the base cost as the original asset had been acquired before 1 April 1982 and sold before 1 April 1988 (when 'rebasing' was introduced).

	£
Anticipated sale proceeds in June 2003	140,000
Less: Cost 70,000 - $\frac{1}{2} \times 31,510$	(54,245)
Unindexed gain	85,755
Less: Indexation allowance $54,245 \times 0.771$	(41,823)
Indexed gain	43,932

(b)   Net proceeds generated

Sales proceeds anticipated	£	£
Land		60,000
Building		140,000
		200,000
Gains chargeable		
Land	3,755	
Building	43,932	
	47,687	
Corporation tax payable on gains @ 30%		(14,306)
Net proceeds generated		185,694

Note: W Ltd's marginal tax rate for the year to 31 December 2003 is 30% - the full rate - as profits are expected to exceed £500,000 - the full rate threshold for three associated companies.

(c)   Borrowings required to meet the acquisition costs:

	£
Acquisition price	250,000
Funds generated by sales	(185,694)
Shortfall to borrow	64,306

APPENDIX B - Corporation tax payable by W Ltd and L Ltd for the year to 31.12.03

	W Ltd £	L Ltd £
Chargeable profits (estimate before gains)	900,000	30,000
Chargeable gains (Appendix A)	47,687	-
	947,687	30,000
Less: Group relief B Ltd to W Ltd		
28,000 × $\frac{6}{12}$ (overlapping period 1.7.03 - 31.12.03)	(14,000)	-
PCTCT	933,687	30,000
CT liability @ 30%/19%	280,106	5,700

APPENDIX C - Relief for W Ltd surplus ACT brought forward

If W Ltd pays a dividend in the current year this generates shadow ACT which reduces the scope to set off real ACT brought forward.

	£20,000 dividend £	£100,000 dividend £
PCTCT @ 20% : 933,687 × 20%	186,737	186,737
Less: Shadow ACT 20,000/100,000 × 25%	(5,000)	(25,000)
ACT set off limit	181,737	161,737

In either case the available surplus ACT brought forward of £30,000 is set off in full.

APPENDIX D - Quarterly instalment pay days for W Ltd

	£
CT liability estimated for the year to 31.12.03 (App B)	280,106
Less: ACT set off (App C)	30,000
	250,106

Pay days		£
14 July 2003	$250,106 \times \frac{1}{4}$	62,526
14 October 2003	$250,106 \times \frac{1}{4}$	62,527
14 January 2004	$250,106 \times \frac{1}{4}$	62,526
14 April 2004	$250,106 \times \frac{1}{4}$	62,527
		250,106

(b)   **Report to the Directors of W Ltd**

Re: Corrected CT liabilities for W Ltd and L Ltd for the year to 31 December 2003

Date: 5 January 2004

This report updates the CT liabilities estimated in my report of 5 June 2003 and considers the tax implications of an alternative method of gaining control of future target companies.

(i)   *Corrected CT liabilities (Appendix A)*

W Ltd's CT liability for the year to 31 December 2003 as reduced by surplus ACT is expected to be about £224,000 compared to £250,000 estimated back in June. This results from over estimation of W Ltd's profits and B Ltd's loss available for group relief.

Similarly L Ltd's CT liability for the year to 31 December 2003 has been revised downward from £5,700 to £3,420 also due to an original overestimate of profit.

The remaining instalments due for W Ltd's CT liability have been revised to take account of the overpayments. The next instalment due on 14 January is reduced to £43,247 (from £62,526) with payment due of £56,100 on 14 April. Interest is receivable on the earlier overpayments which totalled £12,853.

(ii)   *An alternative method of gaining control of future target companies.*

B Ltd and L Ltd's businesses were acquired by share purchase. An alternative method of acquisition would be to buy the underlying business and assets from the target company. The tax implications of this alternative method are as follows:

♦ Tax relief in the form of capital allowances may be available for certain assets such as plant and industrial buildings. Tax relief is also available for any goodwill which is written off after the acquisition. By contrast there is no tax relief for acquiring shares.

♦ The assets acquired could be used to rollover group gains.

♦ As no new company is being brought into the group there is no increase in the number of associated companies with dilution of the small company bands.

♦ W Ltd would be acquiring just the assets desired and not the liabilities (some of which may be unknown at the time of purchase) as would apply on a share purchase. Thus there is no necessity to obtain warranties and indemnities as there are when shares are acquired.

Please let me know if I can be of further assistance.

APPENDIX A - for report dated 5 January 2004

(a)   Revised CT liabilities for W Ltd and L Ltd for the year to 31 December 2003

	W Ltd £	L Ltd £
Revised chargeable profits	860,000	18,000
Less: group relief $\frac{6}{12} \times £24,000$	(12,000)	-
PCTCT	848,000	18,000
CT liability @ 30%/19%	254,400	3,420
Less: Surplus ACT b/f	(30,000)	-
	224,400	3,420

(b)   Pay days for W Ltd and L Ltd

For W Ltd, a large company, the CT liability is due by instalments. The next instalment due, on 14 January 2004 has to be adjusted for overpayments of the two previous instalments which were based on higher estimates of liability.

	£	£
Due on 14.1.04: 224,400 × $\frac{1}{4}$		56,100
Paid to date: 62,526 + 62,527	125,053	
Due to date: 2 × 56,100	112,200	
Overpaid to date	12,853	(12,853)
Payment to make on 14.1.04		43,247
For L Ltd: Due on 1.10.04		3,420

Answer 46

L plc group

(a) **REPORT**

> **To:** The Board of Directors of L plc
>
> **Re:** Group CT liability for the year to 31 March 2004
>
> **Date:** 10 May 2004
>
> **From:** Chief Accountant

The purpose of this report is to show the corporation tax (CT) liabilities for the group for the year just ended and to cover a number of related issues.

1 CT liabilities

Taking maximum advantage of the available group losses the CT liabilities calculated in Part C of the attached Appendix are as follows:

L plc	:	£14,900
S Ltd	:	£7,283
C Ltd	:	£109,140
P Ltd	:	£Nil

All the tax for L plc and S Ltd is payable on 1 January 2005. C Ltd's liability is payable by four equal quarterly instalments on 14 October 2003, 14 January 2004, 14 April 2004 and 14 July 2004.

Estimated amounts for the first three payments for C Ltd have already been made and overpayment (or underpayment) will be accounted for against the final instalment of £27,285 ($109,140 \times \frac{1}{4}$) due 14 July 2004.

L plc's CT liability includes tax due on T SA's profits. T SA is a 'controlled foreign company' (CFC) so we have to self-assess CT at the full rate (30%) on our apportioned share (30%) of T SA's profits but are entitled to a tax credit for the foreign CT suffered on the apportioned profits.

2 Related issues

> *(a) Associated companies*
>
> Each company in the group (L plc, W Ltd, S Ltd, C Ltd, P Ltd and Z Inc) has five associated companies. This is because L plc controls each of the other companies.
>
> As six companies are associated together the small company rate and starting rate marginal relief bands have to be divided by six. This is important when deciding how to allocate losses around the group. For example any losses applied to reduce profits in the band £50,000 to £250,000 will save tax at 32.75%. Losses applied to profits between £8,333 and £50,000 save tax only at 19%.
>
> *(b) Relief for group losses*
>
> The application of group losses is shown with explanations in parts A and B of the Appendix.

As far as trading losses are concerned the group has benefited from the following three reliefs:

(i)   *s393A relief.* A company can set its trading loss for an accounting period (AP) against its other profits for the same AP.

(ii)   *Group relief.* A company can surrender its trading loss to another company in the same 75% group. If there are several potential claimants the loss can be surrendered in whichever proportion and to whichever company or companies to maximise its tax saving.

(iii)   *Consortium relief.* A consortium company is a company owned by other companies such that at least 75% is owned by companies each holding at least 5% but not as much as 75% of the shares. Note that W Ltd is thereby a consortium company.

         The loss of a consortium company can be surrendered to a consortium member in proportion to the member's shareholding.

The actual reliefs claimed to maximise tax relief have been made as follows:

(i)   W Ltd, a consortium company, has to relieve its own profits before its loss can be claimed. Even if it fails to do so it is deemed to have done so. An actual claim to use £30,000 against its own profits is therefore advisable as there is no other use for it.

(ii)   L plc holds 60% of W Ltd directly and 6% (20% × 30%) indirectly via T SA. The fact that T SA is not UK resident is not relevant. L plc can claim up to 66% of W Ltd's remaining loss of £70,000 (100,000 - £30,000). Again, with no other use for the loss apart from carrying it forward in W Ltd this claim is advisable.

(iii)   P Ltd's loss is available in full to S Ltd as it was 75% of S Ltd throughout the period but only half of the loss (6 out of 12 months) is available to L plc as it was only grouped with L plc from 1 October 2002. Up until then it only controlled 72% (80% × 90%) ie less than 75%. When T SA acquired a 20% holding, L plc's holding in P Ltd increased by 6% (20% × 30%) ie now over 75%. Thus the priority use of the loss is as follows:

- ♦ £140,000 (280,000 × $\frac{6}{12}$) by group relief to L plc saving tax at 30%/32.75% (preferable to surrender to C Ltd where it only saves tax at 30%).

- ♦ £121,667 by group relief to S Ltd saving tax at 32.75%/19% and leaving just sufficient for P Ltd to set against other income

- ♦ £18,333 by s393A relief saving tax at 19%/23.75%.

(iv)   Z Inc's trading loss of £200,000 can be group relieved against L plc, S Ltd or C Ltd in any combination. As it has the greatest degree of freedom it is left until last. By this stage it appears that L plc requires another £63,800 of group relief to reduce it to the top of the 19% band thereby saving tax at 32.75%. The balance of £136,200 is most effectively relieved in C Ltd saving tax at 30%.

Finally, C Ltd has realised a capital loss of £90,000 and S Ltd has a gain of £80,000. As both companies are in a 75% group – L plc being the principal company owning 75% of each – they can make a joint election by 31 March 2006 to deem that the disposal by S Ltd had been made by C Ltd – thereby matching the loss and the gain.

(c)   *The effect of T SA*

The 30% holding of T SA by L plc gives access to group relief of P Ltd's loss (via an indirect holding of 6%) and a further 6% of W Ltd's loss through consortium relief. Both of these advantages are referred to above.

However, T SA is a controlled foreign company as it is controlled (over 50%) by UK resident companies and its profits are taxed at less than 75% of the rate that would apply if it were UK resident. As L plc has a holding of at least 25% it must self-assess its holding proportion of T SA's profits and tax them at the full CT rate. This applies even though the profits are not remitted to L plc and L plc's marginal tax rate is other than 30%.

(b)   **REPORT**

To: The Managing Director of L plc

Re: Overseas Matters

Date: 14 May 2004

From: Chief Accountant

This report covers two issues you raised with me recently in discussion on overseas matters.

Operating in overseas countries

If a profitable business is operated overseas as a branch of L plc, the profits will be assessable to UK corporation tax whether or not they are remitted to the UK. The profits will be adjusted under the Schedule D Case I rules and capital allowances will be available on plant and industrial buildings just as apply to the existing UK trade. Double tax relief will be given for any foreign tax suffered limited to the UK rate of corporation tax. Any excess foreign tax can be carried forward for relief against UK corporation on future profits of the same branch.

If instead the overseas activities were operated through non-UK resident subsidiaries the profits would only be taxable when dividends are remitted to the UK, or if L plc fell foul of the CFC rules as already apply with T SA. L plc would be entitled to double tax relief on any foreign tax (withholding or underlying) suffered on the foreign dividends but not exceeding the UK CT payable on the dividends.

Transferring the management of Z Inc

At present Z Inc is UK resident and its trading losses are available for group relief. If Z Inc's management was transferred overseas it would become non-UK resident and any trading losses (other than of a UK permanent establishment) would not be available for group relief. If the objective is to avoid high UK rates of CT, this would probably be frustrated by the CFC rules.

APPENDIX

A   Final corporation tax chargeable profits for group (profit making) companies.

Loss memo (**B**)

	L plc £	S Ltd £	C Ltd £	P Ltd £	W Ltd £
Schedule D Case I	200,000	160,000	450,000	-	-
Other income	100,000	-	50,000	20,000	30,000
Profit before loss reliefs	300,000	160,000	500,000	20,000	30,000
(i) Less: S393A relief in W Ltd					(30,000)
					-
(ii) Consortium relief W → L	(46,200)				
(iii) Group relief P → L	(140,000)				
(iv) Group relief P → S		(121,667)			
(v) s393A relief in P				(18,333)	
(vi) Group relief Z → L	(63,800)				
(vii) Group relief Z → C			(136,200)		
PCTCT	50,000	38,333	363,800	1,667	-

Notes:

1   Each company has five associates (six including itself) so group's marginal tax rates are:

Profits

over	£250K (1,500,000 ÷ 6)	30%
	£50K - £250K	32.75%
	£8,333 - £50,000	19%
	£1,667 - £8,333	23.75%
under	£1,667	Nil%

Unless otherwise restricted losses should be used against the highest marginal tax rates in priority.

2   S Ltd and C Ltd are in the same capital gains group so the capital gain and capital loss can be matched by election leaving a net loss of £10,000 (£90,000 - £80,000) to carry forward in the group.

B   Memorandum of losses

	P Ltd £	Z Inc £	W Ltd £
Trading losses for the y/e 31.3.04	280,000	200,000	100,000
Less: s393A relief for W Ltd (takes priority over consortium relief)			(30,000) (i)
			70,000
Utilising W Ltd's loss by consortium relief			
Maximum percentage of loss:			
L plc holds 60% direct and 6% (20% × 30%) indirect			
Consortium claim 66% to L plc			(46,200) (ii)
Balance unavailable to L plc			23,800

Utilising P Ltd's loss (grouped with S Ltd
for whole period but only grouped with
L plc for 6 months)

Maximum to L plc $\frac{6}{12}$	(140,000)	(iii)
Surrender to S Ltd	(121,667)	(iv)
S393A in P Ltd (the balance)	(18,333)	(v)

‑

Utilising Z Inc's loss

Group relieve sufficient to L plc
to reduce to bottom of 32.75% band   (63,800) (vi)

Balance group relieved to C Ltd
where it saves tax at 30%   (136,200) (vii)

‑   ‑

Tutorial note:

W Ltd's loss of £46,200 surrendered by consortium relief to L plc could be used by other group companies such as C Ltd. L plc is known as a 'link' company and the loss could 'flow through' to other group companies. 'Flow through' is excluded from the syllabus, however, and does not affect the overall strategy to maximise the use of available losses in this situation.

C   Corporation tax liabilities for group companies

	L plc £	S Ltd £	C Ltd £	P Ltd £
PCTCT (see A above)	50,000	38,333	363,800	1,667
CT @ 19%/19%/30%/Nil%	9,500	7,283	109,140	-
Add: CT on T SA's allocated profit as a CFC (always the full CT rate) 30% × 120,000 × 30%	10,800	-	-	-
Less: 15% foreign tax credit	(5,400)			
CT payable	14,900	7,283	109,140	-

Note

L plc's and S Ltd's CT liability is payable on the normal due date of 1 January 2005 as their profits are not large.

C Ltd is large and was large in the previous AP so its CT liability is due by instalments.

May 2002 Exam Answers

Answer 47 (1 of Exam Paper)

47.1   C

The end of year return to the Revenue is Form P35.

47.2   B

If the period of account exceeds 12 months the first AP is for the 12 months from commencement of the period and the second AP is for the balance.

47.3   A

Starting rate marginal band limits:

$10,000 \times \frac{9}{12}$ =   7,500

$50,000 \times \frac{9}{12}$ =   37,500

$\therefore$ P of £35,000 is marginal.

FY straddle: but rates for FY02 and FY03 are the same.

GCT:	$30,000 \times 19\%$	5,700
	Less: $\frac{19}{400} \times (37,500 - 35,000) \times \frac{30}{35}$	(102)
		5,598

47.4   C

Basic tax point is date of delivery (10/10/03) but actual tax point is invoice date as this falls within 14 days after the basic tax point.

47.5   C

Regardless of the length of the AP, the final quarterly instalment is due 3 months and 14 days after the AP end on 14 December 2003.

47.6   D

Actual gain : 6,600 – 3,800 = £2,800.

As the asset is a chattel, marginal relief restricts the gain chargeable to $\frac{5}{3} \times (6,600 - 6,000) =$ £1,000.

47.7   A

	General pool £	Expensive car £	CA summary £
Year to 31 March 2004			
Tax wdvs b/f	360,000	24,000	
Sale		(12,000)	
Balancing allowance		12,000	12,000
25% WDA	(90,000)		90,000
	270,000		
Additions with FYA	90,000		
Less: 40% FYA	(36,000)		36,000
	324,000		138,000

Note: 100% FYA not available for computer as company not 'small'. To be 'small' it must satisfy two of the following:

Turnover   ¡Ì   £2.8m

Assets   ¡Ì   £1.4m

Employees   ¡Ì   50

Answer 48 (2 of Exam Paper)

A Ltd and B Ltd

REPORT TO THE DIRECTORS OF A LTD

Re: Estimated corporation tax liabilities for the 15 months to 31 March 2004

Date: 1 November 2003

Synopsis

As the company will be changing its accounting reference date from 31 December to 31 March by preparing a 15 month period of account to 31 March 2004, corporation tax will be chargeable separately for the 12 month period to 31 December 2003 and the 3 month period to 31 March 2004.

At a recent meeting you advised me of several proposed transactions which could take place independently at any time from September 2003 to 31 March 2004. The following report explains the optimum timing for each transaction for minimising the company's tax liabilities.

Assuming that the optimum timing is adopted, the corporation tax liabilities and pay days are as follows (see Appendix D):

12 month period to 31 December 2003   £300,005 due 1.10.04
3 month period to 31 March 2004   £193,028 due 1.1.05

Timing of transactions

(1)   *Acquiring an 80% holding in B Ltd*

At present A Ltd has no associated companies so pays less than the full 30% rate of corporation tax (CT) if its profits for a 12 month period do not exceed £1,500,000.

If more than 50% of B Ltd's ordinary shares are acquired, B Ltd becomes an associated company and the full CT rate applies where profits exceed £750,000 for a 12 month period. In other words as there are two associated companies, A Ltd and B Ltd, the £1,500,000 threshold is halved (see Appendix C).

The threshold would be halved for the year to 31 December 2003 if B Ltd was acquired at any time in that year.

As A Ltd's profits for the year are estimated to fall between £750,000 and £1,500,000 it would be advisable not to acquire an associated company before 1 January 2004. This advice is not dependent upon the choices over the timing of the two other proposed transactions (see below).

As B Ltd is expected to have losses in the year to 31 December 2004, there is scope to benefit from group relief. If B Ltd is acquired early in the year it can group relieve up to 3 months of loss as A Ltd's 3 months to 31 March 2004 will 'overlap' with 3 months of B Ltd's period of 12 months to 31 December 2004.

Group relief is possible because A Ltd will hold at least 75% of B Ltd's ordinary shares.

Recommendation: Acquire B Ltd not before 1 January 2004 but as soon as possible on or after that date.

(2) *Investment of £90,000 in a new computer system*

Taking account of the level of turnover and number of employees, the company is a 'medium' size business but not a 'small' business. The significance is that the company can claim a 40% rate of first year allowance but not 100% first year allowance on the cost of the computer.

The allowance is available in the accounting period in which the expenditure is incurred. The balance of expenditure attracts 25% writing down allowances.

Appendix A shows the capital allowances available depending on whether the computer is purchased before the end of the current period or in the 3 month period to 31 March 2004. Although the earlier purchase results in slightly higher overall allowances for the two periods (£134,375 compared to £131,000) the advantage of the earlier purchase lies in the significantly higher allowances in the current period.

As shown in Appendix D, A Ltd's profits fall in the small company marginal relief band for the 12 months to 31 December 2003 where the marginal rate of CT is 32.75%.

In the following period profits are 'large' so the marginal tax rate is 30%.

Recommendation: Purchase the computer system before 1 January 2004 as it results in a higher rate of tax savings and delays the pay day.

(3) *Sale of office blocks*

The computation of the gains on the office block disposal is shown in Appendix B. Delaying the disposal from December 2003 to March 2004 reduces the gain slightly as the indexation allowance will increase.

If the gain occurs in the current period (ie December disposal) it is taxed at the current marginal rate which, as explained above, is 32.75%. Delaying to the next period sees a marginal tax rate of 30% as well as a 3 month delay in paying the CT liability.

Recommendation: Delay the disposal until after 31 December 2003.

Other tax issues

1   *Pay days*

A Ltd will be paying CT at the full 30% rate for the 3 months to 31 March 2004. However, the quarterly instalment regulations will not apply as A Ltd was not paying the full rate for the previous period.

2   *VAT group registration*

A Ltd and B Ltd could elect for VAT group registration whereby only one registration would cover both companies. However, B Ltd is principally an exporter and (if this is to non-EU countries) will be in a regular VAT repayment position. It may be preferable to keep separate registrations so that B Ltd can submit monthly returns to recover input tax thereby improving cash flow.

3   *Capital gains*

A Ltd and B Ltd will be in a capital gains group as A Ltd will own at least 75% of B Ltd. This allows assets to be transferred between A Ltd and B Ltd on a no gain/no loss basis and would allow group wide rollover relief.

Please let me know if you require any further explanation of the above matters.

Chief Accountant
Arnie Andersen

Appendix A – Capital allowances on plant

(i)   **Assuming computer system purchased by 31 December 2003**

	Pool £	CA summary £
Y/e 31.12.03		
Tax wdv b/f 1.1.03	320,000	
25% WDA	(80,000)	80,000
Addition with FYA	90,000	
40% FYA	(36,000)	36,000
		116,000
3 months to 31.3.04		
Tax wdv b/f 1.1.04	294,000	
25% WDA × ³⁄₁₂	(18,375)	18,375
	c/f 275,625	Total 134,375

(ii)   **Assuming computer system purchased post 31 December 2003**

	Pool £	CA summary £
Y/e 31.12.03		
Tax wdv b/f 1.1.03	320,000	
25% WDA	(80,000)	80,000
3 months to 31.3.04		
Tax wdv b/f 1.1.04	240,000	
25% WDA × ³⁄₁₂	(15,000)	15,000
Addition with FYA	90,000	
40% FYA	(36,000)	36,000
	c/f 279,000	51,000
		Total 131,000

Appendix B – Sale of surplus office block

Date of sale:	*Dec 2003* £	*March 2004* £
Anticipated proceeds	600,000	600,000
Less: Cost	(120,000)	(120,000)
	480,000	480,000
Less: Indexation allowance – 120,000 × 0.818/0.835	(98,160)	(100,200)
	381,840	379,800

Appendix C – The impact of acquiring B Ltd on tax rates

Starting with the AP in which B Ltd was acquired, the small company marginal relief band limits for A Ltd (and for B Ltd) would have to be divided by two.

(i)   *For acquisition in y/e 31.12.03*

Limits become	£750,000	(1.5m ÷ 2)
and	£150,000	(£300k ÷ 2)

(ii)   *For acquisition in 3 months to 31.3.04*

Limits become	£187,500	(£1.5m ÷ 2 ÷ 4)
and	£37,500	(£300k ÷ 2 ÷ 4)

Appendix D – Computation of CT liabilities

	£	*AP 12 months to 31.12.03* £	*AP 3 months to 31.3.04* £
Trading profits	1,500,000		
Add: Patent royalties receivable (25,000 + 5,000)	30,000		
Less: Patent royalties payable	(70,000)		
Apportioned 12 : 3	1,460,000	1,168,000	292,000
Capital allowances (Note 3)		(116,000)	(18,375)
Schedule D Case I		1,052,000	273,625
Schedule D Case V – 17,000 × $\frac{100}{85}$			20,000
Capital gain (Note 2)			379,800
Less: Gift Aid (Note 3)		(10,000)	-
		1,042,000	673,425
Less: Group relief from B Ltd			
'Overlapping' loss $\frac{3}{12}$ × 80,000			(20,000)
		1,042,000	653,425
Small company limits (Note 4)		£300k/£1.5m	£37,500/£187,500
GCT: £1,042,000/£653,425 × 30%		312,600	196,028
Less: SCMR (1st AP only)			
$\frac{11}{400}$ (1,500,000 – 1,042,000)		(12,595)	
Less: DTR			(3,000)
		300,005	193,028
Due dates		1.10.04	1.1.05

Notes:

1   The computer is acquired by 31.12.03 to enable the 40% FYA resulting to achieve relief at the 32.75% marginal rate (instead of the 30% marginal rate relevant in the 3 month period).

2   The capital gain is deferred to the 3 month period where the marginal tax rate is 30% (not 32.75%).

3   The Gift Aid payment should be made before 31 December 2003 to maximise the relief.

4   The acquisition of B Ltd is deferred to 1 January 2004 to maximise the small company marginal relief in the year to 31 December 2003.

Answer 49 (3 of Exam Paper)

P Ltd and T Ltd

(a) **Recoverable input tax for the quarter to 30 September 2003**

	£
Input tax attributable to standard rate sales	4,000

Proportion of unattributable input tax:

$$2,000 \times \frac{\text{Standard rate turnover}}{\text{Total turnover}}$$

$$= 2,000 \times \frac{90,000}{120,000}$$

	£
	1,500
	5,500

Non-recoverable input tax: 2,200 + (2,000 – 1,500) = 2,700.

This is greater than £625 per month so the de minimis rule does not apply.

At the end of each year the calculation would be reworked on an annual basis and any over or under recovery of input tax would be adjusted for.

(b) **Report to the Directors of T Ltd**

   Re: The operation of the tax favoured employee share schemes introduced by FA 2000

   Date: 1 November 2003

   Introduction

   The FA 2000 introduced two new schemes giving tax advantages where shares and share options are provided as part of an employee remuneration package.

   The first scheme is called the Share Incentive Plan (SIP). Essentially employees obtain shares in the company – usually allocated at no cost to them – and the gains eventually realised on sale can be free of all taxes. There are conditions and restrictions (see below) and the scheme has to be available to employees generally.

   The second scheme is called the Enterprise Management Incentive (EMI) scheme and can be targeted to benefit selected employees. The scheme allows the company to grant share options which the employees can exercise in due course without a tax charge. Again there are conditions and restrictions (see below). The main problem is that it only applies to relatively small companies as it is designed to help companies attract and keep key employees who might otherwise prefer better career prospects with a larger company.

Share Incentive Plans – Summary

The plans are operated through a trust. The trustees hold the shares for the employees until they are taken out of the plan or sold.

- Employers can give employees up to £3,000 of shares each year free of tax and NIC.

- Employees can buy up to £1,500 of 'partnership' shares each year out of their pre-tax salary.

- Employers can match partnership shares by giving up to two free shares for each partnership share the employee buys. These 'matching' shares are also free of IT and NIC at that point.

- Employees cannot normally withdraw shares from the plan for three years.

- Shares are subject to tax on their initial value if taken out of the plan between years three and five.

- Shares held for more than five years are completely free of IT and NIC.

- Any increase in value in the shares while they are in the plan will be free of tax and NIC.

- The plan must be available to all employees. Variations are permitted for length of service, etc.

- Employees or directors with a material interest of 25% or more must be excluded.

Enterprise Management Incentives (EMI) – Summary

This scheme allows small high risk UK trading companies to reward selected employees with share options worth up to £100,000 each at the date of grant.

- There is normally no tax or NIC on the grant or exercise of the option.
- Employees or directors with a material interest of 30% or more must be excluded.
- The option must be capable of being exercised within 10 years.
- The total of EMI options issued must not exceed £3 million.

Chief Accountant
Ernie Enron

Answer 50 (4 of Exam Paper)

IB Ltd

Maximum IBAs that may be claimed for the year to 31 March 2004

		£
Building 1	The 25 year tax life expires on 31 March 2003 so no further IBAs would be available.	
Building 2	The qualifying cost excludes the land leaving £120,000 of construction cost. It also excludes the cost of the administration offices £35,000 as this is 29.16% of the cost, ie exceeds 25% de minimis. WDA 4% × 85,000	3,400
Building 3	Qualifying cost is lower of original cost (£110,000) and second-hand price (£160,000) ie £110,000. Tax life remaining: 25 – (1.4.90 – 1.4.82) = 17 years. WDA: $^{110,000}/_{17}$	6,471
Building 4	Year to 31 March 2002 - 60% Year to 31 March 2003 - 25% Year to 31 March 2004 - 15% balance of £100,000 ──── 100%	15,000

c/f 24,871

Second-hand buildings available:

(a)   No IBAs available as outside 25 year tax life.

(b)   Qualifying cost remaining : £100,000
Tax life left: 25 – (1.4.2003 – 1.4.1980) = 2 years

WDA : $^{100,000}\!/_2$ 50,000

(c)   Qualifying cost remaining: £120,000

Tax life left: 23 years

WDA: $^{120,000}\!/_{23}$ £5,217

If building (b) is acquired total IBAs : 50,000 + 24,871 =   £74,871

Answer 51 (5 of Exam Paper)

L Ltd and E Ltd

(a)   **L Ltd – profit adjustment**

		£
Profit per accounts		60,000
Add back:	Non-trade loan written off	50,000
	Loan costs written off	6,000
		116,000
Less:	Non-trade interest credited	(3,000)
Schedule D Case I		113,000

L Ltd – loan relationship items under Schedule D Case III

		£
Interest receivable		3,000
Less:	Loan and costs written off	(56,000)
Schedule D Case III deficit		53,000

As L Ltd controls at least 75% of the ordinary shares of S Ltd, L Ltd could group relieve the non-trade loan deficit to S Ltd.

For the year to 31 March 2004 (FY 2003), the bands for two associated companies are reduced to:

Lower limit	300,000/2	=	£150,000
Upper limit	1,500,000/2	=	£750,000

The marginal tax rate for S Ltd is 32.75% and this would apply on its top £70,000 of profit (£220,000 - £150,000). Therefore the deficit should be surrendered to S Ltd where it would save tax of £17,357 (£53,000 × 32.75%).

By contrast, using the deficit in L Ltd saves tax of £10,070 (53,000 × 19%). Thus the decision to group relieve saves additional tax of £7,287 (£17,357 - £10,070).

(b)   **Report to the Chairman of E Ltd**

Re: UK tax implications of takeover for E Ltd

Date: 1 May 2004

You have requested a brief report on the tax implications for E Ltd of being acquired (80%) by a company resident in the USA.

1   If E Ltd joins a group comprising of 37 associated companies, the small company marginal relief band thresholds become: £8,108 (300,000 × $\frac{1}{37}$) and £40,540 (1,500,000 × $\frac{1}{37}$).

2   This makes it more likely that E Ltd will pay the full 30% rate of CT instead of 19%.

3   Where E Ltd pays the full CT rate for two consecutive accounting periods it will be liable to pay its CT liability by quarterly instalments for the second and subsequent accounting periods.

4   There will be scope for group relief claims between E Ltd and the other 75% owned UK companies in the group.

5   Similarly the 75% UK group companies will form a capital gains group with automatic no gain/no loss treatment on transfers of chargeable assets and scope for group wide rollover relief.

6   The UK group companies could elect for VAT group registration. This would save administration costs and would defer accounting for VAT if there were taxable inter-company transactions.

Signed: Financial Controller

Answer 52 (6 of Exam Paper)

G Ltd

Computation of gains and losses for the year to 31 March 2004

(1)   *Grant of sub-lease – May 2003*

		£	£
(i)	Schedule A position:		
	Premium charged		36,000
	Deduct capital element: 2% × (5 – 1) × 36,000		(2,880)
			33,120
	Deduct allowance for premium paid	50,000	
	Less: 2% × (40 – 1) × 50,000	(39,000)	
		11,000	
	$\frac{5}{40}$ thereof		(1,375)
	Assessable under Schedule A		31,745

(ii)   Capital gains position:

Premium received   36,000

Less: Cost depreciating over 5 years of sub-lease

$$50,000 \times \frac{(91.981 - 87.330)}{95.457}$$ (2,436)

                                                                        33,564
Less: Indexation allowance 2,436 × 0.105   (256)

                                                                        33,308
Deduct amount charged under Schedule A   31,745

Capital gain   1,563

(2)   *Sale of plot of land – June 2003*

Proceeds   80,000
Less: Cost as reduced by small proceeds (15,000 – 12,000)   (3,000)

                                                                        77,000

Less: Indexation allowance

On cost (April 85 – June 03) 15,000 × 0.904   (13,560)

    Less: On small proceeds (May 88 – June 03)
             12,000 × 0.700   8,400

                                                                        71,840

(3)   *Sale of factory – August 2003*

			Cost £	31.3.82 MV £
Proceeds			180,000	180,000
Less:	Cost/31.3.82 MV		(30,000)	(40,000)
	Enhancement	June 1978	(8,000)	N/A
		May 1981	(12,000)	N/A
		August 1990	(8,000)	(8,000)
		September 1998	(15,000)	(15,000)
			107,000	117,000
Less:	Indexation allowance			
	50,000 × 1.281		(64,050)	(64,050)
	8,000 × 0.415		(3,320)	(3,320)
	15,000 × 0.102		(1,530)	(1,530)
			38,100	48,100
Lower gain applies			£38,100	

(4)   *Deferred gain crystallising – September 2003*

August 1995	Gain on building	50,000
	Unreinvested proceeds (200,000 – 180,000)	(20,000)
	Gain deferred	30,000
September 2003	As the reinvestment was made in depreciating assets the gain is merely put in suspense until the plant is either sold or scrapped.	
	Gain crystallising on scrapping	£30,000

Summary

		£
(1)	Sub-lease	1,563
(2)	Land	71,840
(3)	Factory	38,100
(4)	Gain crystallising	30,000
		141,503
Add:	Schedule A amount	31,745
Additional profits for the year to 31.3.04		173,248

Additional CT

With three associated companies (G Ltd + 2 others) the band limits become: £100,000 (£300,000 ÷ 3) and £500,000 (£1,500,000 ÷ 3).

As the profits, other than the amounts calculated, are £200,000 the additional profits are all taxed at the marginal rate of 32.75%.

Additional CT: 173,248 × 32.75% = £56,739

November 2002 Exam Answers

Answer 53 (1 of Exam Paper)

53.1   B

Tutorial note: The basic tax point is the date of despatch but if the payment is made before that date the payment date becomes the actual tax point.

53.2   A

Tutorial note: A 4 part Form P45 is raised when an employee ceases employment. The 3 copies given to the employee show such details as the tax and earnings in the tax year to date. The employee keeps one copy for his own records and is supposed to give the other copies to his new employer.

53.3   C

Tutorial note: The final instalment is always due 3 months and 14 days after the end of the accounting period. However, where the AP is so short that this date falls before the first instalment date (6 months and 13 days from the start of the AP) the tax falls due on the first instalment date (ie 6 months and 13 days after the AP start).

53.4   A

Tutorial note:

	£	£
Personal allowance		4,615
Less: Car taxable benefit	2,400	
Gross equivalent of underpaid tax $110 \times \frac{100}{22}$	500	(2,900)
		1,715
Translates to PAYE code		171L

By restricting the allowances by £500, a basic rate taxpayer effectively pays a further £110 (£500 × 22%) of tax under PAYE.

53.5   D

Tutorial note: To commence an enquiry, the Revenue must issue a written notice within 12 months of the filing date (ie by 30 June 2003) or, if later, within a year of the 31 January, 30 April, 31 July or 31 October following the actual delivery date of the return (ie by 31 October 2004).

53.6   D

Tutorial note: FYA at 40% is only available to a small or medium sized company. As L Ltd's turnover exceeds £11.2 million and its workforce exceeds 250, it is not a medium sized company and therefore does not qualify for FYA. There is a 100% FYA for expenditure on computer equipment but only for small companies.

53.7   C

Tutorial note:

Loan to acquire subsidiary	-	Not for T Ltd's trade so allowable instead under Schedule D Case III.
Bringing a tax appeal to the High Court	-	Not for purposes of trade.
Obtaining planning permission	-	Capital so disallow.

Answer 54 (2 of Exam Paper)

TD Ltd

(a) **REPORT TO THE DIRECTORS**

Re: 1 Trading profits liable to Corporation Tax (CT) for the year to 31 December 2003
2 Main adjustments to profit
3 The company's CT liability for the year to 31 December 2003

Date: 6 April 2004

From: Chief Accountant

1 Trading profit

The final adjusted trading profit for TD Ltd for the year to 31 December 2003 is calculated at £1,310,000 (see Appendix 1). Note that the provisional figure before final adjustments as shown in the Appendix is the profit per the accounts after certain standard tax adjustments. Note also that in the capital allowance computation (Appendix 2) no relief is claimed for first year allowances as the company is not a medium or small company.

2 Main adjustments to profit

I have explained the rules regarding the tax treatment of transactions associated with loans in a separate report. In this section of this report I have explained four of the main non-loan adjustments as follows:

(a) The repairs to the second-hand printing press have to be treated as part of the capital cost of purchase since the press was not acquired in working order. This follows the precedent set many years ago in the Law Shipping case where a newly acquired unseaworthy vessel required a refit before it could be used.

(b) The misappropriation by the senior employee is disallowed following the case of Bamford v ATA Advertising Ltd as the loss does not relate to the company's trading activities. Petty theft by junior employees would normally be an allowable tax expense. The issue is the seniority of the employee.

(c) The UK dividends are not taxable and have therefore been deducted from trading profit. This exemption is logical as the dividends will be paid out of UK company profits which have already been subject to UK CT.

(d) The capital gain is excluded from trading profit although it is subject separately to CT after adjustment for indexation allowance and rollover relief.

3 The company's CT liability

As shown in Appendix 3, the final CT liability for the year to 31 December 2003 is £387,300. This has been reduced by a 20% tax credit under the Corporate Venturing Scheme for the £30,000 investment in an EIS company.

Note that the company pays CT at 30% since it has two associates, albeit non-UK resident, and the small company upper band limit of £1,500,000 has to be divided by three to £500,000.

The company is subject to the quarterly instalment payment regulations as it is due to pay CT at 30% in the current year and was also taxable at the full rate for the previous year. In the previous year there was only one associate but the final profits of £850,000 still exceeded the upper band limit of £750,000 (£1,500,000 ÷ 2).

As the initial estimate of profit for the current year was only £1,000,000 the initial instalments were insufficient. The final instalment is due next week on 14 April and will be adjusted to settle the outstanding balance. I should point out that the Revenue will charge interest on the earlier underpayments and could question why we did not review our estimate of profits as the year progressed. We have a defence in that profit did not out-perform expectation until the final quarter.

Please let me know if I can provide further explanations.

Chief Accountant

Appendix 1 – Adjustment of trading profit for the year to 31 December 2003

		£
Provisional figure for adjusted trading profit		1,320,000
Add back over deducted capital allowances (see Appendix 2)		23,500
		1,343,500
Items charged against financial profits but disallowed for tax purposes (ie add back):		
(B)*	Repairs categorised as capital	40,000
(D)	Legal costs of share issue	12,500
(E)	Misappropriation expense of senior employee	35,000
(F)	Non-trading loan written off	40,000
(H)	Capital cost of share acquisition	30,000
(I)	Loan interest paid for non-trade purpose	28,000
		1,529,000

Items credited to financial profits but not taxable as trading income (ie deduct)		£	
(K)	Non-trading loan interest received	5,000	
(L)	UK dividends received	60,000	
(M)	Capital gain	130,000	
(N)	Letting income	24,000	
			(219,000)
Schedule D Case I profits			1,310,000

*Letters in brackets refer to first draft working Appendix – not included.

Appendix 2 – Computation of capital allowances for the year to 31 December 2003

(i) **General plant**

	General pool £	SLA (1) £	SLA (2) £	Allowances £
Tax wdvs brought forward	650,000	20,000		
Disposal		(25,000)		
Balancing charge		(5,000)		(5,000)
Additions:				
Repairs to second-hand plant	40,000			
New computer			250,000	
	690,000		250,000	
Less: WDA @ 25%	(172,500)		(62,500)	235,000
Tax wdv carried forward at 31.12.03	517,500		187,500	

(ii)   **Expensive cars**

	Car (1) £	Car (2) £	Car (3) £	
Tax wdv brought forward	28,000			
Disposal	(12,000)			
Balancing allowance	16,000			16,000
Additions		32,000	24,000	
Less: WDA (max £3,000)		(3,000)	(3,000)	6,000
Tax wdvs carried forward at 31.12.03		29,000	21,000	
Total of capital allowances				252,000
Allowances incorrectly calculated and used to determine provisional figure of adjusted profits				(275,500)
Over claim of capital allowances				23,500

Appendix 3 – Computation of CT liability for the year to 31 December 2003

	£
Schedule D Case I (Appendix 1)	1,310,000
Schedule A	24,000
Capital gain (Appendix 4, W2)	40,000
	1,374,000
Less: Schedule D Case III deficit (Appendix 4, W1)	(63,000)
Profits chargeable to corporation tax (PCTCT)	1,311,000
Add: UK dividends $60,000 \times \frac{100}{90}$	66,667
Profits for determining rate of CT	1,377,667

There are three associated companies so the upper limit of £1,500,000 is reduced to £500,000. As profits exceed £500,000 the full rate of CT applies.

	£
CT liability £1,311,000 × 30%	393,300
Less: Corporate venturing relief 30,000 × 20%	(6,000)
	387,300

This is due for payment in four equal quarterly instalments commencing 14 July 2003.

The first three payments were based on a profit estimate of £1,000,000 which, at 30%, gives CT of £300,000.

Payment schedule:

14 July 2003	$300,000 \times \frac{1}{4}$	75,000
14 October 2003	$300,000 \times \frac{1}{4}$	75,000
14 January 2004	$300,000 \times \frac{1}{4}$	75,000
14 April 2004	Balance	162,300
		387,300

Appendix 4 – Working notes on non-trading items

1   **Schedule D Case III – non-trading interest**

	£
Interest received	
Loan interest received from supplier	5,000
Interest paid and expenses	
Loan to supplier written off	(40,000)
Interest on loan to buy subsidiary	(28,000)
Schedule D Case III deficit	(63,000)

2   **Capital gain**

Proceeds	340,000
Less: Cost	(220,000)
Unindexed gain	120,000
Less: Indexation allowance: 220,000 × 0.146	(32,120)
	87,880
Proceeds unreinvested (340,000 – 300,000)	40,000
Gain rolled over (balance)	47,880
	87,880
Gain remaining chargeable	40,000

(b)   **REPORT TO THE DIRECTORS**

Re: Tax treatment of loan related transactions

Date: 6 April 2004

From: Chief Accountant

Background

Where a company borrows or lends money in virtually any form – eg bank loan, overdraft, debenture, loan stock, casual borrowing to or from directors – any expense or income arising therefrom is subject to the loan relationship rules.

If the borrowing relates to a trading purpose, any debit or credit is dealt with under Schedule D Case I on a normal accruals basis. Otherwise debits and credits are dealt with under Schedule D Case III, also on an accruals basis.

Specific treatment of items in the 31 December 2003 accounts

1   The loan interest of £15,000 paid to a UK finance company on the loan to buy plant and machinery is allowed as a trading expense as it is clearly for a trading purpose.

2   The costs of raising this loan are similarly allowed as a trading expense. Strictly we should write this off over the period of the loan.

3   The loan of £40,000 to the UK supplier which had to be written off is categorised as a non-trading loan because TD Ltd does not conduct a trade of money lending. The loan may have been made in the course of trading but it is not strictly a trading loan. The write-off and the interest of £5,000 received is therefore dealt with under Schedule D Case III.

4   Similarly, the loan to acquire a controlling interest in the French subsidiary is not for a trading purpose – the company is not trading in shareholdings. The interest payable is therefore debited under Schedule D Case III.

In respect of the non-trading loans there is a deficit. This is allowed against the company's total income for the same year. You might comment therefore that it has made no practical difference in our situation as to where the debits and credits are shown!

Please let me know if I can provide further details.

Chief Accountant

Answer 55 (3 of Exam Paper)

Hols Ltd

(a)   **Computation of Class 1A NIC**

    1   **The Manager**

If the refurbishment cost of £8,000 relates to redecoration and repairs, there should be no benefit charge on the employee.

However, if the £8,000 cost relates to furniture, there would be a benefit charge of £8,000 × 20% = £1,600 for a full year.

It is reasonable to assume the manager has to live in, so the accommodation is job related and there is therefore no charge for the use of the flat.

The relocation expenses are exempt from a benefit charge for qualifying expenses up to £8,000. The excess (£4,000) is an assessable benefit. Although the costs appear to be reimbursed to the manager and would normally fall under Class 1 NIC, this could be difficult to administer as Class 1 is not charged on a cumulative basis. Instead, the legislation provides for the benefit to be charged under Class 1A.

Summary

	£
Refurbishment (unless mere decoration)	1,600
Excess relocation expenses	4,000
	5,600
Class 1A @ 12.8%	£717

    2   **The Senior Chef**

Class 1A is 12.8% of the value of his benefits as calculated for income tax:

	£
Excess relocation expenses (10,000 – 8,000)	2,000
Gross annual value of house	12,000
Expensive accommodation charge (140,000 – 75,000) × 5%	3,250
Interest free loan: 8,000 × 5%	400
Maintenance and heating costs	5,000
	22,650
Class 1A @ 12.8%	£2,899

As the house is not job-related accommodation, the accommodation charge applies (12,000 + 3,250) and the running costs are not limited to 10% of his other remuneration and benefits.

3   **The Assistant Chef**

Taking a simplistic view, the £7,000 accommodation cost is probably exempt if it relates solely to the GAV. However, if any part relates to running costs, leasing, etc there would be a benefit charge limited to 10% of this remuneration. We are not told this figure so assume the full £7,000 is exempt.

The school fees of £6,000 would be assessable under Class 1 if the contract for the education was between the school and the Assistant Chef. In this case the company is discharging the employee's liability and the normal Class 1 charge arises. However if, as is very unlikely in practice, the school agrees to contract directly with the employer the charge would be under Class 1A.

Relocation expenses of £5,000 fall within the £8,000 benefit exemption, therefore would not be liable to Class 1A (or Class 1). This assumes that the expenses qualify. Not all types of relocation expenses count.

Summary

School fees (assume) £6,000 × 12.8%   £768 Class 1A

4   **Free meals to staff**

If all members of staff are provided with free meals on broadly similar terms, there is no assessable benefit so there can be no Class 1A charge.

Summary

1	The Manager	717
2	The Senior Chef	2,899
3	The Assistant Chef	768
	Total Class 1A	4,384

(b)   **Reporting and paying Class 1A**

The company is required to submit a form P11D(b) by 6 July following the tax year (ie by 6 July 2004 for 2003/04). The form shows the total of the figures in the 'Class 1A boxes' of Forms P11D for all the P11D employees. Just a raw total which, at 12.8%, gives the Class 1A NIC due. Strictly, the benefits themselves are reported on Forms P11D due also by 6 July following the tax year.

The Class 1A NIC is then payable by 19 July following the tax year (ie by 19 July 2004 for 2003/04).

Answer 56 (4 of Exam Paper)

New Ltd

Computation of corporation tax for the first three periods

	Year to 30 June 2002 £	3 months to 30 Sept 2002 £	Year to 30 Sept 2003 £	Year to 30 Sept 2004 £
Schedule D Case I 12:3; (W1)	748,000	187,000	–	870,000
Less: S393(1) relief (W2)				(370,000)
				500,000
Less: S393A(1) relief (W2)	(561,000)	(187,000)		
	187,000	–		
Less: Non-trade charges				
Gift Aid	(20,000)	–		(15,000)
PCTCT	167,000	–		485,000
CT @ 19%/30%	31,730			145,500
Less: $^{11}/_{400}$ (1,500,000 – 485,000)				(27,912)
Corporation tax payable	31,730			117,588
Due date				1 July 2005
CT originally due (W3)	197,170	50,930		
CT repayable	165,440	50,930		

Workings

1 Adjustment of trading results

	15 months to 30 September 2002 £	Year to 30 September 2003 £	Year to 30 September 2004 £
Trading profit/(loss)	900,000	(1,100,000)	860,000
Add: Patent royalties receivable	65,000	12,000	40,000
Deduct: Patent royalties payable	(30,000)	(30,000)	(30,000)
Adjusted trading results	935,000	(1,118,000)	870,000

Tutorial note:

From 1 April 2002 patent royalties paid or received are dealt with for tax purposes in line with their accounting treatment – ie the accruals basis. Provided they are paid or received for a trading purpose, they are debited or credited to trading profits under Schedule D Case I (otherwise they are dealt with under Schedule D Case VI).

2   **Loss memorandum**

		£
Year to 30 September 2003 (W1)		1,118,000
Less:	Used under S393A(1)	
	3 months to 30.9.02	(187,000)
	9 months to 30.6.02 $\frac{9}{12}$ × 748,000	(561,000)
		370,000
Less:	Used under S393(1) in year to 30.9.03	(370,000)
		-

3   **Corporation tax originally payable**

	Year to 30 June 2002 £	3 months to 30 Sept 2002 £
Total profits	748,000	187,000
Less: Gift Aid	(20,000)	-
	728,000	187,000
CT @ 30%	218,400	56,100
Less: $\frac{11}{400}$ (1,500,000 – 728,000)	(21,230)	
$\frac{11}{400}$ (375,000 – 187,000)		(5,170)
	197,170	50,930
Due date	1 April 2003	1 July 2003

Answer 57 (5 of Exam Paper)

H Ltd and S Ltd

(a)   (i)   **Computation of Schedule A amount for the year to 30 September 2004**

1 October 2001 – Grant of lease

	£
Premium	60,000
Less: 2% (20 – 1)	(22,800)
Schedule A charge on H Ltd	37,200

S Ltd is entitled to an annual deduction of 37,200/20 = £1,860.

1 October 2003 – Grant of sub-lease

		£
Premium		15,000
Less:	2% (5 – 1)	(1,200)
		13,800
Less:	$\frac{5}{20} \times 37,200$	(9,300)
		4,500
Add:	Rent receivable for the year to 30 September 2004	12,000
		16,500
Less:	Rent payable by S Ltd on lead lease	(20,000)
Schedule A loss		(3,500)

(ii)   On the grant of a short lease, 2% of the premium for every complete year that the lease can last is treated as a capital receipt. The balance is taxed as income.

The 'cost' is found by valuing the landlord's interest in the property immediately after the lease is granted. This is known as the freehold reversionary interest and takes account, inter alia, of the future stream of rents receivable under the lease.

The proportion of 'cost' to apply against the capital receipt is given by the following formula.

$$\frac{\text{Capital element of premium}}{\text{Total premium + Freehold reversionary value}}$$

(b)   **REPORT TO THE DIRECTORS**

Re: Group VAT registration matters

Date: 8 November 2004

From: Chartered management accountant

Introduction

The company intends to acquire a number of other UK companies and requires a report on the most efficient way of organising the group's VAT registration.

Background

Where companies are under common control they can be covered by a single VAT registration. In this case Customs treat the representative member as the registered person and require a single VAT return per period covering all the companies within the VAT group. This has the advantage of needing fewer VAT returns and avoids the need for VAT on inter-company sales. There is a practical disadvantage in that the VAT return may be difficult to complete on time if the accounting records are diverse. This can be minimised if the representative member provides the central accounting function but may still be dependent on information from the subsidiaries.

There is no requirement to include all the companies within the group registration. For example, if a group company is in a repayment position (eg where it exports all its output), it should remain outside the VAT group and elect for a monthly return period. However, the cash flow advantage should be balanced against the extra administration.

There is another consideration where a company makes only exempt supplies. Including it within the group registration could enable its input VAT to be recovered and would avoid irrecoverable VAT on a management charge to the company. However, its inclusion in the VAT group could result in the group losing VAT recovery under the partial exemption rules. The figures would have to be considered before including an exempt company.

Customs have powers to control the entry to and exit from VAT groups to prevent the rules being manipulated to avoid VAT.

Recommendation

A group registration should include all companies making taxable supplies (standard or zero rated) although consideration should be given to excluding companies which are in a regular VAT repayment position. Whether or not to include companies which make only exempt supplies would depend on their impact on the group's partial exemption position.

Please let me know if I can provide further details.

Chartered Management Accountant

Answer 58 (6 of Exam Paper)

E Ltd

Computation of capital gains for the year ended 31 March 2004

Charge on leaving group within 6 years of earlier inter-company transfer:

	£
Proceeds (MV at transfer)	350,000
Less: Cost (March 1992)	(200,000)
	150,000
Less: Indexation allowance 200,000 × 0.200	(40,000)
Chargeable gain	110,000

This gain crystallises in the AP in which E Ltd leaves the group (ie when parent company's holding falls below 75%).

1 **31 July 2003 – Sale of 30,000 K Ltd shares**

FA 1985 pool:

		No	Cost £	Indexed cost £
May 1990	Purchase	15,000	40,000	40,000
June 1990	1 for 2 bonus	7,500	-	-
		22,500		
June 1996	Indexed rise £40,000 × 0.212			8,480
				48,480
	Purchase	5,000	15,000	15,000
		27,500	55,000	63,480
July 2003	Indexed rise 63,480 × 0.182			11,553
				75,033
	Sale	(27,500)	(55,000)	(75,033)
		-	-	-

Capital gain:

Proceeds	$^{27,500}/_{30,000} \times 120,000$		110,000
Less:	Cost		(55,000)
			55,000
Less:	Indexation allowance (75,033 – 55,000)		(20,033)
			34,967

Balance of disposal from FA 1982 holding:

		No	Cost	31.3.82 MV
Jan 1980	Purchase	5,000	6,000	
Jan 1982	Purchase	10,000	15,000	
Jun 1990	1 for 2 bonus	7,500	-	
		22,500	21,000	31,500 (@1.40)
July 2002	Sale	(2,500)	(2,333)	(3,500)
		20,000	18,667	28,000

Proceeds	$^{2,500}/_{30,000} \times 120,000$	10,000
Less:	31.3.82 MV (clearly applies)	(3,500)
		6,500
Less:	Indexation allowance 3,500 × 1.277	(4,470)
		2,030

2 **30 September 2003 – Sale of warehouse**

Disposal in March 1986:

Proceeds		60,000
Less:	Cost	(30,000)
		30,000
Less:	Indexation allowance 30,000 × 0.218	(6,540)
Gain rolled over		23,460

Disposal in September 2003

		£	£
Proceeds			180,000
Less:	Cost	60,000	
Less:	Half gain rolled over 23,460	(11,730)	
			(48,270)
			131,730
Less:	Indexation allowance 48,270 × 0.875		(42,236)
			89,494

3   **25 December 2003 – Gift of painting**

This would be exempt provided the gallery is maintained by a local authority (or university). The question is somewhat ambiguous on this point but it is assumed the examiner meant the gallery to be an appropriate recipient for the gift to be exempt.

Disposal by a fellow subsidiary in October 2003

The question states that E Ltd leaves the group in the year to 31 March 2004. If its actual leaving occurred after H Ltd realised the £30,000 loss, it would be possible for E Ltd and H Ltd to elect that the disposal had been made by E Ltd – effectively transferring the loss to E Ltd. It is assumed that the examiner intended this to be possible.

Summary

		£	£
Crystallised gain			110,000
K Ltd shares	FA 1985 pool	34,967	
	1982 holding	2,030	
			36,997
Sale of warehouse			89,494
Gift to gallery			-
Less: From H Ltd			(30,000)
			206,491

(b)   **Corporation tax payable on chargeable gains**

There are 6 associated companies so the upper limit is 1,500,000 ÷ 6 = 250,000.

Gains attract CT as follows:

		£
250,000 – 120,000 =	130,000 × 32.75%	42,575
	76,491 × 30%	22,947
	206,491	
Additional CT		65,522

May 2003 Exam Answers

Answer 59 (1 of Exam Paper)

59.1 **A**

		£
Benefits:	GAV	15,000
	Expensive charge: $(200,000 - 75,000) \times 5\%$	6,250
		21,250
	Less: contribution 500×12	(6,000)
		15,250
	Add Council Tax	2,500
		17,750

59.2 **C**

59.3 **D**

$(25,000 + 3,000) = 28,000 \times 28\% \ (15\% + 3\% + (205 - 155) \times \frac{1}{5})$

59.4 **D**

$4,615 - 3,300 - (80 \times \dfrac{100}{40}) = 1,115 \therefore 111L$

59.5 **C**

If the return is delivered after the filing date the enquiry time limit is 12 months from the 31 January, 30 April, 31 July or 31 October whichever next follows the day the return was delivered.

59.6 **A**

From 1 April 2002, patent royalties payable are allowed as a trading expense assuming they are paid for the purpose of the trade. The debenture interest payable is allowed as the loan was taken out for a trading purpose. However the loan to acquire a subsidiary does not count as a trading loan – the interest payable is allowed instead under Schedule D Case III.

59.7 **B**

The final instalment is always due three months and 14 days after the end of the AP.
It is $240,000 - 2 \times (240,000 \times \frac{3}{8}) = £60,000$.

59.8   **D**

$$\text{Portion recoverable} = \frac{\text{Taxable supplies}}{\text{Total supplies}} = \frac{30,000}{36,000}$$

59.9   **D**

	General Pool £	Jaguar Car £	Bentley Car £	CA Total £
01/04/03 Tax wdvs b/f	840,000	11,000	48,000	
Disposal			(24,000)	
Balancing allowance			24,000	24,000
100% FYA on new low emission cars				45,000
WDA @ 25%	(210,000)	(2,750)		212,750
	630,000	8,250		281,750

59.10   **C**

Nine months to 30 September 2003 straddles FY02 and FY03 but separate calculations are not required as rates unchanged.

Starting rate limits:

$10,000 \times \dfrac{9}{12} \times \dfrac{1}{2}$	3,750
$50,000 \times \dfrac{9}{12} \times \dfrac{1}{2}$	18,750

CT:

$9,000 \times 19\%$	1,710
Less $\dfrac{19}{400} \times (18,750 - 9,000)$	(463)
	1,247

Answer 60 (2 of Exam Paper)

BJD Ltd

REPORT

To:	Mr D
Re:	Taxation matters raised in a meeting in January 2004
Date:	25 January 2004
From:	Chief Accountant

The purpose of this report is to supply the figure for the corporation tax (CT) liability for BJD Ltd for the year just ended and to cover certain other specific taxation matters raised at a meeting earlier this month.

1   CT liability for the year to 31 December 2003

As shown in Appendix 1, I calculate the CT liability for BJD Ltd for the year to 31 December 2003 to be £58,276. As we discussed earlier, although you own 75% of TEC Ltd as well as a 60% holding in BJD Ltd, there is no scope to claim relief in BJD Ltd for TEC Ltd's trading losses. However, because you have a controlling interest in both companies, they are treated for tax purposes as 'associated' and therefore the CT rate band limits have to be divided by two.

If BJD Ltd had no associates it would only pay CT at 19% on its current level of profits (ie £236,000 × 19% = £44,840). Your holding of TEC Ltd has resulted in an extra CT liability in BJD Ltd of approximately £13,500.

You should note that the income tax of £4,400 deducted from the patent royalties received from individuals during the year may be deducted from your corporation tax liability, leaving tax payable of £53,876. This is due for payment by 1 October 2004.

2   Short-term interest free loan to your son

A short-term interest free loan of £40,000 to your son to be repaid during the current year will require reporting on his form P11D as he is an employee of the company. His employment income benefit is based on the interest foregone, and will be calculated at the rate of 5% while the loan remains outstanding. The income tax would probably be collected by restricting his PAYE code although it could be collected through self-assessment.

The company will be liable to a Class 1A NIC charge calculated at 12.8% of the amount of the benefit. This is payable by 19 July following the tax year of the benefit. Thus if the loan is made before 5 April 2004 but not repaid until after that date there will be a benefit for 2003/04 and a benefit for 2004/05, and a Class 1A liability for both of those years.

BJD Ltd is a close company, being controlled by its directors, and a loan made to a participator (ie a shareholder) will therefore attract a liability to 'penalty' tax. This is an enforced loan to the Revenue equal to 25% of the amount of the loan. However, this is only payable nine months after the accounting period (AP) in which the loan is made and if the loan is repaid before the tax falls due, the liability to pay the tax is cancelled. Therefore if the loan is made in 2004 and repaid by 30 September 2005 there is no penalty tax to pay. I would stress that if the loan is not repaid until after that date, the tax is payable in full and is only refunded nine months after the end of the AP in which the loan is repaid.

3   Research and development (R&D) expenditure

Expenditure on R&D by a small or medium sized company enjoys a tax incentive. The company is entitled to deduct 150% of the expenditure as a trading expense. Your intended expenditure in 2004 appears to meet the criteria for this uplift. The company has less than 250 employees and a turnover of less than £25 million so fits the size definition. There is a minimum qualifying spend of £10,000 but as £50,000 expenditure is intended again the condition for the uplift is met. Note however that the expenditure must be on staff costs and consumables and must relate to the company's trade.

4   Overseas branch or subsidiary

♦   *As an overseas branch.* A branch (UK or overseas) is just an extension of BJD Ltd's existing activities so that any trading profits or losses would be automatically included in BJD Ltd's chargeable profits as they arise regardless of whether they are remitted to the UK. The company would be entitled to capital allowances on the expenditure on plant etc for use in the overseas branch subject to the normal capital allowance rules. Any foreign tax paid would be allowed as a credit against the corporation tax liability on the branch income. Unrelieved foreign tax may be carried forward for relief against future tax liabilities on the branch profits.

♦   *As an overseas subsidiary.* An overseas (ie non-resident) subsidiary is a separate entity in its own right. Careful steps would have to be taken for the company to be non-resident. It would have to be incorporated overseas and not controlled from the UK This requires its 'central management and control' to be located outside the UK and would normally require directors to hold board meetings overseas.

The profits of an overseas subsidiary would only be subject to UK CT when they were remitted as a dividend to the UK (under Schedule DV). The underlying foreign tax would be allowed as a credit against the UK CT, with any excess foreign tax being carried forward for future relief.

As the foreign tax rate is higher than the UK CT rate at present, the overseas company would not be treated as a controlled foreign company (CFC). However, if the overseas rate fell below 75% of the UK CT rate the CFC provisions could apply. BJD Ltd would then be taxed on the subsidiary's profits as they arose as they would be notionally apportioned to the company. They would be taxed at the full 30% rate although credit would be given for foreign tax paid by the subsidiary.

♦   *Choice of commencement date.* If a subsidiary starts trading before 31 December 2004 BJD Ltd will have a further subsidiary and would have further reduced CT band limits. As shown above, at current profit levels, this can have a significant effect on the company's rate of CT. If the choice is between starting just before the current year end or just after, the latter is to be preferred for its effect on BJD Ltd's tax rate.

If the unit starts trading as a branch, it may be advisable to set it up before 31 December 2004 so that tax relief for the set up costs is obtained against the UK profits of the year to 31 December 2004.

It is possible to commence as a branch and to incorporate the business at a later stage when it has become profitable.

5   Proposed acquisition of a non-resident company

Usually a controlled foreign company is thought of as a company controlled by UK resident persons. However, a foreign company can still be a CFC if a UK resident and a non-UK resident control the company between them and

♦   The UK resident holds at least 40% of the joint holding and

♦   The non-UK resident holds at least 40% but not more than 55% of their joint holding.

If the proposal proceeds as planned, BJD Ltd will hold 40% and Z Ltd, a non-UK resident will hold another 40%. Control is held between the two companies and as each has 50% of the joint 80% holding the CFC provisions potentially come into play.

As the foreign CT rate that the target company will pay is clearly less than 75% of the corresponding UK rate, the CFC rules apply and 40% of the company's profits will be apportioned to BJD Ltd. BJD Ltd will have to self-assess these profits, pay UK CT at 30% regardless of its level of profits but it will be entitled to a corresponding apportioned foreign tax credit.

There are five exclusion tests under which apportionment of the CFC's profits is not required:

♦   If the overseas company distributes at least 90% of its profits within 18 months of the end of the profit period;

- If it is engaged in exempt activities – ie, conducts at least 50% of its business with unconnected persons;

- At least 35% of its shares are publicly owned (clearly not here);

- Profits are less than £50,000 pa; or

- Avoidance of UK tax was not the main purpose of setting up the company.

I trust this report covers all the questions you have raised but please let me know if you require further information.

Chief Accountant

APPENDIX 1

Corporation tax liability of BJD Ltd for the year to 31 December 2003

		£	£
Schedule D Case I Profit			254,000
Schedule A			18,000
Capital gain		80,000	
	less capital loses brought forward	(95,000)	
	Excess capital losses carried forward	(15,000)	-
			272,000
Less	Schedule D Case III deficit:		
	Interest receivable	6,000	
	Loan written off	(30,000)	(24,000)
			248,000
Less:	Gift Aid		(12,000)
PCTCT			236,000
Add:	FII		20,000
Profits			256,000

CT rate:

Mr D controls BJD Ltd and TEC Ltd therefore there are two 'associated' companies and the band limits are halved.

GCT:	$236,000 \times 30\%$	70,800
	Less: $\dfrac{11}{400}(750,000 - 256,000) \times \dfrac{236}{256}$	(12,524)
CT liability		58,276
Less:	Income tax suffered $20,000 \times 22\%$	(4,400)
MCT payable on 1 October 2004		53,876

Note: it is assumed that the patent royalties were received as trading income. If not, they would instead be assessed under Schedule D Case VI, although this does not alter the CT liability.

Answer 61 (3 of Exam Paper)

G Ltd

(a)   *Computation for the manager*

(i)   *Cash position of using own car*

		£	£
Additional income:			
Salary £300 × 12			3,600
Mileage allowance 20,000 × 20p			4,000
			7,600
Deductions:			
Income tax: Salary	3,600		
Expense allowance under AMAP			
10,000 × (40 – 20)	(2,000)		
10,000 × (25 – 20)	(500)		
	1,100		
IT : 40%	440		
Lease costs	3,600		
Insurance and repairs	1,200		
Petrol $\dfrac{24,000}{35} \times £3.50$	2,400		
Class 1 NIC 3,600 × 1%	36		
			7,676
Net cost of using own car			76

(ii)   *Cash position of being supplied with a company car*

	£
Car benefit £18,000 × 24%	4,320
Fuel benefit £14,400 × 24%	3,456
	7,776
Income tax @ 40%	3,110

(iii)   *Conclusion*

The manager will save over £3,000 pa if he chooses to use his own car rather than a company car.

(b)   *Computation for the directors*

(i)   *Cost of paying manager to use his own car*   £

Salary	3,600
Class 1 NIC : 12.8%	461
Mileage allowance	4,000
	8,061
Less: CT : 19%	(1,532)
Net annual cost to the company	6,529

(ii)   *Cost of providing a company car*

It is assumed that the company leases the car and incurs the same running costs as would apply if the manager himself provided the car. Otherwise a number of assumptions would have to be made if the company bought the car – eg intended length of ownership, resale value etc.

Lease costs	3,600
Insurance and repairs	1,200
Petrol	2,400
Class 1A on car/fuel benefit 7,776 × 12.8%	995
	8,195

Amount on which CT relief given is restricted for 'expensive car' leasing:

Disallow: $3,600 \times \dfrac{\frac{1}{2}(18,000-12,000)}{18,000} = £600$

CT relief: 8,195 – 600 = 7,595 × 19%	(1,443)
Net cost to company	6,752

(iii)   *Conclusion*

The costs of the two alternatives are fairly close – just a £200 odd advantage if the employee uses his own car. From both the company's viewpoint and the manager's viewpoint it would be beneficial if the manager provided his own car.

Tutorial note:

The examiner's answer did not make the (albeit minor) adjustment for 'expensive car leasing' when calculating the CT relief (see part (b) (ii) above), although this does not alter the overall conclusion.

Answer 62 (4 of Exam Paper)

CCD Ltd

(a)   *Capital allowances computation*

    (i)   Plant and machinery

	General pool £	Jaguar car £	BMW car £	SLA £	CA Total £
Tax wdvs b/f 1.1.03	740,000	18,000	34,000	25,000	
Less disposals	(21,000)	(12,000)	(28,000)	(4,000)	
Balancing allowances		6,000	6,000	21,000	33,000
	719,000				
WDA @ 25% × $\frac{10}{12}$	(149,792)				149,792
	569,208				
Additions with 100% FYA					
08.01.03					45,000
11.04.03					16,000
24.04.03					18,000
Addition with 40% FYA	60,000				
Less: 40% FYA	(24,000)				24,000
Tax wdv c/f 31.10.03	605,208				
					285,792

    (ii)   Flat conversion allowances: 120,000 × 100%   120,000

    (iii)   Industrial buildings allowance:

First factory   £

		£
AP to 31.12.99		
Qualifying cost		210,000
Less WDA 4%		(8,400)
AP to 31.12.00	WDA 4%	(8,400)
AP to 31.12.02	Notional WDAs 2 × 4%	(16,800)
AP to 31.10.03	Tax wdv b/f	176,400
Net cost 210,000 – 180,000		30,000

Adjusted net cost:

Net cost × $\dfrac{\text{Industrial usage}}{\text{Total ownership}} = 30,000 \times \dfrac{2\frac{1}{2}}{4\frac{1}{2}} =$ 16,667

Compare to IBAs given   16,800

Balancing charge   133   (133)

Second factory:

Original qualifying cost	£140,000	

(less than second-hand price)
Tax life of building remaining
25 – 13½ = 11½ years

WDA = $140{,}000 \times \dfrac{1}{11\frac{1}{2}}$ = £12,174 pa

For 10 months AP: $12{,}174 \times \dfrac{10}{12}$ 10,145

Total of allowances   415,804

Tutorial note:

The examiner comes to a slightly different answer because he puts the low emission car into a separate column as an 'expensive car'. As it is sold in the AP of purchase for £1,000 (£16,000 - £15,000) less than cost, he arrives at a balancing allowance of £1,000. By contrast the above answer allocates 100% FYA and, as the car is a general pool item, sets the £15,000 proceeds against the general pool. This is correct because S.74(2) (c) CAA 2001 specifically exempts low emission cars from the 'expensive car' single asset pool treatment.

(b)   *Treatment of low emission cars and new computer*

The company is a medium sized company as its turnover on an annual basis is £9.6 million (£8 $\times \dfrac{12}{10}$) which is less than the £11.2 million limit and the number of employees are less than 250.

However, the company is not small as the 'small' turnover and staff limits are £2.8 million and 50.

Low emission cars registered on or after 17 April 2002 attract 100% FYA regardless of the size of company.

A computer only attracts 100% FYA if purchased by a small company. As the company is medium sized it qualifies for 40% FYA as on all plant. It would be possible to elect for short life asset treatment on the computer and whether or not this is an advantage should be reviewed before the two year time limit elapses. No advantage applies in the AP of purchase so a SLA election can be ignored for the current AP.

Answer 63 (5 of Exam Paper)

PGD Ltd

(a)   *Computation of gains chargeable for the year ended 31 March 2004*

Gain on building crystallising when PGD Ltd de-grouped

Gain as at October 1999:	£
Market value	200,000
Less: cost (May 1995)	(140,000)
	60,000
Less: indexation allowance 140,000 × 0.113	(15,820)
	44,180

Other disposals

(1) August 2003 – Sale of 10,000 TD Ltd shares.

Share history:

April 1987: 2,000 shares cost £2,400

May 1997: Reorganised:

	Value £	Cost apportioned £
12,000 50p ords : 2.20	26,400	2,018
5,000 25p prefs : 60p	3,000	229
£1,000 5% debentures	2,000	153
	31,400	2,400

Proceeds:	36,000
Less: cost $\frac{10}{12} \times 2,018$	(1,682)
	34,318
Less: indexation allowance $1,682 \times 0.780$	(1,312)
	33,006

(2) November 2003 – Sale of marble statue

	£
Proceeds (deemed)	6,000
Less: cost	8,000
Allowable loss	2,000

(Indexation allowance cannot increase a loss)

(3) December 2003 – sale of land (part disposal)

Proceeds	280,000
Less cost: $60,000 \times \dfrac{280,000}{280,000 + 160,000}$	(38,182)
	241,818
Less: indexation allowance $38,182 \times 0.921$	(35,166)
	206,652

Total gains: (44,180 + 33,006 + 206,652 – 2,000)	£281,838

(b)   *Deferral of gains*

Gains on land and buildings can be rolled over against the cost of business assets acquired in the period 12 months before to 3 years after the disposal.

The asset sold must have been used for the purpose of the disposing company's trade and the asset acquired must similarly be used from acquisition for the acquirer's trade.

The company acquired a building in March 2004 for £210,000. Assuming this building is to be used for PGD Ltd's trade and the building on which the gain crystallised is also used for the trade all the gain can be rolled over. The gain is deemed to crystallise at the start of the period in which PGD Ltd leaves the group (ie falls below 75% owned) – 1 April 2003.

However, if the landscaped gardens had been occupied by PGD Ltd for the purpose of its trade the gain could instead be rolled over. As only £210,000 is reinvested, leaving £70,000 (£280,000 - £210,000) of surplus proceeds, £70,000 of the gain cannot be rolled over.

This still leaves £136,652 (£206,652 - £70,000) rolled over which is preferable to rolling over all the 'crystallised' gain of £44,180. The roll over claim depends therefore on whether the gardens can be said to be occupied for the trade.

Answer 64 (6 of Exam Paper)

O Ltd

(a)   *Computation of CT payable for the year ended 31 March 2004*

	UK profits £	X SA £	Y Inc £	Z PG £
			---- overseas profits ----	
Schedule A	25,000			
Schedule DV (WN1)		180,000	200,000	187,500
Gains	30,000			
	55,000			
Less: s393A(1)	(55,000)	(95,000)		
	-	85,000	200,000	187,500
Less: Gift Aid	-	(5,000)	-	-
	-	80,000	200,000	187,500
GCT @ 30% (WN2)		24,000	60,000	56,250
Less: Double tax relief (WN1)		(18,000)	(56,000)	(56,250)
UK CT payable : total £10,000	Nil	6,000	4,000	Nil

The S393A(1) relief has been set primarily against UK income, and then against the foreign income with the lowest rate of DTR. Similarly, the Gift Aid is set against the UK income with the lowest rate of DTR.

(b)   *Controlled foreign companies*

A non-UK resident company would be identified as a controlled foreign company (CFC) if over 50% of its share capital was held by the UK resident persons and the foreign corporation tax on its profits is less than 75% of the amount which would have been payable if the company had been UK resident.

There are exclusions from CFC treatment – principally if the overseas company has an acceptable distribution policy, ie it distributes at least 90% of its profits within 18 months of the end of a profit period.

If a company is a CFC, its profits are notionally apportioned to the UK resident shareholders in proportion to the shareholdings. This only applies where the UK resident has 25% or more entitlement to profits. As none of the three companies shown are held at this level, no apportionment would apply to O Ltd.

Working notes

1 *Schedule DV income*

	X SA £	Y Inc £	Z PG £
Net dividend	162,000	144,000	120,000
Add withholding tax (WHT)			
$\frac{10}{90}$; $\frac{28}{72}$; $\frac{20}{80}$	18,000	56,000	30,000
	180,000	200,000	150,000
Add underlying tax (ULT)	n/a	n/a	
$\frac{150,000}{960,000} \times 240,000$			37,500
Foreign tax credit available	18,000	56,000	67,500
Overseas tax rate	10%	28%	36%

2 *UK corporation tax rate*

There are five associated companies so the small company marginal relief bands are reduced to:

Lower limit   300,000 ÷ 5 =   £60,000

Upper limit 1,500,000 ÷ 5 =   £300,000

Profits chargeable £467,500 (80,000 + 200,000 + 187,500) exceed the upper limit so the full 30% rate applies.

November 2003 Exam Answers

SECTION A

Answer 65 (1 of Exam Paper)

65.1 **B**

			£
Turnover	Oct 2003 – Jan 2004	4 × £7,000	28,000
	Feb 2004 – Apr 2004	3 × £10,000	30,000
			58,000

N Ltd exceeded the threshold of £56,000 on 30 April 2004, must notify Customs by 30 May 2004 and will be registered from 1 June 2004.

65.2 **C**

			£
Personal allowance			4,615
Add:	Professional subscription		200
			4,815
Less:	Unpaid tax	£220 × 100/22	(1,000)
			3,815

Code 381L

65.3 **A**

		£
CT due for year		500,000
Instalments due 14 Oct 2003, 14 Jan 2004 and 14 Apr 2004		
	¾ x £500,000	375,000
Less:	Paid	(300,000)
Due 14 Apr 2004		75,000

65.4 **B**

		£
(i)	Trading purposes	-
(ii)	Interest paid	(15,000)
	Costs of securing loan	(2,000)
(iii)	Interest received	8,000
(iv)	Bad debt	(50,000)
	Collection costs	(3,000)
Non-trade loan deficit		(62,000)

65.5   **D**

	£
PCTCT	160,000
FII	10,000
Profits	170,000
Small companies lower limit £300,000/2 =	£150,000
Small companies upper limit £1,500,000/2 =	£750,000
CT £160,000 × 30%	48,000
Less: SCMR	
(750,000 – 170,000) × 160,000/170,000 × 11/400	(15,012)
	32,988

65.6   **C**

	£	Pool £	Expensive Car £	Capital Allowances £
Tax WDV b/f		36,000	13,000	
Disposal			(8,000)	
Balancing allowance			5,000	5,000
WDA @ 25%		(9,000)		9,000
Additions with 40% FYA	16,000			
FYA @ 40%	(6,400)			6,400
		9,600		
Additions with 100% FYA				
Computer	12,000			
Low emission car	14,000			
FYA @ 100%	(26,000)			26,000
		-		
		36,600		46,400

65.7   **A**

65.8   **A**

No taxable benefit arises as the maximum loan outstanding for each employee does not exceed £5,000, so no Class 1A NICs are due.

65.9   **B**

The filing date for the return is 30 June 2004. the return is over three months late.

65.10 **C**

		£
First	10,000 miles @ 40p	4,000
Balance	10,000 miles @ 25p	2,500
		6,500
Less:	Paid 20,000 miles @ 15p	(3,000)
Deduction		3,500

SECTION B

Answer 66 (2 of Exam Paper)

R Ltd

REPORT TO THE DIRECTORS OF R LTD

(i) **Corporation tax liability of R Ltd, year ended 31 March 2004**

The corporation tax payable by R Ltd for the year to 31 March 2004 is £192,600, as shown in appendix 1.

The computation assumes that a joint election is made with S Ltd that S Ltd should be treated as if it had disposed of the shares in V Ltd. The consequence of the election is that the gain of £29,760 (working 1) arises in S Ltd. S Ltd has capital losses brought forward of £50,000 which can be set off against the gain arising. The losses remaining unused of £20,240 are carried forward for relief in future accounting periods.

The computation also assumes that R Ltd has claimed R&D tax relief. R Ltd is a member of a group which is a small or medium sized enterprise under EU law (less than 250 employees and turnover less than €40 million) and may claim a deduction of 150% of qualifying R&D expenditure.

The computation also allows a deduction for the patent fees paid of £8,000. If these were paid for trading purposes, the deduction is made from trading income. Otherwise a deduction is allowed from profits generally for any deficit on non-trading intangibles. In this case there is no difference in the deduction allowed in this instance.

There is also a deduction of £20,000 for the irrecoverable loan to the supplier. The deduction is made from interest and other profits from non-trading loans. Any overall deficit may be deducted from profits generally. If there were no interest and profits on non-trading loans it would be possible to group relieve the deficit. This would achieve a tax saving if group relief were claimed by S Ltd as tax relief would be obtained at S Ltd's marginal tax rate of 32.75% compared to R Ltd's marginal tax rate of 30%.

(ii) **Quarterly payment system**

R Ltd is a "large" company as it pays corporation tax at the full rate and so is required to pay its corporation tax by instalments. A company is not required to pay by instalments in the first year that it become large, but this is not the case here as instalments were payable for the previous year.

The instalments are payable on the 14th day of months 7 and 10 in the accounting period, and of months 1 and 4 following the accounting period. They must be based on the directors' best estimate of the corporation tax payable for the year.

At 14 October 2003, the date of the first instalment, the estimated profits were £600,000, and the corporation tax liability would be £180,000. Thus the first instalment due was £45,000 as shown in appendix 2.

At 14 January 2004 the estimated profits had been revised to £800,000, and the corporation tax liability would be £240,000. In addition to paying the second instalment, the company must pay sufficient to top up the first instalment to the revised amount. The payment due was £75,000 (as shown in appendix 2).

At 14 April 2004, the due date of the third instalment, no revision had been made to the estimate of the corporation tax payable. The third instalment was thus one quarter of the estimated liability, £60,000 (as shown in appendix 2).

The fourth and final instalment is due on 14 July 2004. The final liability for the year has been calculated as £192,600. Deducting the total of the three instalments already paid results in a final payment of £12,600.

It should be noted that interest is charged on underpaid instalments, and will be paid by the Revenue on overpaid instalments.

(iii) **Moving the management of T SA to Switzerland**

T SA is currently wholly managed in the UK and consequently is treated as resident in the UK for corporation tax purposes.

Its profits are liable to UK corporation tax, but T SA may claim group relief for losses realised within the group, and may also surrender its own losses as group relief. Capital assets may be passed between T SA and other group members without giving rise to a chargeable gain, and T SA can enter into a joint election for an asset sold by another group member to be treated for chargeable gains purposes as if sold by T SA, and vice versa.

If the management of T SA is moved to Switzerland then, as T SA is not incorporated in the UK, it will become non UK resident for corporation tax purposes.

T SA will then not be within the charge to UK corporation tax, will not be able to claim or surrender group relief, capital assets cannot be passed to T SA without a chargeable gain arising, and no election may be made to treat an asset as sold by T SA rather than by another group member. (This assumes that T SA does not trade through a permanent establishment in the UK – the advantages of group membership would still apply to any such branch.)

Any dividends paid by T SA to R Ltd will be liable to UK corporation tax. Double tax relief will be available for any withholding tax on the dividend and for underlying tax.

If Switzerland is a low tax country (ie the foreign tax is less than 75% of the UK corporation tax), then the controlled foreign company rules could apply. This would result in the profits of T SA being apportioned to, and taxed on, R Ltd, subject to relief for Swiss tax paid. If most of T SA's trade is with non-group companies apportionment may be avoided under the exclusion for exempt activities.

The transfer pricing rules may also be in point. If any transactions between T SA and UK resident group companies are not on an arm's length basis the transfer pricing rules require the profits of the UK resident company to be calculated as if an arm's length price had applied.

(iv) **Surplus ACT**

Surplus ACT may have arisen in respect of dividends paid by R Ltd before 6 April 1999. Such surplus ACT can be carried forward and set against R Ltd's corporation tax liability until it has been fully utilised.

The maximum surplus ACT that may be set off for any accounting period is limited to 20% of profits chargeable to corporation tax.

If R Ltd pays a dividend during the accounting period then the ACT set off is restricted by shadow ACT. Shadow ACT is calculated as 25% of the excess of dividends paid over dividends received during the accounting period, ignoring dividends from other group companies. The maximum ACT set off is thus:

$$\text{PCTCT} \times 20\% - \text{shadow ACT}$$

The payment of a substantial dividend in the near future may therefore restrict the amount of surplus ACT that R Ltd can offset against its corporation tax liability.

Management Accountant

APPENDIX 1

Corporation tax computation

Year to 31 March 2004

	£
PCTCT (given)	730,000
Qualifying R&D expenditure £40,000 × 150%	(60,000)
Patent fees	(8,000)
Loan to supplier	(20,000)
Capital gains	-
Revised PCTCT	642,000
FII	10,000
Profits	652,000

R Ltd has three associated companies, so the small companies limits are divided by 4:

Lower limit £300,000/4 = £75,000
Upper limit £1,500,000/4 = £375,000

R Ltd is therefore a large company.

Corporation tax payable

£642,000 × 30%	192,600

W1 Capital gains

Disposal of one third of V Ltd shares

	£
Proceeds	120,000
Less: Cost 1/3 × £240,000	(80,000)
	40,000
Less: Indexation 0.128 × £80,000	(10,240)
Capital gain	29,760

An election should be made that the disposal should be treated as made by S Ltd. The gain will be covered by S Ltd's loss brought forward of £50,000, and £20,240 of loss will be carried forward.

No degrouping charge arises on the disposal of V Ltd shares even though V Ltd leaves the R Ltd group, since the transfer of the property was **to** R Ltd, so the property remains in group ownership.

APPENDIX 2

Schedule of corporation tax payments

Year to 31 March 2004

	£
First instalment due 14 October 2003	
¼ × £600,000 × 30%	45,000
Second instalment due 14 January 2004	
Due to date 2 × ¼ × £800,000 × 30%	120,000
Less: Paid	(45,000)
Payable	75,000
Third instalment due 14 April 2004	
Due to date 3 × ¼ × £800,000 × 30%	180,000
Less: Paid	(120,000)
Payable	60,000
Fourth instalment due 14 July 2004	
Corporation tax due for year	192,600
Less: Paid	(180,000)
Payable	(12,600)

Tutorial note:

Although the ACT brought forward of £60,000 would in practice be deducted in the calculation of the corporation tax liability, the examiner has stated that no ACT computations will be required.

SECTION C

Answer 67 (3 of Exam Paper)

CCD Ltd

(a)   The roof of the factory was destroyed before it was acquired by CCD Ltd, and the factory would have been unusable in that condition. The new roof is capital expenditure, and is not allowable as revenue expenditure under Schedule D Case I (see Law Shipping Co v CIR). It is instead treated as part of the acquisition cost for capital gains purposes. The expenditure may be eligible for IBA at the rate of 4% pa.   ADD BACK £45,000

(b)   The costs were incurred in raising a loan which was used for a non-trading purpose (ie the acquisition of an investment property). Although the expenses of raising a loan are allowable, the deduction is made under Schedule D Case III. The expense is not allowable under Schedule D Case I.   ADD BACK £3,000

(c)   The interest paid on the loan is also an expense of a non-trading loan relationship and is an allowable expense under Schedule D Case III. It is not allowable under Schedule D Case I.   ADD BACK £8,000

(d)   Where a car costing more than £12,000 is leased, the allowable leasing expense is restricted. There is, however, no restriction for low emission cars, so the full cost of leasing the Audi A2 of £4,800 is allowable.

The disallowable expense in the case of the Lexus 300 is:

$$\frac{\frac{1}{2} \times (32,000 - 12,000)}{32,000} \times £7,200 = £2,250 \qquad\qquad \text{ADD BACK £2,250}$$

(e)   Although redundancy payments would not be allowable under general rules as they are not incurred for the purposes of a trade which is being carried on, statutory and contractual redundancy payments are specifically allowable. Ex gratia payments are only allowable to the extent that they do not exceed three times the allowable redundancy payment.

If the whole payment of £10,000 is contractual redundancy pay, it would be wholly allowable. On the assumption that the £8,000 excess over the statutory redundancy pay of £2,000 is ex gratia, the allowable amount per employee is restricted to statutory redundancy pay of £2,000, plus three times £2,000, ie a total of £8,000. The balance of £2,000 per employee is disallowed.

ADD BACK £20,000

(f)   The payment of a lease premium is normally capital expenditure, but where the term of the lease does not exceed 50 years, a proportion is taxed on the landlord as income, and the tenant can claim a deduction for that amount spread over the term of the lease. The balance of the lease premium is taken into account in computing any capital gain if the lease is disposed of before it expires.

The amount charge on the landlord is $(51 - 5)/50 \times £20,000 = £18,400$.

The annual amount allowable as a trading expense = £18,400/5 = £3,680.

The deduction in the accounts of £4,000 must be added back.

ADD BACK £(4,000 – 3,680) = £320

(g)   The cost of the repairs has been allowed as an expense, and the insurance recovery must be treated as income. The recovery of £9,600 in respect of the factory is trading income, and requires no adjustment.

The recovery of £5,400 in respect of the let property is treated as income from the property letting business, and is taxed under Schedule A. It is not trading income taxable under Schedule D Case I.

SUBTRACT £5,400

(h)   The loan to a major supplier company is a non-trading loan, and interest on the loan is taxed as non-trading income under Schedule DIII. It is not included as trading income under Schedule D Case I.

SUBTRACT £6,000

Answer 68 (4 of Exam Paper)

H Ltd

(a)   (i)   The following companies are associated: H Ltd, A Ltd, B Ltd, E Ltd, C SA, F Ltd, D Ltd.

The revised thresholds for corporation tax purposes for each of those companies are:

Starting rate lower limit	£1,429
Starting rate upper limit	£7,143
Small companies lower limit	£42,857
Small companies upper limit	£214,286

(ii)   The following groups exist for group relief purposes:

H Ltd, B Ltd, C SA, F Ltd
B Ltd, E Ltd

H Ltd, B Ltd and F Ltd can surrender losses between themselves. C SA is not UK resident and cannot surrender or claim group relief (unless it trades through a permanent establishment in the UK, and then only to the extent of the profits and losses of that branch). It is, however, a member of the group, thereby enabling its subsidiary, F Ltd, to be a group member.

F Ltd only became a member of the group on 1 October 2003, so that losses may only be surrendered in respect of the period 1 October 2003 to 31 March 2004.

B Ltd and E Ltd can surrender losses between themselves. E Ltd is not a member of the H Ltd group as H Ltd has only a 80% x 90% = 72% holding (ie less than 75%).

(iii)   H Ltd, L Inc and D Ltd form a consortium as H Ltd and L Inc hold at least 75% of D Ltd, and each company holds at least 5%. H Ltd and L Inc are the consortium members, and D Ltd is the consortium company. In determining the existence of the consortium it is immaterial that L Inc is not UK resident.

D Ltd can surrender 60% of its losses to H Ltd, and H Ltd can surrender losses to D Ltd, but only against 60% of D Ltd's profits. L Inc cannot surrender or claim consortium relief (unless it trades through a permanent establishment in the UK, and then only to the extent of the profits and losses of that branch).

(b)

	H Ltd £	A Ltd £	B Ltd £	D Ltd £	E Ltd £	F Ltd £
Trading profits	-	-	420,000	140,000	-	110,000
Group relief E to B (1)			(90,000)			
Group relief H to F (2)						(55,000)
Group relief H to B (3)			(330,000)			
Consortium relief H to D (4)				(84,000)		
PCTCT	-	-	-	56,000	-	55,000

(1)   E Ltd may only group relief losses to B Ltd.

(2)   F Ltd only joined the group on 1 October 2003, and may only claim group relief against $6/12 \times £110,000 = £55,000$.

(3)   B Ltd's remaining profits are only sufficient to group relieve £330,000 of H Ltd's loss.

(4)   D Ltd may only claim consortium relief for H Ltd's loss against 60% of its profits, ie $60\% \times £140,000 = £84,000$. The loss available for consortium relief is calculated after group relief, assuming all group relief claims are made.

(5)   H Ltd's loss remaining unrelieved is £(480,000 – 84,000 – 55,000 – 330,000) = £11,000.

Note: It would also be acceptable for E Ltd to group relieve £79,000 against B Ltd's profits, enabling H Ltd to claim group and consortium relief for the whole of its loss. E Ltd would have an unrelieved loss carried forward of £11,000. Claims between these two amounts would also be possible. In practice the claims would be set so as to achieve the soonest possible relief for the carried forward loss, ie depending on whether E Ltd or H Ltd was expected to become profitable in the future.

Tutorial note:

In practice, B Ltd's claim for group relief from H Ltd could be restricted by £1,429 so as to utilise the starting rate band. This complication has been ignored in this answer as the tax saving wasted is not material.

Answer 69 (5 of Exam Paper)

MD Ltd

(a)   **Total benefits assessable**

			£	£
(1)	Mercedes car: benefit = list price x benefit percentage. £45,000 × 32%			14,400
	Car fuel benefit applies as private use fuel is provided. Benefit = car fuel benefit figure x car benefit percentage. £14,400 × 32%			4,608
(2)	Wife's car. This is provided by reason of Mr D's employment, and is taxed on him. Benefit = list price × benefit percentage. There is a 3% uplift in the petrol benefit percentage for diesel cars. (25 + 3)% = 28% × £17,000			4,760
(3)	Mr D is taxed on the annual value of the suits, ie 20% of cost. 20% × £(700 + 500)			240
(4)	The subscription is a benefit, based on cost to the employer, but Mr D can claim a deduction from his employment income for the expense.			
(5)	The benefit is the higher of:			
	Market value		1,500	
	and			
	Cost to employer		3,600	
	Less benefit assessed in 2001/02 and 2002/03 2 x £3,600 x 20%		(1,440)	
	ie		2,160	2,160
(6)	The benefit of the school fees paid is the cost to the employer. £2,100 × 2			4,200
(7)	The benefit from the garden furniture is the cost to the employer			2,800
(8)	There is no net benefit to Mr D from attending the conference (although the cost is taxable, an equal deduction may be claimed). The costs for his wife's travel and accommodation are taxable.			2,200
				35,368

(b)   **Mr D's PAYE code**

	£
Personal allowance	4,615
Less: Assessable benefits	(35,368)
	(30,753)

PAYE code 3,074K

The effect of having code 3,074K is that additional income of £30,749 × 1/12 = £2,562.42 will be added to Mr D's salary each month, and tax calculated on the combined amount. Mr D will therefore pay tax on his benefits evenly over the year, at his marginal tax rate.

Each payday there is an overriding limit on the total tax that can be deducted of 50% of actual pay. This prevents the use of a K code leading to excessive deductions on any one payday.

(c) **Additional cost**

The company will pay Class 1 or Class 1A NICs on the benefits provided, as follows:

	Class 1 £	Class 1A £
Mercedes car		14,400
Car fuel benefit		4,608
Wife's car		4,760
Suits		240
Home cinema system		2,160
School fees (note 1)	4,200	
Garden furniture		2,800
Wife's travel and accommodation (note 2)		2,200
	4,200	31,168
Class 1 / 1A NICs @ 12.8%	537.60	3,989.50

Class 1 NICs are due within 14 days of the end of the tax month in which the payment was made.

Class 1A NICs are due by 19 July following the end of the tax year in which the benefit was provided.

Notes:

1   School fees are normally the liability of the parent, so payment by the employer is the settlement of the employee's liability. This is a payment of earnings for Class 1 purposes. Had the schooling been arranged by the employer, a Class 1A liability of the same amount would have arisen instead.

2   The answer assumes that the employer arranged the travel and accommodation. If the employer had reimbursed Mr D, or Mr D had arranged the travel and accommodation and his employer merely settled his liability, then a Class 1 NIC liability would have arisen instead.

Answer 70 (6 of Exam Paper)

J Ltd

(a)   J Ltd left the HC Ltd group on 30 September 2003 as on that date HC Ltd's shareholding was reduced below 75%.

A gain arises in J Ltd as at the start of the accounting period in which J Ltd left the group. The gain is:

		£	£
Market value at transfer (May 1999)			180,000
Less:	Cost	75,000	
	Indexation July 1993 – May 1999 0.177 x £75,000	13,275	
	Legal fees	3,000	
			(91,275)
Chargeable gain			88,725

An election may be made for the chargeable gain arising from degrouping to be transferred to another member of the HC Ltd group. The election must be made jointly by J Ltd and the company to which the gain is transferred, and must be made within two years from the end of J Ltd's accounting period, ie by 31 March 2006. The election can apply to all or part of the gain.

It would be advantageous for an election to be made transferring the whole gains to the subsidiary with capital losses brought forward of £100,000. The gain would be wholly covered by the loss, and the remainder of the loss unused of £11,275 would be carried forward.

Any payment by J Ltd for the transfer of the gain is not taxable in the recipient company, provided it does not exceed the amount of the gain transferred.

(Note that the gain by HC Ltd on the sale of the J Ltd shares will be exempt, provided J Ltd is a trading company and HC Ltd is the holding company of a trading group under the rules for the sale of substantial shareholdings.)

(b)   **Transaction 1**

The proceeds from the sale of rights exceed 5% (5% x £(280,000 + 20,000) = £15,000) and so must be treated as a part disposal.

		£	£
Proceeds			20,000
Less:	Cost £180,000 x 20,000/(280,000 + 20,000)	12,000	
	Indexation £12,000 x 0.289	3,468	
			(15,468)
Chargeable gain			4,532

Transaction 2

		Cost £	MV 31.3.82 £
Proceeds		200,000	200,000
Less:	Cost May 1976 & May 1980	(48,000)	
	Market value 31 March 1982		(60,000)
	Improvements September 1993	(20,000)	(20,000)
	Improvements July 2002	(24,000)	(24,000)
		108,000	96,000
Less:	Indexation		
	3.82 – 1.04 £60,000 × 1.307	(78,420)	(78,420)
	9.93 – 1.04 £20,000 × 0.292	(5,840)	(5,840)
	7.02 – 1.04 £24,000 × 0.042	(1,008)	(1,008)
		22,732	10,732
Take lower gain			10,732

Total gains £(4,532 + 10,732) = £15,264

In the accounting period to 31 March 2004 J Ltd had three associated companies (HC Ltd and its two other subsidiaries). The small companies lower and upper limits are reduced to £75,000 and £375,000. L Ltd is a marginal company, and pays corporation tax at a marginal rate of 32.75%.

Corporation tax on chargeable gains = £15,264 x 32.75% = £4,999

(Note it is assumed that the degrouping charge has been reallocated within the HC Ltd group. If not a further £88,725 x 32.75% = £29,057 of corporation tax would arise.)

Exam Kit Review Form

CIMA PAPER 5 KIT – BUSINESS TAXATION (FA 2003)

We hope that you have found this Kit stimulating and useful and that you now feel confident and well-prepared for your examinations.

We would be grateful if you could take a few moments to complete the questionnaire below, so we can assess how well our material meets your needs.

	Excellent	*Adequate*	*Poor*
Depth and breadth of technical coverage			
Appropriateness of coverage to examination			
Presentation			
Level of accuracy			

Did you spot any errors or ambiguities? Please let us have the details below.

Page	**Error**

Thank you for your feedback.

Please return this form to:

The Financial Training Company Limited
4 The Griffin Centre
Staines Road
Feltham
Middlesex TW14 0HS

Student's name: ....

Address: ....

....

....

CIMA Publications Student Order Form

ftc
The Financial Training Company
A **Kaplan Professional** Company

To order your books, please indicate quantity required in the relevant order box, calculate the amount(s) in the column provided, and add postage to determine the amount due. Please then clearly fill in your details plus method of payment in the boxes provided and return your completed form with payment attached to:

THE FINANCIAL TRAINING COMPANY, 4 THE GRIFFIN CENTRE, STAINES ROAD, FELTHAM, MIDDLESEX TW14 0HS
OR FAX YOUR ORDER TO 020 8831 9991 OR TELEPHONE 020 8831 9990

For examinations in May 04 ☐ Nov 04 ☐ (please tick)

FOUNDATION

PAPER	TITLE	TEXT ORDER	PRICE £	EXAM KIT ORDER	PRICE £	FOCUS NOTES ORDER	PRICE £	AMOUNT £
1	Financial Accounting Fundamentals		21.00		11.00		6.00	
2	Management Accounting Fundamentals		21.00		11.00		6.00	
3a	Economics for Business		21.00		11.00		6.00	
3b	Business Law		21.00		11.00		6.00	
3c	Business Mathematics		21.00		11.00		6.00	

INTERMEDIATE

PAPER	TITLE	TEXT ORDER	PRICE £	EXAM KIT ORDER	PRICE £	FOCUS NOTES ORDER	PRICE £	AMOUNT £
4	Finance		21.00		11.00		6.00	
5	Business Taxation [FA 2003] (May & Nov 2004)		21.00		11.00		6.00	
6a	Financial Accounting (UK Standards)		21.00		11.00		6.00	
6b	Financial Accounting (International Standards)		21.00		11.00		6.00	
7a	Financial Reporting (UK Standards)		21.00		11.00		6.00	
7b	Financial Reporting (International Standards)		21.00		11.00		6.00	
8	Management Accounting - Performance Management		21.00		11.00		6.00	
9	Management Accounting - Decision Making		21.00		11.00		6.00	
10	Systems & Project Management		21.00		11.00		6.00	
11	Organisational Management		21.00		11.00		6.00	

FINAL

PAPER	TITLE	TEXT ORDER	PRICE £	EXAM KIT ORDER	PRICE £	FOCUS NOTES ORDER	PRICE £	AMOUNT £
12	Management Accounting - Business Strategy		21.00		11.00		6.00	
13	Management Accounting - Financial Strategy		21.00		11.00		6.00	
14	Management Accounting - Information Strategy		21.00		11.00		6.00	
15	Management Accounting - Case Study		21.00						
							Sub Total	£

Postage, packing and delivery (per item) – please note a signature is required on delivery

Textbook & Exam Kit	First	Each Extra	Focus Notes	First	Each Extra		£
UK	£5.00	£2.00	UK	£2.00	£1.00		
Europe (incl ROI and CI)	£7.00	£4.00	Europe (incl ROI and CI)	£3.00	£2.00		
Rest of World	£22.00	£8.00	Rest of World	£8.00	£5.00		
						POST & PACKING	£
						TOTAL PAYMENT	£

The following section **must be filled in clearly** so that your order can be despatched without delay.

TO PAY FOR YOUR ORDER TICK AN OPTION BELOW

A. I WISH TO PAY BY   MASTERCARD ☐   VISA ☐   DELTA ☐   SWITCH ☐

CARD NO. ☐☐☐☐ ☐☐☐☐☐☐☐ ☐☐☐☐ ☐☐☐☐ (Some cards don't need all boxes)

EXPIRY DATE ☐☐☐☐   ISSUE No. ☐☐ (Switch only)   All cards - last 3 digits on signature strip ☐☐☐

Cardholder's Signature _____

Cardholder's Name & Address: _____

Cardholder's Tel. No. (Day): _____

B. I WISH TO PAY BY CHEQUE ☐ Cheques should be made payable to *The Financial Training Company Ltd* and must be attached to your order form. **Personal cheques cannot be accepted without a valid Banker's Card number written on the back of the cheque.**

STUDENT NAME: _____

DELIVERY ADDRESS: (Must be the same as cardholder's address. Please contact us if you wish to discuss an alternative delivery address).

POST CODE: _____   TEL. NO. (Day): _____